A HISTORY OF
SMALL BUSINESS
IN AMERICA

W9-BSZ-446

THE
LUTHER
HARTWELL
HODGES
SERIES

ON
BUSINESS,
SOCIETY,
AND THE
STATE

William H. Becker, editor

A HISTORY OF SMALL BUSINESS IN AMERICA

Second Edition

MANSEL G. BLACKFORD

WITHDRAWN

THE UNIVERSITY OF NORTH CAROLINA PRESS
Chapel Hill and London

© 2003 The University of North Carolina Press
All rights reserved

Design by Jacquline Johnson
Set in Minion
by Tseng Information Systems, Inc.
Manufactured in the United States of America

The paper in this book meets the guidelines for permanence and
durability of the Committee on Production Guidelines for Book
Longevity of the Council on Library Resources.

Library of Congress Cataloging-in-Publication Data
Blackford, Mansel G., 1944–
A history of small business in America / by Mansel G. Blackford.— 2nd ed.
p. cm. — (The Luther Hartwell Hodges series on business, society, and the state)
Includes bibliographical references and index.
ISBN 0-8078-2780-0 (cloth : alk. paper) —
ISBN 0-8078-5453-0 (pbk. : alk. paper)
1. Small business—United States—History.   2. Small business—
Government policy—United States—History.   I. Title.   II. Series.
HD2346.U5 B56   2003
338.6′42′0973—dc21
2002151277

cloth   07 06 05 04 03   5 4 3 2 1
paper   07 06 05 04 03   5 4 3 2 1

For my wife, Vicki,

with great thanks

for her continued support

CONTENTS

TABLES

I have long been fascinated by the history of small business in America. Some of my interest has been personal. My father was involved in the formation of several small businesses, one of which was quite successful, another of which was not. His work—for there was always lots of work—intrigued me as I grew up and made me wonder just what motivated him and others of his ilk. Similarly, my daughter owned and operated an independent bookstore for five years, juggling business responsibilities with those of raising a family.

My interest has also stemmed from professional concerns. My major field of research and teaching has been business history. I have chosen to work in this field because it has seemed to me that a fruitful way to understand the cultural, political, and social, as well as economic, evolution of the United States is through an examination of the development of its business institutions. Central to an understanding of America's business system, although a topic long overlooked by most scholars, has been small business. Most business historians have focused their energies mainly on trying to unravel the development of big business. I hope my study will help redress this imbalance and thereby add to our understanding of both business institutions and broader patterns of culture and politics in the United States.

In light of both the expanding interest in small business in general and our growing understanding of small firms, the time is ripe for a study that pulls together and makes sense of the history of small business in America. This volume presents a comprehensive, chronological account of the history of small business in the United States, focusing on two interrelated issues: the changing place of small business in America's business system, including an examination of managerial strategies and the institutional growth of small firms, and the evolution of public attitudes and public policies toward small business. This book describes and analyzes the changing fortunes of small businesses in farming, manufacturing, sales, and services from colonial times to the present. While always focusing on small business, this study of necessity examines changing relationships between big business and small business after the 1880s, when big business began developing in a major way.

I have incurred many intellectual debts in my ongoing study of small business. Carol Chin, Thomas Dicke, John Ingham, Edwin Perkins, and Philip Scranton provided valuable comments on drafts of the first edition of this work. Jonathan Bean was especially helpful with insights into an earlier draft of the second edition; David Stebenne and Paul Watkins critiqued drafts of Chapter 9 of this edition. I would also like to thank the two anonymous readers for the University of North Carolina Press for their valuable comments. As always, I have benefited from conversations with my colleagues in history at The Ohio State University, especially William Childs and Austin Kerr. I remain, of course, responsible for any errors of fact or interpretation this study may contain.

A HISTORY OF
SMALL BUSINESS
IN AMERICA

Observing the American scene in the early 1830s, the French writer and social commentator Alexis de Tocqueville noted in his 1835 book *Democracy in America*, "What astonishes me in the United States is not so much the marvelous grandeur of some undertakings as the innumerable multitude of small ones." As this statement suggests, small businesses have long been central to American life. In fact, from the founding of the first colonies in the 1600s to the present day, small businesses have been integral to the economic, political, and cultural development of the United States. Over the past three decades or so, there has been an awakening of interest in small businesses on the part of historians, social scientists, and business school faculty members. As big businesses seemed to falter as engines of economic growth in America in the 1970s and 1980s, some observers came to see smaller firms as likely sources for economic rejuvenation—a hope not always borne out in reality.

What Is Small?

Despite the progress made in scholarly understanding of small business, there exists no agreement upon what is meant by "small." The law that created the U.S. Small Business Administration (SBA) in 1953 stated that a small business was a firm that was "independently owned and operated . . . and not dominant in its field of operation." Since its establishment, the SBA has defined small businesses in different ways. In the late 1950s, the agency included the following as its focus: small industrial establishments with fewer than 250 employees, wholesalers whose annual sales amounted to $5 million or less, and retail and service businesses with yearly sales of $1 million or less. Thirty years later, reflecting the growing sizes of businesses in the United States, the SBA was defining any firm with 500 or fewer employees as small, though the acceptable maximum number of employees might vary by industry group. For instance, in retail sales only firms with 100 or fewer employees were considered to be small. While many scholars have accepted the definitions of the SBA, others have focused upon functional characteristics, rather than upon absolute measures of size: the nature of firms' management setups (whether or not there are managerial hierarchies, different levels of management), the nature of relationships between firms and their labor forces, and the types of arrangements firms have with their local communities.

To me the functional approach makes sense, for most small businesses seem to share several common characteristics. Their management arrangements are usually simple. The chief executive officer, who is often also the owner, runs the business personally. He or she knows the other managers and most of the workers. In one small company that I have studied, a director recalled that in the firm's formative years its management setup consisted simply of "a gang" of friends fighting for their lives. In small companies the elaborate hierarchies of top, middle, and lower management that normally exist in big businesses are not present. Moreover, most small businesses are single-unit enterprises. They do not have plants or offices in more than one locality. As locally oriented companies, small businesses commonly recruit their workforces from their communities and are deeply involved in community affairs. They are also more apt than larger firms to purchase their raw materials locally and to produce for local rather than national or international markets.

Nonetheless, the question of just what constitutes a small firm must be approached with caution. It is important to recognize that neither large nor small firms constitute homogeneous groups and to realize that a "gray" intermediate area exists between the two groups. There are many gradations of "smallness." Certainly, conceptions of small businesses have varied from one time period to the next, as demonstrated by the shifting definitions offered by the SBA. Firms that are today seen as small businesses by the SBA would have been viewed as large by most mid-nineteenth-century Americans. Finally, it is important to note that many differences exist in trying to define what is meant by small business across national boundaries. In fact, in many countries, small and medium-sized enterprises (SMES), not small businesses, are differentiated from big businesses, with the dividing line often set at about 300 employees.

Wherever possible, I have taken the functional approach in defining small businesses in this study. However, my work is a synthesizing study relying in large part upon the studies of other scholars and upon investigations by federal government agencies. Since others have often taken approaches based upon absolute measures of size—most commonly, the number of employees in a firm—I have had to be eclectic in my approach to definitions of "small," "medium," and "big" business.

The Importance of Small Business in America

Small businesses have always played important roles in America's economic evolution. Before about 1880, small businesses were the norm. Thousands of small firms handled the production and distribution of goods and services in the American economy. Only from the middle of the nineteenth century did big businesses emerge in fields where new technologies permitted economies of scale in the production and/or distribution of goods. When they did develop—first in railroads, a bit later in some industrial fields—big businesses came to dominate those sectors of the economy in which they arose and were sustained. Small businesses did not, however, disappear. They adjusted to the presence of big businesses. While their relative share of America's industrial output declined, small businesses continued to grow in absolute numbers, even in manufacturing. By developing market niches ignored by large manufacturers or by becoming intermediate goods suppliers to larger industrial firms, small businesses persisted in the industrial segment of America's business system. Only in farming did small businesses dramatically decrease in importance. In most other fields—in the sales and service sectors, especially—small firms, while losing market shares to larger concerns, remained important.

The years after World War II witnessed fluctuations in the fortunes of small businesses. While the number of businesses in the United States, nearly all of which were small enterprises, rose from about 11 million in 1958 to nearly 17 million in 1980, the relative importance of small businesses fell. Something of a resurgence in small business occurred in the late 1970s and the 1980s. Particularly noticeable was the growing role of small business in manufacturing. In a reversal of its previous decline relative to big business, small business increased its share of America's manufacturing output from 33 to 37 percent between 1976 and 1986. However, there were signs that this resurgence stalled in the 1990s; small firms did not prove to be the robust sources of growth and employment dreamed of by many Americans.

If small businesses have been vital to America's economic development, they have been perhaps even more important as a component of American culture. More than the cultures of other nations, that of the United States has developed as a business culture; and the love affair of most Americans with business has focused especially upon small business. From the time of Thomas Jefferson to the present, many Americans have seen the owners of small businesses as epitomizing all that is best about the American way of life. Even as they embraced what they viewed as the superior efficiency and productivity of big businesses, Americans continued to revere small business people for their self-reliance and independence. Indeed, twentieth-century Americans have frequently differentiated between small businesses, which they have seen as inefficient and backward, and small business people, whom they have continued to admire. In the period after World War II, the small business owner was often pictured as a bastion of political as well as economic democracy in the Cold War between the United States and the Soviet Union.

The importance of small business to the development of America's business system and cultural values carried over into the political realm as well. Small businesses have often received special treatment in state and national legislation. A major reason for the enactment of America's first antitrust laws, the Sherman Act in 1890 and the Clayton Act in 1914, was a generalized desire to protect small firms from the perceived "unfair" encroachments of larger companies, even though the larger businesses were usually more efficient in their production and distribution of goods to consumers. In the 1920s and 1930s, large chain store operations extended their reach throughout the United States. Competing with smaller "mom-and-pop" grocery and drug stores, the chains frequently benefited from economies of scale and were able to sell at prices lower than those of their smaller rivals. Responding to this threat to small businesses, a number of states passed legislation heavily taxing chain stores, and Congress enacted the Robinson-Patman Act of 1936 and the Miller-Tydings Act of 1937 to shield small retailers from the competition of larger firms. Most recently, Congress created the SBA in 1953 as a federal government agency charged with the goal of encouraging small business development in the United States and, through the Regulatory Flexibility Act of 1980 and other measures, exempted small firms from many aspects of federal government regulation of business.

However, the expressed desires of Congress and the state legislatures usually have not succeeded. In fact, some of the legislation—the Sherman Act and, perhaps, the Robinson-Patman Act—has aided larger concerns at the expense of smaller ones, and other pieces of legislation designed to help small firms have been largely ineffective. Moreover, actions of the federal government, such as its defense procurement policies, have often favored large businesses over small ones. Thus, a paradox has existed. Americans have generally admired the owners of small businesses and have desired the preservation of small enterprises, even at the expense of economic efficiency. Nonetheless, governmental policies have often directly or indirectly furthered the development of big businesses in the United States. There has been a discrepancy between political rhetoric and reality, one that continues to the present day.

Scholarship Dealing with Small Business

Until recently, most historians have neglected the evolution of small business in favor of looking at the development of big business. Although lamentable, this emphasis on the study of big business is understandable. The rise of big businesses did transform parts of the business systems of the United States and the world. Change occurred most rapidly in the realm of big business; and so historians, generally more interested in chronicling change than in recording continuity, have focused upon the larger companies and the executives who have run them. In addition, there are practical difficulties that hinder those wanting to study small businesses: most small firms last for only a few years and fail to preserve the types of records historians need to examine and review.

Nonetheless, while generally most interested in big businesses, some historians have been concerned with the development of small businesses. Retailing, a field long dominated by small firms, attracted much of the early attention given to small business, with a lot of that attention going into the study of country stores. These studies emphasized the importance of the stores, not simply as retail outlets, but also as sources of credit and business information for people in their localities. Initially, small business in manufacturing attracted less attention from historians, but early case studies — of cutlery making in the Connecticut Valley and of the Smith & Griggs Company's brass fabricating business — pointed to directions that later historians would follow.

Going beyond these two studies, the economic and business historian James H. Soltow examined the evolution of small metal fabricating and machine-making companies in New England in a pathbreaking work first published in 1965. Soltow found that a leading reason for the persistence of small businesses over several generations lay in their ability to carve out market niches for their products. His extended essay showed that small businesses, even in manufacturing, could successfully adjust to the rise of big businesses in the United States.

Historians' interest in small businesses heightened in the 1970s and early 1980s, as it became apparent that America's big businesses were having increasing trouble with foreign competition. The seventeen essays comprising *Small Business in American Life*, edited by Stuart Bruchey and published in 1980, illustrated the wide variety of social and economic roles that small business people have played in the development of the United States. Rich in the diversity of its offerings, this volume pointed out the need for additional scholarly work on the history of small businesses. Most recently, a number of historians have paid special attention to the interactions among technological changes, managerial strategies, and labor relations in small manufacturing firms. Particularly important has been research and writing on the development of industrial districts, often composed mainly or exclusively of small and medium-sized firms, in the United States, Europe, and Japan. In these districts, which scholars such as Philip Scranton have recently shown were much more important than was previously realized, manufacturing ventures used flexible production techniques rather than mass-production methods to compete successfully with much larger firms for long periods of time.

Social scientists, as well as historians, have contributed to our growing understanding of the development of small business in America. Looking especially at the years since World War II, political scientists and sociologists have probed the contributions of small business to the evolution of American culture, often in the hope of influencing government policies. They have also examined the impacts of public policies on small business. Until very recently, most economists pictured big businesses as benefiting from scale economies that made their development nearly inevitable, with small firms pictured as relics from the past. The most current economic studies, however, have significantly altered our view of the roles small firms have played in America's development and the relationships between large and small firms in the United States. Some economists looking at the problems faced by American manufacturers in the 1970s and 1980s argued that the solution to America's economic crisis lay in moving out of the standardized mass production of homogeneous products into a system of flexible production by smaller companies linked together in industrial communities.

Faculty members at colleges of business administration, and business writers in general, have also dealt with small business. In their writings, small business owners have often been pictured as entrepreneurs. For example, since 1980 the Center for Entrepreneurial Studies at Babson College has sponsored an annual conference on entrepreneurship, and many of the papers presented at the conferences have focused on small businesses. While recognizing that only a minority of small businesses survive their infancy to grow to maturity, authors of these types of studies have stressed the contributions these firms have made to the economic advance of the United States in recent years. In several very controversial studies, David Birch has expressed well the feelings of this school of thought. Birch and scholars like him have attributed nearly all of the jobs and technological innovations generated in modern America to small businesses. Not all scholars accept Birch's findings, however, and the varied roles of small firms in the creation of jobs and the making of innovations remains unclear.

The Scope of this Study

Building on the growing number of works on small business by a variety of scholars, the second edition of this study differs from the first edition in important respects. Most obviously, this edition incorporates information from the numerous studies about small business published in the 1990s. Particularly important has been new literature on the significance of small businesses for minorities and women. The second edition melds that information with data from earlier studies to reach a new synthesis. The second edition also does more to address complex relationships among small, medium-sized, and large firms in many fields, in recognition of the diversity of firm sizes in America. Then too, the second edition goes much farther than its predecessor in comparing the experiences of small businesses in the United States to the experiences of those in some other countries, as a way of pointing out both commonalities and situations unique to the United States.

This study combines general narrative chapters with chapters that contain case studies of individual small business firms and their industries. While the general, narrative chapters describe and explain the changing roles of small businesses in the overall economic system of the United States, the case-study chapters focus on the histories of individual firms, industries, and regions. The book thus links examinations of general business trends with detailed investigations of specific small business situations.

Five chapters carry the story of small business through World War II. Chapter 1 looks at small business development up to about 1880, when big businesses first began emerging in large numbers in the manufacturing sector of the economy. In these early years small businesses were the norm in all fields, and a small business ideology began developing. General stores, this chapter shows, were especially important in holding parts of America's emerging economy together. Chapter 2 examines how small businesses coped with the rise of big businesses, especially in manufacturing, up to about 1920. Small firms sometimes operated independently, but they also often worked together (even as they competed with each other) in industrial districts, such as Philadelphia's textile district. Chapter 3, the first chapter to deal with a case study of business enterprise, presents the history of small businesses in metal making in the late nineteenth and early twentieth centuries. This chapter shows how one independent steelmaker, the Buckeye Steel Castings Company, developed on its own in Columbus, Ohio; but it also looks at how scores of small and medium-size iron and steel companies, loosely linked together in the Pittsburgh region, successfully coexisted for decades with their larger brethren there. Chapter 4 analyzes the changing fortunes of small firms during times of boom and bust for the American economy between 1921 and 1945. During these years small firms faced growing competition from big businesses in sales as well as in manufacturing and responded by trying to protect themselves through state and national legislation. Chapter 5 examines in a case-study format one small business that emerged from World War II as a very prosperous enterprise: Wakefield Seafoods of Alaska. Pioneering in a brand-new industry, selling king crabs as frozen food, Wakefield became the industry leader in the 1940s and 1950s. The company's story demonstrates how some small firms continued to succeed by exploiting niche markets for specialty products.

Four chapters examine developments over the past fifty years. Chapter 6 analyzes the status of small firms during what was a prosperous period for most Americans, the years 1946 through 1971, a time during which small firms nonetheless generally lost ground relative to their larger competitors. Chapter 7 describes how one group of small firms, those composing California's Silicon Valley, fared during those years, focusing on the importance of entrepreneurship and regional propinquity. This case-study chapter also investigates why it has been difficult to replicate the success of the Silicon Valley elsewhere. Chapter 8 looks at business developments since 1971, a time marked by growing foreign competition for American businesses and a period in which there have occurred significant changes in relations between large and small firms. This chapter explores, in particular, the thorny issues of job creation and technological innovation. Chapter 9 investigates in a final case study how one small business, K&M Books of

Cleveland, Ohio, tried to deal with consolidations occurring in the publishing and book-selling industries in the 1990s. In existence for five years, that small business closed its doors in early 2002. The trials this company faced illuminate well the difficulties that small retailers encounter in trying to compete with their "big box" competitors in modern-day America. Finally, this book's conclusion looks at the changing place of small business in the American economy over several centuries.

Additional Reading

Richard John, "Elaborations, Revision, Dissents: Alfred D. Chandler Jr.'s *The Visible Hand* after Twenty Years," *Business History Review* 71 (Summer 1997): 151–206; and Daniel Nelson, "The History of Business in America," *OAH Magazine of History* 11 (Fall 1996): 5–10, are valuable introductions to how historians have approached the study of business. Will Hausman, ed., *Business and Economic History* 26 (Fall 1997), contains sixteen essays by business historians on new approaches to research and writing in the field of business history. Mansel G. Blackford, "Small Business in America: A Historiographic Survey," *Business History Review* 65 (Spring 1991): 1–26; and Thomas Dicke, "The Small Business Tradition," *OAH Magazine of History* 11 (Fall 1996): 11–16, examine how scholars have written about small businesses. Leah Hertz, *In Search of a Small Business Definition: An Exploration of the Small Business Definitions of the U.S., the U.K., Israel, and the People's Republic of China* (Washington, D.C.: University Press of America, 1982), looks at how and why "small" businesses have been defined in different ways in different nations.

Several collections of essays survey the development of small business. Konosuke Odaka and Minoru Sawai, eds., *Small Firms, Large Concerns: The Development of Small Business in Comparative Perspective* (Oxford: Oxford University Press, 1999) is international in scope; Stuart Bruchey, ed., *Small Business in American Life* (New York: Columbia University Press, 1980) examines small business developments in the United States. To the extent that they have succeeded in business in America, minorities and women have generally done so, at least until very recently, in smaller firms. Angel Kwolek-Folland, *Incorporating Women: A History of Women and Business in the United States* (New York: Twayne, 1998) is a valuable survey. Virginia G. Drachman, *Enterprising Women: 250 Years of American Business* (Chapel Hill: University of North Carolina Press, 2002), offers another survey of the roles played by women. For more detail, see the essays comprising Mary Yeager, ed., *Women in Business* (Cheltenham, U.K.: Edward Elgar, 1999); fifty-seven of them deal with women in American business. Juliet E. K. Walker's *The History of Black Business in America: Capitalism, Race, Entrepreneurship* (New York: Twayne, 1998) is an excellent overview; her edited volume, Walker, ed., *Encyclopedia of African American Business History* (Westport, Conn.: Greenwood, 1999), offers more detail.

1

Small Business before 1880

Writing in 1849, John Beauchamp Jones, a small-scale Missouri store-keeper, captured well the importance of merchants in mid-nineteenth-century American life: "Wherever the surges of 'manifest destiny' scatter the seeds of civilization—whether it be in the solemn shade and solitude of the dark forests bordering the 'Mad Missouri,' or on the interminable prairies beyond the woods—the merchant or trader is always found in their midst." Whether operating from offices called "counting houses" in major cities, running small country stores, or roaming the backwoods as peddlers, merchants held together the business systems of colonial America and the early United States. Thousands of small, personally owned and operated firms—such as Jones's country store—formed the glue of America's business system.

In the years before 1880, small business assumed myriad forms in America's merchandising, farming, manufacturing, and service industries. Small businesses were the norm in most fields of endeavor, with single-unit, nonbureaucratic firms dotting the American landscape. Only in the 1880s and later was the dominance of small businesses challenged by the rise of big business in some fields. Small businesses were important to Americans in noneconomic as well as economic senses. From the first, America was a land settled by business people imbued with business values. Setting off for Arrow Rock, Missouri, then a frontier region, in the early 1830s, Jones expressed sentiments common in America: "I now determined to be a merchant, a millionaire, and nothing else," he exclaimed. "I resolved to make my way in the world, and to obtain wealth." Getting ahead in America meant succeeding in the world of business, and at a time when few large firms existed, business success meant success as a small business person.

Not surprisingly, a national ideology favorable to business, especially small business, developed from the time of the founding of the first colonies.

Economic Growth and Limitations on Business Development

Rapid economic growth characterized the development of the American colonies and the new nation of the United States, and this economic expansion created opportunities for the small business people who came to compose America's expanding commercial network. Technological, market, and financial limitations precluded the development of big businesses, except in a few fields, until after about 1880. Until these restrictions began to be lifted in the mid- and late-nineteenth century, small firms made up America's business system.

Economic growth came from several sources in colonial America. The production of goods for foreign markets was a prime engine of growth. Throughout the colonial period the Atlantic Ocean served as a bridge connecting the colonies to overseas markets. By the 1760s and 1770s, the colonists were sending abroad a substantial share of the crops they raised and the handicraft items they made, to the extent that perhaps 20 percent of the income of the colonists came from these exports. Domestic developments, as well as foreign trade, drove the colonial economies. As time progressed, trading networks based upon major cities such as Boston, Philadelphia, New York, and Charleston penetrated inland, and local and regional commerce came to rival and then surpass overseas trade as a stimulus for economic growth.

Domestic commerce became still more important as the United States developed as an independent nation. As people moved west across the Appalachian Mountains, the focus of economic activity moved inland, and internal development replaced foreign trade as the most powerful force driving the American economy. An agricultural revolution greatly increased America's output of staple crops, especially cotton and wheat, and the beginnings of the Industrial Revolution in America spurred the production of manufactured items. Meanwhile, the construction of turnpikes, canals, and railroads encouraged local, regional, and interregional trade. The emergence of America as the world's largest domestic free-trade region provided the single most powerful stimulant to the business development of the United States throughout the nineteenth century and well into the twentieth.

As the United States developed an increasingly unified business system, the individual firms making up that system became more and more specialized. For most of the colonial period, the largest merchants and other business people were generalists. Markets were too small and fragmented and financial facilities too poorly developed to permit them to specialize very much. From about the 1750s on, however, the growth of commerce, industry, and agriculture, together with transportation improvements, allowed business people to begin specializing. Merchants, who had previously dealt in a wide variety of goods and markets, found it possible to specialize as brokers handling specific products, such as cotton, wheat, or iron. Others became involved in financing and insuring America's growing commerce, while still others entered the world of industry. This transformation was, nonetheless, far from complete at the time of the Civil War. Especially in frontier areas, business people operating as generalists continued to run country stores and to work as peddlers.

Most colonial Americans were eager participants in the development of a commercial economy. Merchants were, as already suggested, one of the key groups—probably the key group—in the business system of colonial America. But, so were artisans (skilled workers), many of whom possessed their own tools and shops and who may well be thought of as the owners of small businesses. Farmers, too, were part of the commercial development of colonial America. Only a relatively small proportion of them was involved in subsistence growing. Perhaps three-quarters produced for the market and, like merchants and artisans, acted as small business people in their economic transactions. With the development of a vibrant business system, colonial Americans experienced a rising standard of living, which reinforced their commercial outlook. By the time of the American Revolution, the colonists (except for black slaves) possessed a standard of living higher in many respects than that of most Europeans. The involvement of Americans in the development of their nation's commercial economy increased in the early and mid-1800s, and most Americans continued to share in a rapidly rising standard of living. Despite economic downturns in 1837, 1857, and 1873, America's real per capita gross national product (GNP) rose by one-third in the twenty years after 1839 and continued to rise in later years.

For all of this economic activity, however, individual businesses remained small. Limitations in both the distribution and production of goods prevented the rise of big businesses on a major scale until after the Civil War. What the dean of business historians Alfred D. Chandler Jr. has called the "throughput" of business, the amount of goods and services passing through a nation's business system in a given period of time, remained so small in the antebellum years — when compared to what would come later — that small businesses, linked together in America's commercial web, could easily handle it. Only after 1880 did large companies arise in substantial numbers to coordinate the greatly increased flow of goods resulting from accelerating industrialization.

Limitations in distribution were those of speed and expense in transportation and communications. Wind and animal power long remained the energy sources in transportation. Ships in the transatlantic trade required months to reach their destinations, while those sailing to China took a year or more. In domestic commerce, roads were so poorly constructed as to be virtually impassable much of the time. Canals, although an improvement, especially in the carriage of heavy and bulky goods such as wheat and coal, were slow and unreliable. Only from the 1830s on did railroads begin hastening the speed of transporting goods over long distances. Similarly, in the 1840s and 1850s the telegraph began to be used by business people for scheduling orders and keeping track of affairs, quickening commercial life. Constraints in technology also limited the production of manufactured items. As long as animal, water, and wind power ran mills and factories, their output remained relatively low. Breakthroughs along the East Coast started in the 1830s, when anthracite coal from Pennsylvania began to come into use as a fuel for steam engines and as a source of heat in processes for the making of sugar, beer, chemicals, and the like. A bit later, producers in the Midwest used bituminous coal mined west of the Alleghenies. Still, the changes in industrialization required decades to complete, and as late as 1880 most industrial firms were still small businesses.

Enterprise in Trade and Commerce

Foreign and domestic commerce held together the economies of the American colonies and the new United States, and it was merchants of various types who handled this trade. Comprising 2 to 5 percent of the workforce in colonial times, and probably a somewhat larger proportion in the early and mid-1800s, the merchants were all small business people. Even the largest and most important conducted their business affairs in single-unit enterprises that lacked managerial hierarchies. They could do so because the pace of business was slow and the volume of business was low. Thomas Hancock, the leading Boston merchant of the mid-eighteenth century, for instance, sent out an average of only sixty-two letters per year.

Nonetheless, while all of the merchants may be considered small business people, gradations appeared within their ranks. Relatively large sedentary merchants operated from offices in seaport cities, importing and exporting goods and selling at wholesale and retail. Smaller storekeepers located in inland towns supplied the countryside with goods and credit. Purchasing their products from the eastern merchants and selling them to farmers in return for their agricultural produce, the country storekeepers were, arguably, the most important small business people of their day. Upon their work pivoted the economies of colonial and early national America. Finally, peddlers owning only the goods upon the backs of their horses or in their wagons reached beyond the areas served by stores to the farthest frontiers.

Personal trust lay at the heart of colonial America's business system, even in that part controlled by the largest merchants. At a time when communications were slow and the risks in business were traditional ones such as shipwrecks, merchants found themselves having to rely upon friends and relatives. Elaborate managerial hierarchies, whether staffed by relatives or not, offered no advantages and were not used. Colonial American trading companies lacked the monopoly powers often granted European trading companies and were, consequently, much smaller. A colonial American merchant ran his business from his (or occasionally her) counting house with the aid of only one or two or, at most, a half-dozen clerks, all of whom he or she knew personally. The merchant often spent each afternoon away from the counting house in nearby coffee houses and inns discussing affairs with other traders. Little in the way of new business methods came into use, for they provided no advantages over traditional ones. The types of risks apt to be encountered in trading were well known and unlikely to vary much from year to year. New ways of doing things could not appreciably lessen the risks, such as storms at sea. Instead, techniques handed down with little change from medieval Europe remained in vogue: the use of single and (occasionally) double entry bookkeeping, promissory notes, bills of exchange, and samples.

When the regional economies of the colonies and, later, the new United States became better developed through transportation and financial improvements, mercantile specialization occurred. Merchants engaged in just one type of trade: importing or exporting, trading with just one rather than many parts of the world, selling at wholesale or retail, but not both. By the late 1850s, for instance, Boston possessed 218 wholesale establishments engaged in importing and selling shoes and another 70 houses doing business solely in hardware. As Americans moved inland, Cincinnati, St. Louis, and Chicago developed as wholesale centers. By 1859, Cincinnati boasted

50 wholesalers specializing in dry goods and another 50 specializing in clothing, leading one news reporter to observe that "within the last eight or ten years Cincinnati has been gaining a position as a great centre of supply, by wholesale, to the country merchants of Ohio, Indiana, Illinois, and Kentucky, of their dry goods, groceries, hardware, boots and shoes, hats, drugs, and fancy goods."

While relatively large merchants controlled the wholesale trade of the nation, smaller retailers brought the goods to customers throughout America. By 1839, there were 57,565 retail outlets in the United States, with the average amount of capital invested in each store coming to $4,350. The most common form of retailer was the country storekeeper. Operating in small towns, the storekeepers generally found their markets too restricted to allow specialization. Most carried a broad assortment of goods, everything from groceries and drugs to hardware and dry goods. A traveler in Pennsylvania remarked upon this feature in 1806: "These storekeepers are obliged to keep every article which it is possible that the farmer and manufacturer [artisan] may want. Each of their shops exhibits a complete medley; a magazine where are to be had both a needle and a anchor, a tin pot and a large copper boiler, a child's whistle and a pianoforte, ring dial and a clock, a skein of thread and trimmings of lace, a check frock and a muslin gown, a frieze coat and a superfine cloth, a glass of whiskey and barrel of brandy, a gill of vinegar and a hogshead of Madeira wine."

For all of the variety in their goods, however, the country stores were very limited in both their physical size and their capital investment. The stores were the archetypal small businesses of their day. Log cabins about twenty feet on a side were the norm into the 1820s and 1830s. The stores contained display counters, open barrels, and shelves for the goods, together with a small office where the storekeeper kept his or her ledgers and accounts. By the mid-1800s, these rude structures were giving way to brick and clapboard stores with bay windows and other amenities in the more settled areas. It was a rare store that stocked more than $10,000 worth of goods at a time (many carried only $1,500 to $3,000 in goods), most of these purchased on credit from wholesalers.

The main economic function of the stores was to facilitate the exchange of goods. Once or twice each year storekeepers made trips to purchase goods from wholesalers in New York, Philadelphia, and Baltimore, or from those in emerging regional centers such as Chicago and St. Louis. The storekeepers usually bought their supplies with a bill of exchange payable in twelve months (no interest was charged for the first six months, but a rate of 6 to 10 percent applied for the second six months). For western storekeepers these buying trips were often arduous, sometimes requiring six weeks or longer to complete. John Allen Trimble, a storekeeper in Hillsboro, Ohio, wrote of his early nineteenth-century experiences, emphasizing that poor transportation facilities made travel difficult. "Turnpikes, rail roads & steam boats were not then in existence," he observed. "The roads over the mountains were the most indifferent wagon ways conceivable," he continued, "without grading, ruts & gutters, mudholes and other obsticles [*sic*], never mended, and being hilly, broken & uncommon mountainous country made it toilsome in the extreme."

Storekeepers sold their items to nearby farmers, accepting goods of all types in payment. Cash was usually in short supply, especially on frontiers, and most storekeepers conducted a portion of their trade on a barter basis. Storekeepers allowed liberal credit terms to their customers, often as long as twelve months, for farmers could settle their accounts only in the fall and winter after they had harvested their crops. Storekeepers accumulated corn, pork, cotton, and wheat—as well as more esoteric products, such as ginseng, beeswax, feathers, and beaver pelts—in their trade. These they either sent east directly to pay off their debts to the wholesalers or processed locally, as in the grinding of wheat into flour, before shipping them east.

Country stores played especially important economic roles in the predominantly rural South. Small farms were at least as important as large plantations in southern development, and country stores grew up at crossroads throughout the antebellum South to serve them. While larger merchants called "factors" operated directly from southern cities such as Charleston and New Orleans to handle the purchasing, marketing, and credit requirements of the planters, country storekeepers took care of the smaller farmers. On average, each storekeeper supplied 300 to 400 farm families with goods, allowing, as in other regions of the United States, up to twelve months' credit on the purchases. Storekeepers also acted as marketing agents for the cotton, tobacco, corn, and other crops taken in trade—selling them in large lots to urban-based factors and commission houses, selling them in other regions or even abroad through partners residing in cities, or sending them out in peddling wagons for sale to whomever would buy them.

Even more than the merchant, the storekeeper found that traditional forms of business organization sufficed. Most storekeepers operated as single-owner proprietors. Almost none of the storekeepers organized their businesses as corporations. Their capital needs were scanty, and working capital could be provided by credit from their wholesalers. Although less common than single-owner proprietorships, partnerships did exist. In the most prevalent form of partnership both partners gave full-time service to one store and contributed to its capital stock. Less commonly, a partnership might control two or more stores, with different partners running the individual stores and acting as agents in eastern cities. Occasionally, family-based partnerships grew to control chains of country stores. In 1803, Andrew Jackson operated three stores in different parts of Tennessee, and in the same year James and Archibald Kane ran four stores in villages around Albany, New York. The Andrews family entered merchandising with a store in Huntsville, Alabama, in 1826, opened a second store in Tuscaloosa three years later, and soon had family members in New York and Philadelphia employed as buying and selling agents for the stores.

In running their businesses, the storekeepers depended upon their own efforts with, perhaps, the help of unpaid family members. Multilevel managerial hierarchies did not exist. At most, a storekeeper might employ a young man as a clerk. Clerking became, in fact, the most commonly followed road to store ownership by the 1840s, at least in the West. Some 70 percent of the storekeepers in that region started as clerks in other people's stores. Another 15 percent entered merchandising directly from agriculture, and 5 percent had first been schoolteachers. Few day laborers or skilled artisans became storekeepers. Most stores opened early and closed late. Nonetheless, stock turnover was slow, sometimes painfully so. When John Jones and his brother opened their first store in Missouri in the early 1830s, they sold $150 worth of goods on their first day of business, but receipts soon fell to less than that per week. As Jones glumly noted, "We had dull days there as well as elsewhere." The average weekly sales of the stores, which varied considerably with the seasons, came to roughly $200 to $300.

In this situation of slow business, traditional bookkeeping methods saw little change. A few storekeepers simply marked their walls with chalked tallies of their accounts; others ran columns of figures on shingles, the forerunner of the visible file. One storekeeper kept his cash account by hanging up a pair of boots, one on each side of a fireplace. Into one boot went the money received during the day; into the other went pieces of paper covering the money paid out. To arrive at a balance, the storekeeper simply emptied the boots! Most found it necessary, however, to maintain more complete accounts based upon single entry bookkeeping. They used two books: a waste or day book, containing a running record of all of their transactions; and a ledger in which accounts were arranged by customer, with a debtor page on the left showing what was owed and a creditor page on the right showing what had been paid. The accounts were usually settled only once a year, generally in December or January.

In retailing, as in wholesaling, specialization began in the antebellum years where markets were large enough and concentrated enough to support it. Although country stores selling a broad range of goods remained important in some rural areas well into the twentieth century, they soon gave way to more specialized outlets in cities. Retail drug stores, bookstores, and jewelry stores made their appearance in the antebellum years. Shoe and furniture stores were less common, but not unknown. Although fully developed department stores came into existence only after the Civil War, forerunners were on the scene in the 1840s. By 1847, one Philadelphia dry goods store had systematized and departmentalized its operations. A contemporary account described its layout:

> Each department of the store is alphabetically designated. The shelves and rows of goods in each department are numbered, and upon the tag attached to the goods is marked the letter of the department. . . . The proprietor's desk stands at the farther end of the store, raised on a platform facing the front, from which he can see all the operations in each section of the retail department. From this desk run tubes, connecting with each department of the store, from the garret to the cellar, so that if a person in any department, either porter, retail or wholesale clerk, wishes to communicate with the employer, he can do so without leaving his station.

Peddlers formed the third type of sellers of goods, after wholesalers and retail storekeepers. Serving regions in which the population was too sparse and dispersed to justify the operation of country stores, peddlers usually offered a wide range of goods for sale from wagons or from packs upon the backs of horses. Peddlers were numerous in the antebellum years: 10,699 in 1850, 16,594 ten years later. Wagon peddlers started each season with goods valued at $300 to $2,000 (about the same as the value of the goods in a small country store) and turned their stock in about three months. While most handled a variety of goods, some in more densely settled regions specialized in such products as tinware, clocks, spices, patent medicines, or hats. In the antebellum years an increasing proportion became manufacturers' representatives, working directly for early industrial companies. In 1828, for example, the Scovil Company of Waterbury, Connecticut, sent representatives into Ohio to peddle its brass buttons and other products. By the early twentieth century, few independent peddlers remained in the United States, as most were tied in one way or another to manufacturers.

In many other modernizing nations merchants and shopkeepers were also essential to economic growth. In Japan, large sedentary merchants in Kyoto, Edo (later Tokyo), and especially Osaka handled the nation's wholesale trades in rice, salt, and other agricultural staples by the 1600s and 1700s; and shopkeepers facilitated retail trade in smaller centers. Both the merchants (or more properly the merchant houses, for in Japan, even more than in America, these were family organizations) and the shopkeepers provided some of the capital needed for early industrialization; and, indeed, a few of the merchant houses such as the House of Mitsui moved into industrialization themselves. In Great Britain many increasingly specialized merchants took care of wholesale trade in agricultural and early industrial products (such as cotton goods) during the same period, with, again, smaller shopkeepers in local and regional centers handling the nation's retail trade. Peddlers were common in both Japan and Great Britain. However, merchants and, to some degree, even the smaller shopkeepers in England and Japan differed from their counterparts in colonial America and the early United States in two ways: first, because their nations had more fully developed financial and communications systems, they could specialize more than most of their counterparts in America; second, for cultural reasons, they lacked the relatively high status that American merchants and shopkeepers had in their communities, with this lack of status being particularly pronounced in Japan.

The Business of Farming

The United States was still mainly an agricultural nation in 1880, and most of the products entering into the nation's internal commerce and foreign trade — cotton, tobacco, wheat, and corn — came from the farm. Despite the beginnings of industry in the late colonial and antebellum years, agriculture remained more important than manufacturing to America's economic advance until the very late nineteenth century. In 1860, the value of the nation's corn, wheat, and hay crops surpassed the value added by manufacturing for all industries combined, and in the same year the value of the nation's farm lands and buildings was six times as great as the capital invested in all industries. On the eve of the Civil War, agriculture employed nearly three times as many people as manufacturing nationwide, and even in the industrializing Northeast farmers greatly outnumbered industrial workers. Only in the 1880s did the value added to goods by manufacturing come to éxceed the value of agricultural products in the United States.

For the most part, colonial and antebellum farming was commercial, not subsistence, agriculture. Even in the 1600s and 1700s most farmers were market-minded, and this orientation heightened in the early and mid-1800s. Only those lacking good transportation to markets lived a subsistence existence. Most agriculturalists ran their farms as small businesses. In only a few areas did large agricultural establishments exist; even in the cotton belt of the antebellum South, small farms, not large plantations, were the most common units of production.

Roughly 85 percent of colonial Americans were farmers, and the owner-occupied family farm was the typical unit of production (tenancy rates were much lower in colonial America than in other agricultural societies of the time). Often about 100 acres in size, the farms had only about 15 to 35 acres planted in crops, the remainder being in forest, pasture, or fallow land. Most colonial farmers engaged in diversified agriculture, raising enough food for their own personal needs but usually also producing for markets at home, in the Caribbean sugar islands, and in Europe. In the southern colonies the market production of such staples as rice, tobacco, and indigo was particularly pronounced, and large plantations based on slave labor did develop. Even in the southern colonies, however, small farms were common, and they too shipped to foreign markets. Farmers in the middle colonies produced surpluses of foodstuffs for export, and colonists from New England to North Carolina gathered forest products for the shipping industry.

The majority of colonial farmers were entrepreneurial in outlook, but most farmers sought economic gain less for themselves as individuals and more for their families. Most put the subsistence needs of their families and the long-run security of their farms ahead of short-run income maximization, but most aimed as well at a steady increase in their property holdings, whenever that was possible. They sought more than a comfortable status quo by clearing new lands, constructing barns and fences, building up livestock herds for later sale, and hiring workers to plant and harvest crops for the market. Massachusetts farmers, for instance, carefully considered the best markets in which to sell their produce, often traveling considerable distances, up to 150 miles, to make the most advantageous sales. Even many tenant farmers were entrepreneurially motivated. For many, tenancy was simply a temporary stage in their lives before they bought their own farms, and they invested a considerable share of their earnings in productive assets, such as slaves and livestock, before coming into possession of their own land.

Changes occurring abroad and within the United States reinforced the profit orientation of American farmers in the antebellum years. A growing European demand for American corn and wheat stimulated the expansion of agriculture in the northern states and pulled an increasing proportion of farmers into market production. Similarly, the expansion of urban markets inside the United States, increasingly linked by canals and railroads to the newly opened farm areas, further spurred commercial grain production. There can be little doubt that most antebellum agriculturalists sought profits from their farming. There was a strong positive correlation between the price of wheat and the sale of public land; when the price of wheat rose, more land was sold, as farmers strove to take advantage of profitable opportunities. By the late 1850s, farmers were raising a considerable crop surplus for sale in American cities and overseas. In 1859, the average midwestern farm grew enough food to support two other families, the average northeastern farm enough for one other family. In that same year, northern farms earned a 12 percent return on their capital investments — more than the 10 percent return then being earned in cotton production but less than the 25 percent return being made in manufacturing. In addition to these operating profits there were returns that could be earned from the sale of farm lands that appreciated in value. In *Democracy in America*, Alexis de Tocqueville observed the growing commercialization of farming, including the involvement of farmers in land speculation, in the early 1830s. "Almost all farmers," he noted, "combine some trade with agriculture; most of them make agriculture itself a trade. It seldom happens that an American farmer settles for good upon the land which he occupies; especially in the districts of the Far West, he brings the land into tillage in order to sell it again, and not to farm it."

At the center of antebellum agriculture in the United States lay the family farm. The expansion of farming, like the growth in trade, was based upon family enterprises. The family farm and family retail store marched across America in tandem. Agriculture based upon grain, in particular, boosted the growth of small family farms. Farm families who owned about 75 to 100 acres, or in some places even less, could produce successfully for the market. Plantation production was not advantageous, for there were few economies of scale. The improvements needed to increase grain and livestock output — such as putting more land into cultivation, laying out new pastures, and spreading manure — could be done adequately by farmers and their families in their off-seasons. Even in the South, as in colonial times, family farms remained important, as farms produced cash crops and foodstuffs for local consumption and long-distance trade. A dwindling proportion of antebellum farms were self-sufficient producers in remote areas. The per capita value of goods manufactured on the farm in America fell from $1.70 in 1840 to only $0.78 twenty years later. Instead of making items for their own use, farmers resorted to country stores where they purchased them. Writing in the early 1850s, the president of the New York Agricultural Society commented upon this trend, noting that the farmer "now sells for money, and it is in his interest to buy for money, every article that he cannot produce cheaper than he can buy. He cannot afford to make at home his clothing, the furniture or his farming utensils; he buys many articles for consumption for his table."

As farming became increasingly market-oriented, farmers became more and more rational in managing their farms as small businesses. While many continued to trust tradition, using almanacs and Benjamin Franklin's maxims to determine how they ran their farms, some began to think in terms of new methods. Farmers experimented with crop specialization, used horses rather than the slower oxen to work their lands, and in general made conscious choices about how to farm. A farm manual published in 1839 captured the growing stress being placed upon the necessity of running a farm along rational principles. "The business or management of a farm," the manual observed, "is a practice that demands constant care and attention, as well as much activity and judgment, to conduct it in a proper and advantageous manner."

Yet, while profits became the primary goal of American farmers, they were not the only goal. Farming, especially on family farms, was a way of life that provided psychic as well as monetary rewards. Americans remained on the farm when they could have earned greater returns on their capital in other fields of endeavor, such as small-scale manufacturing. Freedom and independence for themselves and their families, as embodied in the security of owning their own land and controlling their own supplies of food, motivated many northern farmers in particular. These values combined with ties to their families and communities to provide farmers with nonentrepreneurial reasons for leading their lives the way they did. Tradition, as well as rationality, lay behind the actions of many colonial and antebellum farmers. Similarly, most farmers saw no conflict between their individual commercial activities (including becoming consumers, as well as being producers for the market) and communal goals. In the Midwest, in particular, farmers did not see market participation as undermining rural solidarity. Farm institutions often encompassed both types of objectives. Such, for example, were the local buying and selling cooperatives set up by the Patrons of Husbandry (the Grange) in the 1870s. Through these institutions, farmers sold their produce as members of groups and likewise bought supplies jointly. The local Grange cooperatives provided farmers with a way to pursue communal morality—they cut out middlemen handling products for farmers at what farmers saw as immoral private profits—while, at the same time allowing farmers to increase their individual profits. Organizational and managerial problems, however, combined with competition from expanding private wholesalers and retailers to undercut the cooperatives, and many failed in the late nineteenth century.

Artisans and Early-Day Manufacturing

Although the United States was still primarily an agricultural nation at the time of the Civil War and for several decades after it, industrialization was beginning to reshape the economic and social contours of the land. Some industry existed in colonial times, but it developed more rapidly after independence was achieved from Great Britain. During the nineteenth century, small businesses were as important as large enterprises in bringing industrialization to America. In the colonial period skilled artisans operated as small business people, producing and selling a vast array of wood, metal, and leather goods. In the antebellum years artisan production continued, and many artisans made the transition to industrial production, setting up firms using new sources of power and production methods. Although some large industrial businesses began to develop in antebellum America, as late as 1870 or 1880 the most typical sort of manufacturing company remained the small firm. Like farms and stores, most of these manufacturing ventures continued to be run as family businesses.

Artisans plying their trades in shops they owned supplied colonists with a wide variety of handicraft goods. Composing about 10 percent of all of the white workers in colonial times, artisans included coopers (barrel makers), tailors, shoemakers, carpenters, tinsmiths, and silversmiths. Many artisans owned their tools and shops, maintained inventories of raw materials and goods-in-process, and handled their own accounts. In short, they operated as small business people. The most successful also often owned a few acres of farm land, and many possessed a few head of livestock. Like country storekeepers, most ran their businesses as single-owner proprietorships, but a few operated them with others in partnership arrangements.

The situation of artisans in pre-Revolutionary Charleston, South Carolina, was probably typical of that in most colonial cities. In Charleston there were two groups of artisans: those who owned their own shops and those who did not. Carpenters, bricklayers, carvers, joiners, and tinsmiths usually did not possess their own shops. However, a large number of saddlers, cabinetmakers, shoemakers, and others did and operated as small business people, fashioning their own wares for sale in their own shops. The second group of artisans often ran their businesses by themselves, but sometimes took in partners to secure needed capital or skills. While all of these businesses were small enterprises (all were single-unit businesses without managerial hierarchies), some became large by colonial standards. In fact, as they became larger and more complex, newspapers carried advertisements offering to bring the account books of artisans as well as those of merchants up to date.

As in farming and shopkeeping, more was involved in the work and lives of artisans than a quest for profits. A concern for family and community matters was also present. The family nature of colonial artisanship was clearest in the practice of apprenticeship. Carried over from the Old World to the New, apprenticeship was widespread until the 1840s. Young boys and girls left their families to live with another family, usually at around twelve years of age. In their new family the head of the household taught the young person farming or a craft (in the case of a girl, cooking and household management). Artisans were expected to initiate their apprentices into all aspects of the "mysteries" of their crafts. In return, apprentices worked for their masters for five to seven years with no pay (the master usually provided his apprentices with new clothes each year, and many apprentices took their meals with the families of their masters). The apprentice system was more than an economic system, for it had social ramifications as well. Masters had a great deal of authority over their apprentices and were expected to insure that they received a basic education and moral and religious training.

While artisans produced a wide range of articles for sale in the colonies, industrial production really began only in the nineteenth century. Industrialization is usually taken to mean the substitution of water and steam power for human and animal power, the increased use of machinery in making products, and the gathering of workforces in central locations called factories. These changes did not necessarily occur simultaneously, however. In some fields, for instance, nonmechanized factories replaced workshops well before new sources of power were tapped. Moving from scattered beginnings, industrialization grew in importance in the mid-nineteenth century. Between 1810 and 1860, the value of manufactured goods produced in the United States rose tenfold, from $200 million to $2 billion. In the same time period, the amount of capital invested in manufacturing facilities increased still more rapidly, from $50 million to $1 billion — signaling that industrialization would spread still more after the Civil War.

Merchants and storekeepers were instrumental in bringing industrial enterprise to America. Using surplus funds earned in trade, the large sedentary merchants of the eastern seaboard financed early industrial projects and were also important in importing the necessary new technologies into the United States. The Rhode Island merchant Moses Brown worked with the British artisan Samuel Slater to establish the first successful cotton textile mill in America in the 1790s. The Boston merchant Francis Cabot Lowell and his friends, calling themselves the Boston Associates, built the nation's first fully integrated cotton textile mills in Waltham, Massachusetts, just after the War of 1812. Operating on a smaller scale, country storekeepers played significant roles in their communities; as small capitalists, they often invested in gristmills, iron forges, fulling mills, distilleries, and so forth.

Artisans were as important as merchants and storekeepers in the industrialization of the United States. While some craft-oriented artisans found themselves unable to compete with businesses using new production methods and left their trade, others made the transition to industrial production. The careers of both individual artisans in specific fields of endeavor, such as Jonas Chickering in piano making in Boston, and groups of craftsmen in particular locales, such as those in the Connecticut Valley and Newark, New Jersey, illustrate how artisans successfully entered and shaped the new industrial world.

Jonas Chickering's career was typical of those artisans who became early-day industrialists. Chickering began as an artisan in Boston. After working in the establishments of several piano makers, he broke away to form his own firm in 1826. Like many artisans moving into industry, Chickering initially depended on the capital and marketing skills of a merchant to help him get started, but within a decade he bought out the merchant's interest and thereafter ran his business as a sole proprietorship, doing so until his death in 1853. An aggressive entrepreneur, Chickering used advertising and business agents to expand his sales beyond Boston to much of America. Chickering transformed piano making from a craft to an industrial operation by building a manufacturing plant that in 1850 employed 100 men to turn out over 1,000 pianos worth $200,000. Within this factory, work was divided into different tasks. There were twenty different departments, each devoted to a different manufacturing process. Outside the factory an additional 100 men prepared the wood and cast-iron frames going into the pianos. Although Chickering set up the first modern production works in the American piano industry, he remained something of a craftsman at heart. Older ways of thinking and acting died hard. Chickering personally checked the quality of each piano before it was sold and continued to spend much of his time on the shop floor rather than in his office. He knew his workers by name, and those workers turned out in large numbers for his funeral.

In some communities groups of artisans came to specialize in one form of manufacturing, a situation that developed in the Connecticut Valley. There many craftsmen went into the industrial production of cutlery. The inventiveness of its artisans in acquiring capital, making technical innovations in the production process, and opening transportation links to markets was a key factor in the development of the industry. Strictly a handicraft operation in the 1820s and 1830s, cutlery making became over the following three decades an industry that relied upon steam-powered machinery to turn out an ever more specialized assortment of knives. No single company emerged to dominate the industry, which continued to be controlled by a group of small businesses into the mid-twentieth century.

By remaining flexible in their production techniques and adjusting their products to take advantage of market niches, the cutlery companies in the Connecticut Valley continued as industry leaders in the United States until after the Second World War. Even as something approaching mass production began, a concern for craftsmanship lingered. Most of the firms, though now organized as corporations, remained closely held family businesses. Their owner-managers continued to be more interested in producing high quality goods than in increasing profits. They also remained closely identified with their communities, in which they were commonly recognized as social and political leaders.

In still other localities large numbers of artisans in a broad range of crafts made the transition to industrialization. One such place was Newark, New Jersey, America's leading industrial city in 1860. There artisans making shoes, saddles, jewelry, trunks, leather goods, and hats transformed their lines of work from craft to industrial production in the mid-nineteenth century. Well-educated by the standards of their day and innovative and flexible in their outlook toward business, these artisans — like their counterparts in the Connecticut Valley — sought and obtained the capital needed to transform their shops into small factories and opened new markets for their products. Possessing a high sense of self-worth and joined together by cooperative institutions — such as the Newark Mechanics Association for Mutual Improvement in the Arts and Sciences, formed in 1828 by 114 craftsmen, and the Mechanics Bank of Newark, many of whose directors were craftsmen — the artisans looked to the future, not the past, for inspiration. Far from opposing mechanization, Newark's artisans embraced and controlled it. In 1840, no factory in Newark used steam power; just six years later more than 100 did.

It was artisans who brought industrialization and the beginnings of big business to Newark. By 1860, some twenty-two firms in the six fields mentioned above possessed capital of at least $50,000 and employed 100 or more people, making them large businesses by the standards of the time; three-fifths of these had started as artisans' workshops. Despite the growth in the size of their enterprises, most of Newark's artisans-turned-industrialists remained faithful to many of their older values. Like family farmers, they continued to honor hard work, thrift, and independence; and they continued to value their work because they saw it as being useful to society.

The cutlery making of the Connecticut Valley and the more generalized industrialization that occurred in Newark were early-day examples of the importance of industrial districts in the economic development of the United States. Over the course of the nineteenth century, many industrial districts would grow up in America. In them small, medium-sized, and large companies turned out a plethora of industrial goods. The companies in the districts competed with each other in making and selling goods, but they also often cooperated — sometimes sharing machinery, workers, and sales agents. Financial and educational institutions sometimes lent a certain amount of cohesion to the districts, which, more often than not, were organized around the production of one type of good.

As was often the case in economic matters, American developments in the growth of early-day industrial districts resembled those in Europe. In European districts, skilled workers, many of whom had often previously labored as artisans, used flexible machinery to produce a variety of goods. Eschewing mass-production methods, they provided a link between older and newer production methods. Industrialization in both Europe and America was achieved as much by incremental as epochal changes. Well-informed about competitors in other areas, they chose production methods designed to work best in their regions, leading to the creation of long-lived industrial districts populated by firms of many sizes, but especially by small and medium-sized ones.

Two examples clarify the meaning of these industrial districts. For instance, a silk-making region developed around Lyons, France, in the late 1600s and early 1700s. Small firms turned out a wide variety of silk goods, such as silk ribbons and fabrics, in small production runs. Designed to capture the latest fashions, the ribbon styles changed often, at least once a year, a situation that made mass production by large firms impractical. The high quality of their fabrics and their product differentiation gave the Lyons firms a competitive edge that lasted for decades. Another example of an early-day industrial district was the Solingen cutlery making area in the lower Rhineland of Germany. Similar to the cutlery district of the Connecticut Valley in America, the Solingen region featured many small, specialized firms that used flexible production methods, not mass-production techniques, to turn out a variety of knives and other items. From origins in the late 1700s, this district grew in importance until it produced over 80 percent of the cutlery made in the German empire at the time of World War I. Of the 18,000 people employed in the industrial region in 1907, only 7,000 were typical factory workers; the remaining 11,000 were either semi-independent outworkers or artisans laboring in their own workshops. One secret to the success of the Solingen district lay in the willingness of its firms to produce cutlery in very small production runs. Made possible by the intelligence and imagination of its skilled artisans, this mode of operation was especially important in developing new grinding methods for the finishing of forged knife blades. It was only due to a decrease in the number of skilled workers after World War I that the Solingen district went into decline.

Since many of the industrial businesses of the United States had their origins in the workshops of artisans, it is not surprising to find that as late as 1870 small businesses dominated the industrial landscape of the nation. Although average plant output rose dramatically in a few industries in the antebellum years, in most manufacturing fields production figures rose more slowly. For example, in cotton textile production the median

TABLE ONE. Number of Employees per Northeastern
Manufacturing Firm, 1820 and 1850

Manufactured Good	1820	1850
Boots and shoes	19	37
Cotton textiles	35	98
Flour and grist milling	2	2
Glass making	57	65
Hat making	8	17
Iron making	20	24
Liquor distilling	3	5
Paper making	14	22
Tanning	4	4
Wool and mixed textiles	11	25

Source: Kenneth L. Sokoloff, "Was the Transition from the Artisan Shop to the Nonmechanized Factory Associated with Gains in Efficiency?: Evidence from the U.S. Manufacturing Censuses of 1820 and 1850," *Explorations in Economic History* 21 (October 1984): 354.

plant output jumped from $5,000 in 1820 to nearly $100,000 fifty years later, and in iron production it soared from just $2,000 to over $200,000 during the same period. In most other leading American industries, however, increases in plant size occurred more gradually. The median output of flour mills rose from $4,500 in 1820 to $6,300 in 1870, and the figures for lumber mills were $590 and $2,200. The median output of boot-making establishments actually fell, from $3,100 in 1820 to only $2,300 fifty years later (see Table 1).

Average plant size remained small, because in most industrial fields the establishment of many small plants offset the growth of a few large ones. In the antebellum years and for a few years immediately after the Civil War, small plants generally held their own with large ones in manufacturing. In most industrial fields in these years, large plant size was generally not needed to obtain full economies of scale. Only in the 1880s and later, as we shall see in Chapter 2, did production breakthroughs and other events occur to spur decisively the growth of big businesses in manufacturing. Even then, small firms, often linked in industrial districts, continued to perform very well in certain fields.

Service Businesses

Service businesses developed concurrently with the growth of farming, trading, and manufacturing enterprises. Banks, insurance companies, and credit-rating businesses were not latecomers to the business scene; their evolution was an essential part of the growth of the business systems of colonial America and the antebellum United States. In fact, service businesses have been important worldwide in stimulating and facilitating production for the market, helping developing nations make the transition from subsistence to commercial economies. Service business became increasingly important to the American economy from the 1840s onward, and, as in other forms of American business endeavor before the Civil War, the service industries were a home of small firms.

Banking had existed in a very informal manner in the colonial period, as merchants and storekeepers loaned funds to each other and to other members of their communities. Robert Morris, a merchant in charge of the finances for the newly formed federal government, set up the first bank in America, when he established the Bank of North America in Philadelphia in 1781 to provide credit services for the government and for merchants. More banks soon followed, often established by merchants seeking profitable forms of business specialization. In addition to commercial banks, the first savings banks and investment banking houses were established. Savings bank deposits totaled $1 million by 1820, but amounted to ten times as much just fifteen years later. Investment bankers began dealing in railroad securities in the 1850s, branching out to the stocks and bonds of industrial enterprises at a later date.

As in banking, merchants were active in developing the field of insurance. Colonial merchants shared risks by operating through partnerships that owned ships and their cargoes on ocean voyages. The merchant Thomas Willing formed the first insurance company in North America in 1757, and by 1807 some forty companies had been set up to insure ships and their cargoes. Fire and life insurance enterprises also grew up in the antebellum period; by 1860 eighty-one general insurance companies, many of which wrote fire insurance, and forty-three life insurance companies were doing business. Merchants were also instrumental in forming the first credit-rating agencies—made necessary by the geographic expansion of the economy, which made it impossible for business people to know personally who were good and poor credit risks on the farms and in the towns springing up across the nation. By 1858, one agency had branches in seventeen cities.

While a handful of credit-rating agencies developed into multi-unit enterprises in the antebellum years, most service businesses did not. Nearly all operated in just one locale, and the vast majority—like most stores, farms, and industrial ventures—were run as family enterprises. Nowhere was this clearer than in banking.

Most antebellum banks, at least in New England, functioned not so much as modern commercial banks, but more as the financial arms of extended kinship groups. Family-controlled banks raised funds through deposits and the sale of stock in their banks to the public; the families, however, retained a controlling share of the ownership of the banks for themselves. The banks then loaned the bulk of their resources to family insiders who, in turn, invested them in their industrial or trading ventures. Whether the banks were privately held or incorporated, the longevity of family control was often great. The Brown, Ives, and Goddard families controlled the Providence Bank from 1791 to 1926; and the Richmond, Chapin, and Taft families dominated the Merchants Bank of Providence from 1818 to 1926. Like their modern counterparts, these family-controlled banks channeled surplus funds in their communities into profitable investment opportunities. In doing so, they successfully adapted traditional ways of doing business—the reliance upon family ties—to new needs.

The only commercial banks to develop any real hierarchical management were the two nationally chartered institutions, the First (1792–1812) and Second (1816–1836) Banks of the United States. Headquartered in Philadelphia, the Banks of the United States had branches in major cities across the nation, eight in the case of the First and twenty-five in the case of the Second. But, the fate of these large banks was sealed when President Andrew Jackson vetoed the rechartering of the Second Bank in 1836. Contrary to the situation in most other nations, where banking normally became oligopolistic in character, banking in America remained atomized. By 1840, there were 901 banks in the United States; by 1860, 1,562; in 1880, 3,355. With few economies of scale adhering to larger banks, banking was conducted as small business everywhere except in the largest cities, such as New York. In addition, America's legal system—the lack of any federal laws that encouraged national banking and the existence of state laws that made interstate banking difficult—contributed to the spread of small, independent banks.

Women in Business

Women were active in nearly all types of preindustrial business in America —as artisans, farmers, and traders—and these businesses were predominantly small ones. Perhaps 10 to 25 percent of women were engaged in entrepreneurship. If involvement in bartering and market farming are added in, the number of women engaged in economic activity may have nearly equaled the number of men. For women, even more than for men, business was largely a family affair. In fact, the legal systems within which they operated assumed that women were dependents of men rather than independent economic or social actors. Those women who succeeded in business as merchants, storekeepers, and artisans rarely did so as individuals on their own, but more commonly as deputy husbands. That is, they took the places of their husbands in business when the husbands were out of town, were disabled, or died. Small shops, inns, and restaurants were especially attractive businesses for women. Perhaps half of all Anglo-American retailers were women. Less commonly, the role of deputy husband carried over into early-day manufacturing. For example, Rebecca Lukens took over the management of her husband's iron mill upon his death in 1825, expanding its operations and laying the foundations for Lukens Steel.

The expansion of a commercial economy and the beginnings of industrialization had a mixed impact on business opportunities for antebellum women. The increased consumption of luxury goods widened possibilities for women artisans—as, for example, more opportunities arose in the millinery (hat-making) and dressmaking trades—and the growth of cities created new opportunities for women as small-scale traders and shop owners. More generally, the increase in incomes and thus in the purchasing power of Americans called forth the creation of many small retail and service businesses, some of which were run by women entrepreneurs. Nor was this situation limited to America. In northern France, for example, economic growth due to industrialization raised incomes enough in the 1800s to create petty business opportunities for women from the lower-middle class and working classes, and they responded by establishing a wide variety of small shops. Changes in state laws across America also favored women as independent actors in some ways, especially by permitting wives to own some property separately from their husbands.

Yet, at the same time, a "cult of domesticity" arose in the United States and parts of Europe, especially in the growing white middle class. According to this idea, women were to be homemakers, that is, mothers and dutiful wives. Their sphere would be the private one of family activity. By contrast, men were to occupy the public sphere of business and politics. While the line between public and private was always fluid, this new concept may have limited women's engagement in business. Just how much this idea limited the business world for women is a matter of debate. It certainly applied more to women of the middle classes than to those of the working classes. Women continued to move ahead mainly in businesses related to their roles as housekeepers and wives—such as food preparation, textile making, and children's clothing. Only a handful, like Rebecca Lukens, came to own factories in heavy industry. Moreover, as market expansion increased the profit potentials of some industries—such as cheese making, shoemaking, and the production of textiles—women sometimes found themselves shouldered aside by better-financed and better-connected male entrepreneurs.

African Americans in Business

Slaves and free blacks developed businesses that paralleled those of mainstream white enterprises. For blacks, as for nearly all Americans before 1880, business participation meant involvement in small business. By 1860, there were about 500,000 free blacks living in the United States, slightly more than half of them in the South. Free blacks established 5,000 businesses nationwide, making their participation rate in business about 1 percent. In addition, about 3 percent of the South's black slaves were self-hired bondsmen and women, meaning that they, too, participated in business enterprises—often as self-employed business proprietors and owners, such as peddlers and market women. Taken together, the slave and free black participation rate in business was higher in 1860 than the black participation rate in business in 1987. Only racism, which made raising capital especially difficult, kept African Americans from developing even more businesses in the United States than they did.

That blacks were active in business should come as no surprise. Most blacks brought to the United States as slaves came from regions of Africa with a strong business culture. Blacks sold into slavery from West and West Central Africa came from areas with well-established market economies in which black men and women had long worked as artisans, merchants, and entrepreneurs. Trade existed at local, regional, and international levels and was often overseen by fairly sophisticated trading guilds. Economic activity was both individually and communally based, with profit making typically involving kinship and community groups—similar, especially, to what we have seen in antebellum American farming. Not surprisingly, blacks—when circumstances allowed—engaged in a variety of business activities in colonial America and in the antebellum United States.

In colonial America, free blacks owned property (occasionally including slaves), established craft enterprises, and opened small stores. The lack of capital and the social barriers arising from racism kept them from owning large plantations, involving themselves in the transatlantic slave trade, and working as large city merchants. Slaves sometimes were able to grow and sell agricultural produce and to work as artisans (with most of the proceeds going to their masters). Both free blacks and slaves were especially active as food vendors, sometimes using their profits to purchase or rent dwellings that served as restaurants or taverns. The drayage business (that is, moving goods by cart) was also attractive. In all of these enterprises, success depended in part on family ties and networks, which provided credit and labor, and on having access to white markets. All-black markets at this time usually were too small in terms of purchasing power to support black businesses by themselves.

In the antebellum years, black business people built on what they had established earlier. Some slaves continued to hire their own time from their masters to allow them to work as craftsmen in urban enterprises that they or others created. Others established personal-service businesses such as barbershops and bathhouses. Food services and drayage continued to attract black business involvement. Still others, although far fewer, acted as "intrapreneurs," captaining ships and running plantations owned by their masters. Free blacks greatly expanded their involvement in business during the early and mid-1800s, paralleling the growing diversity of American business in general. Like slaves, free blacks worked as artisans. Free blacks were also active in the formation of catering businesses, restaurants, and hotels. Barbershops, tailor shops, and dress shops attracted considerable black business attention. As in the colonial period, these establishments catered primarily to white customers, for blacks alone lacked the purchasing power to support them. Black mutual aid societies formed insurance and banking institutions, which catered mainly to blacks. Lacking capital, few blacks owned factories, large plantations, or internationally oriented merchant houses. As before, they found their opportunities in smaller businesses.

Nor did this situation change much in the half century after the Civil War. Mutual aid societies developed more banks, saving and loans institutions, and insurance companies. Craft enterprises, small stores, and service businesses such as hotels and restaurants continued to win the attention of blacks looking for business opportunities. In the West, some blacks, like their white counterparts, engaged in town formation as a way to earn profits, with black towns springing up especially on the southern Great Plains. On the other hand, at a time when some whites were moving into the creation of large manufacturing businesses, no blacks succeeded in doing so, for they lacked the necessary capital and, moreover, had little experience in the management of such enterprises. Like their white counterparts, black entrepreneurs often used inherited wealth, connections, and apprenticeships in family enterprises to get ahead. As before, black efforts in small business paralleled those of whites.

Toward a Business Ideology

The United States has developed as a nation with a business culture, and business people have generally been admired and looked up to as leaders in American society. As we have seen, many colonists were eager participants in the expanding commercial economy of the British Empire, and the economic growth of the nineteenth century brought still more Americans into the commercial arena. Country storekeepers, farmers, artisan-industrialists, and bankers all sought material gain. De Tocqueville was struck by this orientation of most Americans during his travels in the early 1830s. "Fortunes, opinions, and laws are in ceaseless variation," he found. The only constant in the new United States was the quest for wealth. "The love of wealth," De Tocqueville concluded, "is therefore to be traced, either as a principal or accessory motive, at the bottom of all that Americans do: this gives to all their passions a sort of family likeness."

The embrace of business by Americans contrasts with the attitudes of people in many other nations. In Great Britain, the first nation to industrialize, business people, especially manufacturers, never achieved the level of acceptance won by their counterparts in the United States. Even as Great Britain industrialized, something of an antibusiness bias lingered from feudal times and may have been reinvigorated in the late nineteenth century. As late as 1927, Samuel Courtauld, whose company was a leading producer of textiles, denounced the profit motive that he associated with the American way of life. "I view the so-called 'Americanization of Europe' with the utmost dislike," he observed. "I doubt whether American ideals of living—purely materialistic as they are—will finally lead to a contented working nation anywhere when the excitement of constant expansion has come to an end." In Japan, the first Asian nation to modernize its economy, business people were long held in low repute because they were seen as seeking private profits, not service to society, as their goal. As the head of the Mitsui Trading Company noted with dismay in 1900, "Men of commerce and industry . . . are not the equal of other classes in social prestige."

Relatively little such antibusiness feeling existed in America. In the colonial period the large sedentary merchants played important social and political roles, sitting on boards of selectmen (city councils), serving as members of colonial legislatures, and acting as advisers to governors. As respected members of their communities, country storekeepers played many of the same roles in the antebellum years. Usually older than the farmers of the surrounding countryside, the storekeepers were accepted as leaders in their communities. Many were deeply involved in politics, often rising from a humble office such as hogreeve, a village official charged with keeping hogs off streets and other common ground, to become a member of the state legislature. About one-quarter of the storekeepers in the antebellum Midwest held some type of political office at one time or another. Storekeepers were also often leaders in church, school, militia, and lodge affairs. John Jones, the Missouri trader, summarized well the importance of the storekeeper to his community: "He is the general *locum tenens*, the agent of everybody, and familiar with every transaction in his neighborhood. He is a counselor without license, and yet is invariably consulted, not only in matters of business, but in domestic affairs." Of course, resentment against shopkeepers occasionally surfaced, when prices paid for farm goods dipped or when merchants raised the prices of their items, but, more than in many nations, merchants had the respect of their compatriots.

There was more to the acceptance of business by Americans than simply a desire to get ahead economically. While most Americans were by choice actively engaged in business activities for commercial purposes, nonmonetary motivations also prompted them. They thought they saw in their businesses a way to achieve or maintain personal independence, security for their families, and strong social ties to their local communities. Throughout the antebellum years and later, a desire for individual advancement through entrepreneurial activities coexisted in a sometimes uneasy alliance with a search for personal and family security.

As we have seen, most colonial and antebellum businesses operated as family enterprises, in which short-term profit maximization often took second place to the long-term goal of family survival and advancement. Moreover, especially through the colonial period, but even into the antebellum years, business people normally got ahead less as individuals and more as members of families. Thus, Thomas Hancock, the Boston merchant, ran his trading firm as the House of Hancock. In these family businesses, management succession was often limited to children or other close relatives. Some aspects of the family nature of business began eroding in the antebellum years. The spread of mechanization in manufacturing destroyed the apprentice system, for example, by devaluing skilled labor. Nonetheless, the family nature of many small businesses persisted into the late twentieth century.

Even as farmers, artisans, and other business people sought upward mobility and family security through business success, they hoped to gain other rewards as well. Beyond economic matters, many Americans adhered to the notion that it was only upon a base of widespread property holdings that a framework of political freedom and morality could stand. And, in fact, there was more economic equality in the United States, at least in the North, before the rise of big business than after. Although he was writing specifically about farmers in his *Notes on the State of Virginia* in the 1780s, Thomas Jefferson provided a classic statement on the value of free enterprise for the inculcation of morality, a notion that small business people would return to time and again in the nineteenth and twentieth centuries, despite vastly changed economic circumstances. "Those who labor in the earth are the chosen people of God," wrote Jefferson, "if ever he had a chosen people, whose breasts he has made his peculiar deposit for substantial and genuine virtue." Jefferson observed further, "Corruption of morals in the mass of cultivators is a phaenomenon [*sic*] of which no age nor nation has furnished an example. It is the mark set on those, who not looking up to heaven, to their own soil and industry, as does the husbandman, for their subsistence, depend for it on the casualties and caprice of customers." Jefferson concluded that "Dependance [*sic*] begets subservience and venality, suffocates the germ of virtue, and prepares fit tools for the designs of ambition."

Small Business by the Time of the American Civil War

The idea that morality and freedom were somehow associated with the flourishing of many independent business enterprises — in Jefferson's case, family farms — would animate much of American life and thought over the next 200 years. Over time, notions of independence would become identified in the minds of many Americans with the ownership of small business units. This situation developed even as economic realities changed.

The business systems of colonial America and the antebellum United States evolved as congeries of small businesses. A tremendous amount of economic growth took place between the time of the founding of the first permanent British colony in North America at Jamestown in 1607 and the beginning of the American Civil War in 1861; but, with just a handful of exceptions, few big businesses arose during these years. With the conflict of the Civil War behind them and with technological and market restrictions lifting, Americans would develop a large number of big businesses in the late nineteenth and early twentieth centuries, as we shall see in Chapter 2. Nonetheless, it was in that time period that the general business ideology of earlier years was transformed into an ideology that specifically glorified the small firm and small business person. Nor, as Chapter 2 also shows, did small business disappear during the late nineteenth and early twentieth centuries. To the contrary, small firms increased in absolute numbers, as economic growth continued. Even in manufacturing, many small businesses prospered — some on their own, some as members of industrial districts that mushroomed across the nation.

Additional Reading

Several works provide solid overviews of business and economic change before 1880. Marc Engal, *New World Economies: The Growth of the Thirteen Colonies and Early Canada* (New York: Oxford University Press, 1998); Robert Gallman and John Wells, eds., *American Economic Growth and Standards of Living before the Civil War* (Chicago: University of Chicago Press, 1992); John McCusker and Russell Menard, *The Economy of British America, 1607–1789* (Chapel Hill: University of North Carolina Press, 1985); and Edwin Perkins, *The Economy of Colonial America*, 2d ed. (New York: Columbia University Press, 1987), explore colonial developments. Thomas Doerflinger, *A Vigorous Spirit of Enterprise: Merchants and Economic Development in Revolutionary Philadelphia* (Chapel Hill: University of North Carolina Press, 1986); and Margaret Newell, *From Dependency to Independence: Economic Revolution in Colonial New England* (Ithaca: Cornell University Press, 1998), are valuable regional accounts. Good places to start in understanding economic changes in the antebellum years are Thomas Cochran, *Frontiers of Change: Early Industrialism in America* (New York: Oxford University Press, 1981); Walter Licht, *Industrializing America: The Nineteenth Century* (Baltimore: Johns Hopkins University Press, 1995); and Charles Sellers, *The Market Revolution: Jacksonian America, 1815–1846* (New

York: Oxford University Press, 1991). Francois Weil, "Capitalism and Industrialism in New England, 1815–1845," *Journal of American History* 84 (March 1998): 1334–54, is also useful.

Luke Shortfield, *The Western Merchant: A Narrative* (Philadelphia: Grigg, Elliot, 1849), which includes the accounts of John Beauchamp Jones, is a valuable firsthand account of what it meant to be an early-day storekeeper. Scholarly accounts of country stores and the roles they played in economic development include Lewis Atherton, "The Pioneer Merchant in Mid-America," *University of Missouri Studies* 14 (April 1, 1939): 1–135; Lewis Atherton, *The Southern Country Store, 1800–1860* (Baton Rouge: Louisiana State University Press, 1949); Gerald Carson, *The Old Country Store* (New York: Oxford University Press, 1954); Fred Mitchell Jones, "Middlemen in the Domestic Trade of the United States, 1800–1860," *Illinois University Studies in the Social Sciences* 21 (1937): 9–81 (the source for the quotations about country stores and department stores); and Fred Mitchell Jones, "Retail Stores in the United States, 1800–1860," *Journal of Marketing* 1 (October 1936): 134–42. The activities of peddlers may be followed in J. R. Dolan, *The Yankee Peddlers of Early America* (New York: Bramhall, 1964); and David Jaffee, "Peddlers of Progress and the Transformation of the Rural North, 1760–1860," *Journal of American History* 78 (September 1991): 511–36.

Considerable debate has developed about just how entrepreneurial and market-oriented colonial and antebellum farmers actually were. On this topic, see especially Jeremy Atack and Fred Bateman, *To Their Own Soil: Agriculture in the Antebellum North* (Ames: Iowa State University Press, 1987); Joyce Appleby, "Commercial Farming and the 'Agrarian Myth' in the Early Republic," *Journal of American History* 68 (March 1982); Martin Bruegel, "Unrest: Manorial Society and the Market in the Hudson Valley, 1780–1850," *Journal of American History* 82 (March 1996): 1393–1424; Steven Hahn and Jonathan Prude, eds., *The Countryside in the Age of Capitalist Transformation: Essays in the Social History of Rural America* (Chapel Hill: University of North Carolina Press, 1985); Allan Kulikoff, *The Agrarian Origins of American Capitalism* (Charlottesville: University Press of Virginia, 1992); Edwin Perkins, "The Entrepreneurial Spirit in Colonial America: The Foundations of Modern Business History," *Business History Review* 63 (Spring 1989): 160–86; and Winifred Rothenberg, *From Market-Places to a Market Economy: The Transformation of Rural Massachusetts, 1750–1850* (Chicago: University of Chicago Press, 1992). David Blanke, *Sowing the American Dream: How Consumer Culture Took Root in the Rural Midwest*

(Athens: Ohio University Press, 2000), shows how midwestern farmers were able to reconcile desires for both moral and commercial economies.

On the roles of artisans in early-day social and economic change, see especially Gary Kornblith, "The Craftsman as Industrialist: Jonas Chickering and the Transformation of American Piano Making," *Business History Review* 59 (Autumn 1985): 349–68; Howard Rock, Paul A. Gilje, and Robert Asher, eds., *American Artisans: Crafting Social Identity, 1750–1850* (Baltimore: Johns Hopkins University Press, 1995); W. J. Rorabaugh, *The Craft Apprentice: From Franklin to the Machine Age in America* (New York: Oxford University Press, 1986); Martha Taber, "A History of the Cutlery Industry in the Connecticut Valley," *Smith College Studies in History* 41 (1955): 1–135; and Sean Wilentz, *Chants Democratic: New York City and the Rise of the American Working Class, 1778–1850* (New York: Oxford University Press, 1984). On the role of small firms in early industrialization, see Jeremy Atack, "Firm Size and Industrial Structure in the United States during the Nineteenth Century," *Journal of Economic History* 46 (June 1986): 463–75; and Kenneth Sokoloff, "Was the Transition from the Artisan Shop to the Non-mechanized Factory Associated with Gains in Efficiency? Evidence from the U.S. Manufacturing Censuses of 1820 and 1850," *Explorations in Economic History* 21 (October 1984): 351–82. The essays comprising Charles Sabel and Jonathan Zeitlin, eds., *World of Possibilities: Flexibility and Mass Production in Western Industrialization* (Cambridge, Eng.: Cambridge University Press, 1997), examine the formation of industrial districts; essays by Carlo Poni and Alain Cottereau look at Lyons, and one by Rudolf Bock examines Solingen. On the important, if underpaid, roles played by women in Lyons, see Daryl Hafter, "Women in the Underground Business of Eighteenth-Century Lyons," *Enterprise & Society* 2 (March 2001): 11–40.

Naomi Lamoreaux, *Insider Lending: Banks, Personal Connections, and Economic Development in Industrial New England* (New York: Cambridge University Press, 1994); and Edwin J. Perkins, *American Public Finance and Financial Services, 1700–1815* (Columbus: Ohio State University Press, 1994), offer solid introductions to the nature of early American banking. On the development of credit reporting, see James Madison, "The Evolution of Credit Reporting Agencies in Nineteenth-Century America," *Business History Review* 48 (Summer 1974): 164–86.

On the roles women played in business developments, see Angel Kwolek-Folland, *Incorporating Women* (New York: Twayne, 1998), and the following studies: Caroline Bird, *Enterprising Women* (New York: W. W. Norton, 1976); Beatrice Craig, "*Petites Bourgeoises* and Penny Capitalists: Women in Retail in the Lille Area during the Nineteenth Century," *Enterprise & Society* 2 (June 2001): 198–224; Wendy Gamber, "A Gendered Enterprise: Placing Nineteenth Century Businesswomen in History," *Business History Review* 72 (Summer 1998)): 188–218; and Laurel Ulrich, *Good Wives: Images and Reality in the Lives of Women in Northern New England, 1650–1750* (New York: Knopf, 1980). Julie Winch, "'A Person of Good Character and Considerable Property': James Forten and the Issue of Race in Philadelphia's Antebellum Business Community," *Business History Review* 75 (Summer 2001): 261–96; Loren Schweninger, "Prosperous Blacks in the South, 1790–1880," *American Historical Review* 95 (February 1990): 31–56; John Ingham, "African-American Business Leaders in the South, 1810–1945: Business Success, Community Leadership, and Racist Protest," *Business and Economic History* 22 (Fall 1993): 262–72; and Juliet E. K. Walker, *The History of Black Business in America* (New York: Twayne, 1998), examine the many roles blacks played in American business. Small businesses, such as storekeeping, sometimes offered avenues for advancement to Jews. See Rowena Olegario, "'That Mysterious People': Jewish Merchants, Transparency, and Community in Mid-Nineteenth Century America," *Business History Review* 73 (Summer 1999): 161–89; and Stella Suberman, *The Jew Store* (Chapel Hill, N.C.: Algonquin, 2001), a firsthand account by the daughter of a Jewish storekeeper in the South during the 1920s. Andrew Godley, *Jewish Immigrant Entrepreneurship in New York and London, 1880–1914: Enterprise and Culture* (New York: Palgrave, 2001), is comparative.

2

Small Business in the Age of Giant Enterprise, 1880–1920

From the 1880s onward, big businesses arose in America, especially in some forms of manufacturing, and small businesses, although continuing to increase in absolute numbers, declined in their relative importance to the American economy. One indication of this shift is that although the number of self-employed Americans rose from 1.2 million in 1880 to 2.6 million in 1920, the percentage of the nation's workforce who were self-employed fell from 8 percent to only 6.5 percent over the same forty years. Even so, small firms remained important to American life. Smaller industrial firms, often working in concert with medium-sized and large companies, were active as members of industrial districts. Some small manufacturers also succeeded on their own, as independents. Farming, sales, and services were strongholds of small business, although in these realms, too, larger companies made inroads. This chapter explores the relationships that evolved between large and small companies in America in the late nineteenth and early twentieth centuries, paying special attention to the strategies that small businesses adopted in their growing competition with their larger counterparts. Since businesses never exist in a vacuum but instead are always a part of their fluid social, political, and legal environments, this chapter examines as well shifting public attitudes toward small business and governmental policies for business development.

Industrialization and the Rise of Big Business
Pushed by merchants and artisans, industrialization began in the United States before the Civil War, but only after the conflict did the process reach maturity. Between 1869 and 1919, the value added to products by manufac-

turing rose from $1.4 billion to $24 billion. Economic growth accompanied the speedup in industrialization. Between 1869 and 1921, the GNP of the United States increased from $9 billion to $72 billion, and per capita GNP tripled, from $223 to $683.

The acceleration in industrialization originated in numerous sources, but of key importance were market developments and technological breakthroughs. The unification of the national market by the completion of America's railroad and telegraph networks — railroad trackage rose from about 30,000 miles in 1860 to nearly 170,000 miles by 1890 — allowed manufacturers to locate their factories in one or two cities and sell throughout the United States. Moreover, the market was there. The U.S. population more than tripled between 1860 and 1920, increasing from 31 million to 106 million people eager to purchase industrial goods. At the same time, technological breakthroughs in key industries — the distilling and refining of liquids and semiliquids such as oil, the processing of agricultural goods, and the making and working of metals — greatly sped up and increased the output of America's industrial plants. The adoption of the Bessemer and open-hearth processes, for example, made the United States the leading steel-producing nation in the world by 1900 — with an output of 10.2 million tons, up from only 500,000 tons in 1876.

With improvements in transportation and communications and with the breakthroughs in manufacturing technologies came the rise of big businesses in America. In the 1850s, aside from a few railroads, cotton textile mills were the largest businesses in the United States. Only a handful, however, were capitalized at more than $1 million or employed more than 500 workers. By way of contrast, when the United States Steel Corporation was formed in 1901 as a merger of Carnegie Steel and several other firms, it was capitalized at $1.4 billion, becoming the first billion-dollar company in American history and employing more than 100,000 workers (by 1929, its workforce totaled 440,000). As late as 1860, no single American company was capitalized at as much as $10 million, but by 1904 more than 300 were.

Big businesses developed especially when companies combined mass production with mass distribution to become vertically integrated enterprises, controlling all or most of the stages in the production and sales of their products. Vertical integration became a hallmark of significant segments of America's industrial system well into the twentieth century. To a lesser degree, big businesses also grew up through horizontal integration, the process through which companies sought to control all of one stage of making or selling their products. Central to vertical and horizontal integration—and some companies engaged in both at the same time—was a quest for control over their operations, a search that took various forms.

As the "throughput" of their businesses rapidly increased, executives in some manufacturing fields found it hazardous to rely upon established market mechanisms to ensure the movement of raw materials to their plants, the flow of the work-in-process through their factories, and the distribution of their finished products throughout the United States. Many manufacturers, like Andrew Carnegie in the steel industry, purchased their own supplies of raw materials—in Carnegie's case, iron ore, coking coal, and limestone. Others experienced particular difficulties with America's established marketing network of wholesalers and retailers in the distribution of their goods and so set up their own national sales systems. In some cases, the issue was the speed of distribution, for makers of perishables required timely sales. Thus, Pabst Brewing established its own distribution system, lest its unpasteurized beer spoil en route to market. In other instances, the growing complexity and rising costs of industrial products made it difficult for independent merchants to demonstrate, finance, and service them adequately. In still other cases, the tremendous increase in the output simply overwhelmed established marketers, again bringing manufacturers into the picture. In all of these instances businesses were, through vertical integration, internalizing transactions that had formerly occurred in the marketplace.

By way of contrast, large, vertically integrated industrial firms were less important in most other parts of the globe. In Great Britain, for example, well-established marketers could generally handle the flow of industrial products, freeing many manufacturers of the necessity of controlling sales outlets. Then, too, markets were more fragmented and tastes more regional in nature, limiting the development of huge, national firms for some decades. In Japan, too, large vertically integrated firms were slower to develop than in America, and for many of the same reasons: the existence of established marketers, the importance of regionalism, and so forth. Different legal traditions were also important. In the United States, common law practice and statute law tended to allow the development of big businesses. In many other nations, laws permitted, and even encouraged, small firms to cooperate in groups called cartels. These cartels could often set prices and engage in other practices that were often illegal in America, allowing small firms in other nations to gain many of the advantages of bigness without actually becoming large concerns.

At the same time that America's business leaders sought to gain control over the internal operations of their firms, they tried to dampen competition in their markets. The development of a national market was a mixed blessing for industrialists: on the one hand, as the largest free-trade area in the world at the time, the United States offered tremendous scope for their entrepreneurial energies; on the other hand, the continental American market brought them into increasing competition with each other across the country. The United States experienced its first major merger movement between 1895 and 1904 as several thousand companies disappeared into consolidations. A desire for market control lay behind many of the mergers: in one-half of them the consolidations accounted for over 40 percent of the manufacturing capacity of their industries; in one-third, over 70 percent.

The giant firms that resulted clustered in just a few fields. Nearly all were in industry. Of the 278 American companies with assets of $20 million or more in 1917, some 236 were manufacturing companies. By way of contrast, only five were agricultural firms. Of the manufacturing businesses, 171 firms, or nearly three-quarters, fell into one of just six groups: 39 in primary metals, 34 in food processing, 29 in transportation equipment, 24 in machinery-making, 24 in oil refining, and 21 in chemicals. These companies shared certain characteristics: they were capital-intensive enterprises that produced large quantities of homogeneous products for mass markets; some 85 percent had integrated production with distribution by the time of World War I; and nearly all were multiunit enterprises with operations spread across the United States.

In their management systems, these industrial companies differed in important ways from the small artisan workshops of the antebellum years. Informal arrangements based upon family and personal ties no longer sufficed, for companies had become too large and too complex for any one person to manage. Bureaucratic organization replaced personal management in big businesses. Functionally departmentalized corporate offices — offices composed of managers grouped together in committees set up to handle the different functions of a company's operations, such as production or sales — emerged to set corporate strategies and coordinate operations. By 1917, four-fifths of America's largest 236 manufacturing ventures had adopted management systems based upon departmentalized corporate offices. At the same time, middle management developed to handle the daily work of the companies. Lower-level managers ran individual plants and factories. Between 1880 and 1920, the number of managerial employees in American firms, mainly middle managers in big businesses, increased from 161,000 to 1 million and from 1.1 percent to 2.6 percent of the workforce. In short, managerial hierarchies, composed of top, middle, and lower management levels, began emerging.

Providing the sinew binding the disparate parts of the companies together was improved financial reporting, which went far beyond the simple double entry bookkeeping that had been adequate earlier. Railroad executives and industrialists developed increasingly sophisticated financial accounting, including the use of operating ratios, capital accounting with provisions for depreciation, and cost accounting methods to keep track of past and current operations and help them plan for the future.

Public Attitudes and Government Policies

The attitudes of Americans toward the rise of big business were complex. From the 1880s well into the twentieth century, Americans' relationship with big business was a love-hate affair. Most Americans associated big business with material abundance, efficiency in production methods, and a rising standard of living. Nonetheless, many also feared big business. The public continued to have a sentimental attraction to small business, to the little guy. The development of big business was so sudden and so disruptive of traditional ways of work and life that most Americans looked upon it with anxiety.

The attitudes of middle-class Americans toward big business passed through three stages between 1879 and 1914. The first generation to come into contact with big business maintained an uneasy acceptance of it into the early 1890s. During these years there was relatively little public hostility to big business among professionals, who viewed the spread of large firms as giving rise to economic efficiency. Farmers, hurt by falling prices and angered by what they saw as the economic depredations of railroads and other "trusts," expressed more hostility, especially in the late 1880s and early 1890s. So did skilled workers concerned about the power that large companies could exert over wages, hours of work, and working conditions. Nonetheless, even many farm and labor groups praised big businesses as stabilizing and progressive forces in the nation's economy. A major depression that devastated the United States in the mid-1890s signaled the start of a second stage, one of heightened hostility of all groups toward big businesses, a hostility that ran deepest among labor bodies. The return of prosperity in the late 1890s and the opening two decades of the twentieth century brought forth a third stage, one marked by a more favorable attitude toward large firms. By 1902, most Americans, even most workers, were resigned to the continued presence of big business in their lives, and many welcomed large firms for the outpouring of goods that they brought. Americans were fast becoming consumers as well as producers. This second generation of Americans to live with big businesses increasingly accepted large firms as a part of their socioeconomic landscape.

In fact, during the Progressive period (roughly the first two decades of the twentieth century), a growing number of Americans viewed small firms as anachronistic, obsolete, and inefficient. Small businesses came to be seen as outdated and vanishing forms of enterprise, and their replacement by larger firms was viewed as a natural evolutionary movement. Even so, Americans expressed concern about the fate of the small business person (as distinct from the small business) and the effects that his/her decline would have upon American society. What would become of economic independence, of economic freedom, as large businesses squeezed out small companies? The ambivalent attitudes that most Americans held toward large firms in the 1890s have persisted to the present day, into the twentieth-first century.

These mixed attitudes found expression in governmental actions. Americans expended considerable effort in seeking to control, and sometimes to break up, big businesses through lawsuits—brought before 1890 under common law, but after that year under the terms of the Sherman Act. Rather than try to destroy or atomize big businesses through antitrust actions, however, the main thrust of government policies was to regulate big businesses, via newly formed independent regulatory commissions at both the state and federal levels.

Control through legal actions was the initial response of Americans to the rise of big business. The common law tradition of the United States encompassed well the ambivalent attitudes most Americans harbored toward big business. While placing restrictions upon how big companies could act, it fell far short of outlawing them. Conversely, the common law tradition protected small firms from some, but not all, of the depredations of their larger competitors. A new level of action began with the passage of the Sherman Act by Congress in 1890. Its supporters intended that the act encompass the common law tradition. The Sherman Act outlawed restraints of trade, but the law's sponsors intended that "reasonable" restraints, those not injurious to the public and not preventing new firms from entering business fields, be allowed to continue. It remained for the courts to decide matters. In a series of cases in the mid-1890s federal courts did permit reasonable restraints, but in another series of cases decided between 1898 and

1911 justices took a narrower view and forbade nearly all types of restraints that came before them. Reversing themselves once again, the justices returned to the common law tradition in cases involving the American Tobacco Company and the Standard Oil Company, both decided in 1911, to declare that reasonable restraints were permissible.

Although Standard Oil and American Tobacco were broken up on grounds that their composition constituted unreasonable restraints of trade, few other big businesses suffered similar fates. In fact, of the 127 actions taken under the terms of the Sherman Act between 1905 and 1915, 72 were filed against loose combinations of smaller firms (such as cartels), 32 against tight combinations (such as trusts), 12 each against labor unions and agricultural produce dealers, and 10 against miscellaneous others. Thus were law, public attitudes, and economics reconciled. As interpreted by the U.S. Supreme Court from 1911 onward, the Sherman Act has generally permitted large firms to exist, as long as they have grown big through reasonable means. Microsoft ran afoul of this reasoning in the 1990s, when it came to be seen as having gotten ahead by unreasonable means, much like Standard Oil.

Final, pre–World War I antitrust actions were worked out in 1914, when Congress passed the Federal Trade Commission Act, which established the Federal Trade Commission (FTC), and the Clayton Act. Like many pieces of business legislation passed during the Progressive era, these acts resulted from compromises between various groups of business people—no single, monolithic business community existed—and politicians. For over a decade, business groups had debated the wisdom of having a governmental body oversee competitive conditions, and by 1914 most agreed that such an agency was needed. Small business people, such as retailers and grain dealers, wanted the creation of an agency that could look into the monopolistic practices of big businesses that they thought were threatening them with financial ruin. Larger firms were interested in bringing predictability to their relations with the federal government and sought the establishment of an agency that would clearly delineate what businesses could and could not do in their competition with each other. Officers of large firms especially wanted the establishment of a government agency that could offer businesses advance legal advice on their proposed actions, such as mergers. The FTC Act partly satisfied each camp. The legislation stated that "unfair methods of competition are hereby declared unlawful," created the FTC and authorized it to decide just which methods were unlawful, and empowered the FTC to order offenders to "cease and desist" from engaging in unfair methods. The Clayton Act, a companion piece of legislation, sought to define more clearly than the vague Sherman Act what constituted restraint of trade. In addition to condemning any forms of price discrimination that limited competition, the Clayton Act forbade certain types of interlocking directorates and "tying contracts," by which large firms prevented their suppliers and customers from doing business with competitors. While protecting small businesses to some degree, these laws also created a more stable political and legal environment for large firms.

Similar compromises characterized much of the business legislation passed during the Progressive period. Unwilling to forgo the fruits of big businesses, most Americans turned to politics to regulate, but not destroy, them. Much of the regulation was undertaken by the federal government through the creation of a new device: the independent regulatory commission (the FTC was one). Once established, these bodies operated with a fair degree of independence from either the legislative or executive branches of government. The Interstate Commerce Act of 1887 set up the Interstate Commerce Commission (ICC) to regulate railroads, and later trucks and buses; and the Elkins Act (1903), the Hepburn Act (1906), and the Mann-Elkins Act (1910) greatly increased the agency's powers. The Meat Inspection Act and the Pure Food and Drug Act, both passed in 1906, gave the federal government responsibility for the regulation of America's food and drug industries, and the Food and Drug Administration was set up in the same year. The Federal Reserve Act of 1913 established the Federal Reserve System to regulate banking practices and the money supply in the United States. Spurred by financial panics in 1903 and 1907, bankers joined politicians in seeking federal legislation to bring stability to their industry. The resulting legislation was a compromise between the desires of big city bankers, especially those in New York, who wanted a centralized banking system and bankers in regional centers and small towns who desired a more decentralized one. The Federal Reserve Act established a Federal Reserve Board composed of five members, each from a different region, appointed by the president. Rather than set up a single central bank, as many New York financiers wanted, the act created twelve district Federal Reserve banks, each owned by the banks in its region. Each Federal Reserve district bank had a nine-member board composed of three members from the national Federal Reserve Board, three from district banks, and three nonbankers. The board for the Washington district sought to coordinate overall banking policies — control of interest rates and the money supply —

for the twelve districts; however, these efforts met with only partial success. The Federal Reserve System would acquire greater powers in the 1930s and later.

While Congress passed much of the most important legislation regulating businesses, state legislatures took significant steps as well. During the Progressive era, they initiated or extended state regulation of railroads, public utilities, insurance companies, oil producers, banks, lumber companies, and some types of farm operations. As was occurring at the national level, much of the business legislation passed at the state level embodied compromises between politicians and competing business groups, often groups of large and small business people. In California, for instance, rifts often separated big-city bankers in San Francisco and Los Angeles from their counterparts in small towns scattered throughout agricultural regions. Only when these two groups of bankers could reconcile their differences, as they did following the Panic of 1907, was the state government able to pass significant regulatory legislation—like the Bank Act of 1909, which for the first time clearly separated commercial, savings, and trust banking in California.

Reflecting public attitudes, the impact of court decisions and political actions upon small business was mixed. Some protection was afforded from the most blatant abuses of large firms, as the federal courts and Congress sought to prevent vaguely defined forms of unfair competition. For the most part, however, few impediments were placed in the way of the development of big business. As long as they grew by reasonable means and as long as they submitted to federal and state regulation, big businesses were permitted to grow and prosper. Small businesses persisted, and in some fields thrived, after 1880 less as a result of protective political actions than because of the important contributions they continued to make to America's evolving business system.

Small Business in Manufacturing

Together, America's large and small industrial firms transformed the nation. From a country based upon farms and small towns in the antebellum years, America became a nation of factories and large cities in the late nineteenth and early twentieth centuries. It was in the 1880s that for the first time more people worked in nonfarm than in agricultural jobs; and it was in the 1920s that more people first came to live in towns and cities than in villages and on farms. Particularly noticeable in the early twentieth century were the decline in the proportion of Americans who earned their living as farmers and the rise in the proportion who were in clerical and sales positions.

With the development of industry, the dominance of the merchant yielded to that of the manufacturer. Small businesses found themselves in an ambiguous position. The opportunities of the nation's expanding industrial economy beckoned to small business owners, and they continued to increase in numbers throughout the late nineteenth and early twentieth centuries. Nonetheless, the proportion of America's industrial output coming from small businesses dropped as large manufacturing ventures rose to prominence. By 1904, corporations—the legal form assumed by most big businesses but by relatively few small businesses (most small firms remained single-owner proprietorships or partnerships)—accounted for three-quarters of America's industrial production. By that year, too, one-third of the income generated from manufacturing came from industries in which the four biggest companies accounted for more than one-half of the sales. Small businesses became relatively less important as employers. By 1914, nearly one-third of all industrial workers found employment in plants with 500 or more in their labor forces, and another one-third in those with 100 to 499. As large vertically integrated companies arose in manufacturing, a growing share of industrial workers found employment in companies that operated more than one plant; at least one-third of the nation's workers did so by 1923.

Small businesses did not, however, disappear from the industrial scene in the United States. The same set of census statistics alluded to above shows that in 1914 one-third of America's industrial workforce found employment in firms with 100 or fewer laborers. If small businesses are defined as those with 250 or fewer workers, 54 percent of those employed by manufacturing concerns worked for small firms. Moreover, some 54,000 little businesses, those with 6 to 20 workers, were still in operation on the eve of the First World War. In Europe, where large vertically integrated firms did not develop as readily as in America, small manufacturers remained still more the norm. For instance, as late as 1906, 58 percent of the industrial labor force in France worked in plants that employed fewer than 10 wage earners; only 12 percent of the labor force was employed in plants with more than 500 workers. Regional tastes and geographic separation kept French markets divided and businesses small.

Those small businesses that survived and prospered in manufacturing did so by following several strategies. In some fields—such as leather working, furniture making, and lumber milling—few economies of scale existed, and big businesses simply did not develop. In these areas small manufacturers continued to turn out their goods much as they had in the antebellum years. In realms in which big businesses did emerge, small industrialists had to adapt to the presence of their larger counterparts or fail. Some small businesses were able to operate on the fringes of an industry dominated by big businesses, one made up of an oligopolistic core, by serving either as suppliers of intermediate parts for the larger firms or as independent producers. Moreover, in some regions, small and medium-sized firms, sometimes joined by their larger brethren, formed industrial districts. Some such districts had existed in the antebellum years, but they became more common and more important after the Civil War. As they had in earlier times, small industrialists in these districts relied on flexible production methods and the employment of skilled workers to carve out niches for specialty products.

The evolution of the flour-milling industry and the men's clothing industry illustrates how smaller firms could sometimes serve as fringe producers. In flour milling the adoption of new technologies, mechanical rollers and purifiers, in the late nineteenth century made the industry more capital-intensive than in earlier times and began a trend toward concentration. Large companies located in Minneapolis came to dominate the industry by taking advantage of scale economies in production and by setting up their own nationwide marketing networks. Many small mills went out of existence, and the flour milling industry came to be dominated by a few giants, such as General Mills. While declining in their overall importance in the flour-milling industry, small businesses remained significant in several respects: as millers turning out special blends of flour, as millers in interior towns away from the big cities, and as national producers during times of peak demand. The men's clothing industry experienced similar changes. Between 1880 and 1920, the industry came to consist of two sectors. A handful of large firms that were organizationally and technologically sophisticated manufactured high-quality garments and operated year-round; thousands of smaller firms that came and went with great frequency composed a secondary sector. These firms were technically more primitive and produced mainly lower-quality and lower-priced clothing. Since the demand for clothing was seasonal and generally unstable, the small firms in the secondary sector, with their low capital investments, were well suited to handle the variable component of demand. By 1927, only 14 firms employed more than 1,000 workers, and only 110 employed more than 300. Yet, one-half of the industry's workers found employment in just the largest 6 percent of the companies.

Industrial Districts

Many of the small and medium-sized businesses that succeeded in manufacturing did so as members of burgeoning industrial districts. In these districts they prospered by differentiating their products from those of their larger counterparts. Doing so often meant producing a wide range of goods for rapidly changing regional and seasonal markets. Part of the ability to accomplish this task lay in the employment of intelligent, innovative workers; another part lay in the flexible use of the most advanced (not primitive) technologies. In short, by carving out market niches, by continuing to be responsive to changing consumer preferences, and by developing new production methods, some smaller businesses could remain independent enterprises, successfully coexisting with larger firms. Among the fields in which small firms prospered well into the twentieth century was textiles.

As the nineteenth century progressed, America's textile industry divided into two sectors. At Waltham and Lowell in Massachusetts, large factories employed unskilled workers to turn out standardized goods for the mass market. The mills quickly became fully integrated in the production of textiles, with all of the steps—preparation, spinning, weaving, and dyeing—being carried out on different factory floors linked by elevators. These milling companies were among the largest businesses of the antebellum period. They each employed hundreds of workers, and their physical plants were large. In 1849, one company possessed five mills, each of which was five stories tall, with each story taken up by one room measuring 40 by 151 feet. By the 1830s and 1840s, all of the companies had adopted the corporate form of organization, and most were run through rudimentary managerial hierarchies. Few small textile firms developed at Waltham or Lowell, for the large businesses controlled the available plant sites and sources of waterpower, denying access to others. By 1850, twelve corporations employed 12,000 textile workers in Lowell. Not even the cotton shortage of the 1860s and the nationwide depression of the mid-1870s changed things much. When pressed by rising expenses for their raw materials and falling demand for their finished goods, the companies contracted their operations, laying off workers and reducing wages in the process, but they did not alter their approach to business.

A very different pattern unfolded at Philadelphia, as related by the historian Philip Scranton. In 1850, some 326 firms employed 12,400 textile workers. Two-thirds possessed 25 or fewer workers, and 28 of the largest 32 employed only between 102 and 225. Though employing as many workers in the aggregate as their counterparts in Lowell, the Philadelphia firms were capitalized at much less — $4.7 million, about one-third of the amount invested in the Lowell companies. Most of the Philadelphia companies were organized as single-owner proprietorships. Only about 17 percent were partnerships, and even fewer, a scant 3 percent, were corporations.

The Philadelphia firms competed successfully throughout the nineteenth century with the much larger mills of New England by stressing specialization and flexibility in production and marketing. Few Philadelphia firms tried to master all aspects of textile production; most specialized in one or two steps which they then did very well indeed, using the most up-to-date machinery and employing skilled workers, often men, at high wages. Their productivity levels were high. In their labor practices, as in their management methods, the Philadelphia mills differed a great deal from the larger mills at Lowell and Waltham. The Lowell and Waltham mills employed young, unskilled farm women as workers and treated them very paternalistically, housing them in company dormitories and strictly supervising their morals. Turnover rates were probably higher at Lowell and Waltham than in Philadelphia, thus probably making productivity lower in the northern mills. With a skilled workforce and modern machinery, the Philadelphia mills could also more rapidly switch to various types of cotton, wool, and other fabrics as needed.

The owners of the Philadelphia textile establishments did not, for the most part, become members of their city's social elite — in sharp contrast to the situation in New England, where mill owners became important in cities like Boston. Instead, the textile men remained close to their work, and a commercial elite of merchants long dominated Philadelphia's affairs. This circumstance paid an unexpected dividend. Although Philadelphia was not immune to labor unrest, bonds uniting managers and workers mitigated disturbances. Workers and managers knew each other personally through work on the plant floor and through membership in the same churches and social organizations. Moreover, many mill owners had started as skilled artisans, often renting space for their nascent ventures and only later expanding their enterprises. Workers and owners talked the same language and respected each other, even when they disagreed.

The flexibility of the Philadelphia firms served them well during the crises of the 1860s and the 1870s. Most adjusted better than their larger counterparts in Lowell to the cotton shortage and the wartime demands of the Civil War by shifting to the production of woolen goods and other items. Similarly, their flexibility allowed the Philadelphia mills to prosper and expand even during the hard times of the mid-1870s, a period during which many Lowell mills encountered severe difficulties. By the early 1880s, Philadelphia possessed 849 textile establishments employing 55,000 workers, the largest such concentration of firms and workers in the nation. These were mostly profitable firms. The return on capital in Philadelphia's cotton textile companies averaged 23 percent in 1890, compared to 6 percent in the Lowell companies and 8 percent in cotton textile firms nationwide. Most of the Philadelphia companies remained what they had been in the antebellum years—small, family firms in which the owner-manager personally supervised every aspect of the firm's operations.

Small size and versatility continued to be hallmarks of the Philadelphia textile firms into the twentieth century. Not even the depression of the 1890s, which ushered in merger movements in many industries, led to concentration in Philadelphia's textile industry. Economic factors militated against mergers—the flexible, batch system of production, the ease of entry into the industry, and the near absence of scale economies—but more important was the character of the men owning the mills. They identified personally with their businesses, which they often viewed as extensions of their families. Philadelphia remained the domain of small firms. In 1905, 728 textile companies capitalized at a total of $100 million employed 60,000 workers within the city of Philadelphia (and there were additional firms in the suburbs and nearby areas). As before, these were flexible, specialized companies attuned to making rapid production changes as markets altered. In 1910, for example, a carpet maker celebrated its twenty-fifth anniversary by bringing out its 25,000th pattern.

If the experiences of the Philadelphia textile makers illustrate continuing opportunities for small business people in manufacturing during the age of giant enterprise, they also reveal limitations. Most unsettling was the growth in the power of the intermediate purchasers of the textiles. In the late nineteenth and early twentieth centuries, chain stores and department stores emerged as big businesses in America. Using their buying power and emphasizing the rapid turnover of their stock, they demanded lower prices and more frequent deliveries from their Philadelphia textile suppliers. Wedded to traditional family business methods (few mill owners understood or adopted new accounting methods, for instance), Philadelphia's textile producers failed to mount an adequate defense. They failed, for instance, to form any sort of trade association to combat the demands of the larger companies buying their goods. Their continuing desire to maintain independent family firms prevented any combined defense of their businesses. The new demands of mass retailers put strains on these small manufacturers and eventually overwhelmed them. Flexibility gave way to rigidity, and the industry went into long-term decline.

When national economic problems joined the particular problems of the Philadelphia mills during the Great Depression of the 1930s, the destruction of the textile businesses was assured. Between 1925 and 1933, Philadelphia suffered a net loss of nearly 300 textile firms. Rather than merge with their competitors, most mill owners used up their capital and went out of existence. A corresponding decline occurred in the number of workers in the city's textile industry. Employment peaked in 1925 with 72,000 workers. From that point on, the course was downhill: 60,000 in 1929 and 42,000 in 1932. Some recovery occurred in the late 1930s and during the Second World War, only to be followed by further decline in the postwar years, until a scant 22,000 textile workers remained in Philadelphia in 1960.

The agglomeration of small industrial firms in manufacturing districts was fairly common in the United States. To be sure, large, vertically integrated companies such as Carnegie Steel turned out vast quantities of mass-produced goods for homogeneous markets. In addition, however, manufacturing firms of all sizes — large, small, and medium — were linked together in industrial districts to produce a dizzying array of products. Like Philadelphia's textile firms, they used flexible production methods (not mass-production techniques) and employed skilled workers (not unskilled or semiskilled ones) to make products for smaller, often rapidly changing seasonal or niche markets. Some of the firms using flexible production methods were large by any standard: the Pullman Company, Baldwin Locomotive, Westinghouse, and General Motors. However, there were also clusters of smaller companies turning out an ever-broadening range of consumer goods. Then, too, some smaller and medium-sized firms provided intermediate materials and services for the big businesses. Big and small businesses were not always antagonistic. For example, industrial districts featuring interlinked companies using flexible production methods developed in jewelry making in New York City and Providence, Rhode Island; tool making in Cincinnati; and furniture making in Grand Rapids. Even in Pittsburgh, smaller specialty steelmakers coexisted with the gigantic United States Steel for many decades in the twentieth century. (For more on the steel industry, see Chapter 3.) As in the case of the Philadelphia textile makers, educational, financial, and marketing institutions sometimes lent coherence to these districts—mechanics institutes that trained skilled workers, banks that loaned money to startup firms, and shared-showcase wholesale and retail outlets.

Nor was this situation limited to the United States. In fact, industrial districts, often composed of small and medium-sized manufacturers, were even more common in Europe. By the 1890s, for instance, the British engineering industry (that is, producers of machine tools) had become, as historian Jonathan Zeitlin has observed, "a congeries of distinct but overlapping sectors linked by a common set of metalworking processes and the manual skills associated with them." Companies in Lancashire, Yorkshire, and the East Midlands made textile machinery; firms in Clydeside, the Northeast Coast, and on the Thames produced marine engines; companies in Lincolnshire and East Anglia made agricultural equipment; and firms in the West Midlands turned out hardware and (slightly later) automobiles. The characteristic business unit in these areas was a small to medium-sized family firm with fewer than 500 employees. Even the larger companies often operated more as collections of workshops than as integrated factories. Another example of an industrial district is found in the Oyonnax Valley of France, where small producers made early-day plastics, first from the natural material of animal horn, later from celluloid. For decades in the late nineteenth and early twentieth centuries, small artisanal production and larger factory production coexisted side by side. A mechanics workshop, opened in 1904, helped supply well-trained workers and gave some unity to plastics production in the valley. Shipmaking in Norway, metalworking and cotton textiles in parts of Italy and Great Britain, and silk reeling in sections of Japan and Italy, among other industries, also attest to the importance of industrial districts.

Agriculture: The Continuing Family Farm
Although the United States was fast becoming an urban-industrial nation in the late nineteenth and early twentieth centuries, agriculture remained an important part of the American economy. At the heart of the agricultural picture lay the family farm, which, despite the growing mechanization and commercialization of agriculture, changed but little from the antebellum years. In 1920, family farms operating as small businesses still dominated farming, yet there were also hints of the beginnings of the agribusi-

ness complexes that would largely supplant family farmers in later years. "Agribusiness" is usually taken to mean a cluster of related farming practices and beliefs. Foremost is the notion of farming for profit, to the exclusion of other motives. Closely related is the idea of making farming scientific and efficient. Doing so often meant, in turn, moving away from the family farm as the primary unit of production. Instead, corporations may own and operate farms much larger than those run by most individual families. Specialized farming almost completely replaces general farming, and, as "factories in the field," agribusiness enterprises are operated by managers who employ gangs of hired farm workers, rather than family members. Moreover, the farms themselves often become simply parts of vertically integrated companies, which raise, process, and market agricultural produce, with most of the profits being earned in processing and marketing.

While growing in absolute importance, agriculture declined steadily in terms of its relative significance to the American economy. The number of farms rose from 1.5 million in 1850 to 6.5 million in 1920, and during the same years the land in farms increased from about 300 million to just under 1 billion acres. Despite these impressive increases, the still more rapid rise of industry insured that agriculture's overall contribution to the economy of the United States would fall. In 1880, self-employed farmers composed 28 percent of the total workforce of the United States; by 1920, they formed a scant 16 percent. If farmers and farm laborers are considered together, the trend is the same. In 1860, about 60 percent of the nation's workers were on the farm, forty years later only 37 percent. In 1860, farm income was 30 percent of the national total, by 1900, only 20 percent. (The per capita income of farm workers, however, rose from $70 in 1859 to $112 in 1900, in constant dollars.) It was not that farming regressed; it was more that agricultural incomes failed to keep pace with the tremendous advances being made in industry and the service sector. Agriculture was successful in terms of its overall efficiency, but it was consumers more than farmers who were the main beneficiaries. The markets for farm products remained highly competitive, forcing the less efficient farmers to shift to the manufacturing or service sectors.

Even as the place of agriculture in the American economy changed, so too did farming methods. The mechanization and technological improvements begun in the antebellum years continued after the Civil War. Technological innovations — haying machines, wheat harvesters, combines, mechanical seed drills, and new types of plows — were particularly important for the spread of agriculture in the Midwest and on the Great Plains. The impact of the innovations was sometimes dramatic. The number of man-hours needed to produce 100 bushels of wheat fell from 233 in 1840 to only 87 eighty years later, and the corresponding number of man-hours required for corn dropped from 276 to 113. The use of new types of farm equipment was less widespread in the South and on the Pacific Coast, for the cultivation and harvesting of the primary crops grown there—tobacco, cotton, fruits, and vegetables—remained labor-intensive.

The partial mechanization of farming was part of a larger trend, the commercialization of American agriculture. Even more than in the colonial period or the antebellum years, American farm goods became deeply involved in the national and international trade in agricultural commodities. Communications and transportation improvements—the telegraph, transatlantic cables, the railroad, and steamships—furthered this trend. Individual family farmers across the nation found themselves enmeshed in market forces they neither understood nor controlled. A rise in the demand for their wheat by British consumers might boost the prices paid Great Plains farmers for their harvests in some years, while bumper crops in the Ukraine or Argentina might lower prices in others. The foreign market remained, as it had been earlier, an important outlet for American farm products. Between 1869 and 1900, nearly one-fifth of the nation's farm goods found overseas markets, and in the same period, despite the expansion of industry, farm goods composed about three-quarters of all American exports.

Family farms, which, as in times past, continued to lie at the center of America's agricultural system, remained much as they had been a century before. In 1900, the average family farm encompassed 146 acres, of which about 72 were improved—a considerable increase, to be sure, from the 100 acres, of which perhaps 35 might have been cultivated, in late colonial times, but not an astronomical rise. Despite the mechanization that had occurred in some fields of agriculture, the average farm still possessed only $131 worth of machinery at the turn of the century. Most farms were diversified to some degree; few specialized entirely in just one crop. Despite the spread of a commercial economy across America, general farming remained the norm, as farmers raised livestock, fruit, and vegetables for their own consumption as well as staple crops such as wheat and corn for the market.

Not all family farms remained general-purpose enterprises, however. In California's Central Valley, specialized fruit and vegetable farms developed from about the 1880s. Whether they grew raisins around Fresno, almonds near Davisville, hops near Wheatland, or pears at Newcastle, family farmers developed nuanced approaches to growing techniques, labor relations (including granting land to Chinese and Japanese immigrants as tenant farmers), and marketing. Reflecting the continued belief in farming as a morally beneficial occupation, California growers also developed an extremely positive self-image of themselves. They saw themselves not simply as profit-hungry farmers but as people aiding in the building of a virtuous society in California. This image remained largely intact through World War I. Only then, as consumers faced high prices and food shortages, did the picture erode.

The tension already apparent in colonial and early national times between a desire for family self-sufficiency and a need to participate in a market economy grew more pronounced in the late nineteenth century. In some areas, perhaps especially in the Midwest, farmers settled in ethnic communities in their attempt to reconcile, as the historian Daniel Nelson has put it, "the individualism of American farming with collective and community-based endeavors." By the 1880s, an "ethnic patchwork" took shape in the rural settlement process. In these regions, farmers traded work and helped each other at harvest time, but they kept close watch over how much work each owed the other. Although profit-motivated, farmers also valued agriculture for nonpecuniary reasons — for what they viewed as their independence, for close personal relationships with their family and local communities, together with nearness to the soil and nature in general. Speaking before the United States Industrial Commission in 1916, a tenant farmer from Texas summarized the nonmonetary aspects of agriculture so important to many family farmers. After telling the commission a story of hard work, poor health, and poverty, he testified that farming, nonetheless, offered a contented life, "a legitimate life, a happy life, a useful life, useful to humanity, useful to all developments of every nature."

The career of Lewis D. McMillen illustrates well the sometimes contradictory aspects of farm life. Raised in an Ohio farm family, McMillen acquired his own farm of 125 acres in northern Ohio in 1891 at the age of thirty-three. Here he and his growing family made a living for the next thirty-five years. After surviving the depression of the mid-1890s, McMillen prospered as a general farmer, raising wheat, corn, livestock, and some fruit.

McMillen took part in the commercial market for farm products in the United States. Like a growing number of American farmers, be bought his farm on credit, paying off his mortgage some years later. He made most of his profits by purchasing sheep and cattle in the Chicago market, fattening them on his corn, and then selling them throughout the nation. A progressive farmer, he practiced crop rotation (wheat or oats, clover, and corn in yearly succession) and was always interested in new types of machinery, farming techniques, and crops, including sugar beets. His son recalled that McMillen paid "particular attention to market reports in the daily paper he received from the Pittsburgh stockyards."

For McMillen, however, farming was more than a commercial enterprise. He valued his farm for the independence that it provided him and his family. As his son remembered, "He had always wanted to be a free American, living on and within his own resources, unobligated to anyone for favors or support. . . . One reason he liked the farm was that it was a business he could run without becoming obligated to others." In fact, the McMillen family raised most of the chickens, eggs, milk, vegetables, fruit, and meat that they consumed, and even in the twentieth century made their own soap. Although he was astute in his trading (he was able to save about $1,000 per year, a large sum then, most of which he reinvested in his farm), a quest for luxury did not dominate McMillen's life. His son recalled, "We did know that people somewhere were richer than we, and perhaps did not have to work so much or so hard, and we heard that many more were poorer than we were. We did not expect to strike it rich and did not know how we could relieve distant poverty. In our neighborhood the range from richest to poorest was not wide."

Not all family farmers were as progressive as McMillen; for many farmers traditional techniques and beliefs remained important arbiters in the conduct of agricultural affairs. For example, "moon farming" continued to be widely practiced across the United States. As one adherent explained, "We plant, we sow, we reap and mow; we fell trees, we make shingles, we roof our houses, secure bacon, make fences, spread manure, when the moon is auspicious." Almanacs showing the phases of the moon were in great demand. Not surprisingly, many farmers resisted the Country Life Movement, which aimed at improving farming in the early twentieth century, because they viewed the campaign as an effort by urbanites to force city ways of life and thought upon them (much of the movement was concerned with introducing urban education practices to rural areas).

Nonetheless, farm practices did change, and in some of the alterations may be glimpsed the faint beginnings of agribusiness and the corresponding origins of the decline of family farming. Although not fully developed until after World War II, agribusiness can be traced to the late nineteenth and early twentieth centuries.

Bonanza farms growing wheat in California and on parts of the northern Great Plains in the 1870s and 1880s provide an early example of agribusiness. By 1880, there were 29,000 farms of over 1,000 acres apiece in the United States, many of them in the West. While some of these operated as large family farms, many were organized as corporations designed to earn quick returns for their stockholders. Typical were the efforts of the Dalrymple interests, which controlled 100,000 acres in North Dakota. In 1880, the company raised wheat on 25,000 acres (most of the rest was still uncultivated), divided into farms of about 6,000 acres of plowed land. Each farm was under the control of a superintendent and was subdivided into three segments averaging 2,000 acres apiece. According to an 1880 federal government census report, "Each subdivision has its own farm buildings, boarding-houses, stables, blacksmith-shop, and so on, this size being considered the most convenient, and as large enough for systematic management." Most of the labor came from harvesting crews that traveled across the Great Plains as migrant workers each year.

Most of the nation's bonanza farms disappeared during the depression of the 1890s (many smaller family farms also failed), but the trend toward larger farms reappeared with the return of agricultural prosperity in the early 1900s. These changing relationships in farm size suggest the growing importance of large-scale farming during the first two decades of the twentieth century. Farms larger than 260 acres experienced a rapid growth rate. The increase in the numbers of farms of less than 50 acres, most of which were probably operated by part-time farmers, also continued, though at a slower rate. The numbers of medium-sized family farms (those between 50 and 260 acres) increased at a still slower rate during the first decade and then declined over the next ten years (see Table 2). These trends suggest the emergence of a skewed pattern of farm landholding that would become more pronounced after World War II: a growth in the proportion of farms that were either small or large and a decrease in the proportion of medium-sized units.

Even medium-sized family farmers discovered that they needed to devise new methods to market their crops. As they were drawn into the commercial economy, they formed selling organizations to deal with the growing complexity of their commercial affairs. Beginning in the 1870s and 1880s, farmers set up cooperatives to market their produce. By pooling their marketing efforts, agriculturalists hoped to limit competition among

TABLE TWO. Farms by Size in America, 1900–1920 (in thousands of farms)

Year	Acreage				
	1–49	50–259	260–499	500–999	1000+
1900	1,931	3,278	378	103	47
1910	2,254	3,489	444	125	50
1920	2,300	3,455	476	150	67

Source: U.S. Bureau of the Census, *Historical Statistics of the United States, Colonial Times to 1957* (Washington, D.C.: U.S. Government Printing Office, 1960), 279.

themselves, thus raising the prices they received for their crops. They also sought through combined actions to assure lower railroad rates and faster service, to get their crops to markets before they spoiled. Finally, they joined forces to open sales agencies in eastern cities and abroad, something they could not afford to do as individuals. Even McMillen, much as he valued his independence, marketed through a cooperative. Some cooperatives went beyond selling by branching into the purchasing of a wide variety of products for farmers, ranging from gasoline to insurance. Despite initial problems and failures in the 1870s and 1880s, cooperatives continued to grow in numbers and importance. By 1907, over 1,000 farm cooperatives were operating in America, mainly in wheat, milk, fruits, and vegetables. Their numbers increased in later years.

Cooperatives proved most useful for the farmers, family and corporate, who turned away from general farming to specialize in just one or two crops. This trend was most pronounced in California, where more and more farmers came to specialize in raising specific fruits and vegetables that they then shipped via fast trains to eastern and midwestern markets. By the time of World War I, California's farmers had set up cooperatives to market oranges, grapefruit, lemons, apples, pears, walnuts, berries, rice, almonds, tomatoes, string beans, lima beans, and cantaloupes. Altogether, cooperatives handled more than one-half of the Golden State's produce and helped farms prosper as small- to medium-scale economic units.

Small Business in Distribution and Services
The rise of big business led to significant changes in the distribution and sales of both agricultural and industrial products. Nonetheless, small-scale merchants continued to thrive; and the distribution of goods, particularly

at the retail level, long remained the domain of small business. The number of Americans working in wholesale establishments rose from 170,000 in 1869 to 1.2 million fifty years later, and in the same period the number employed in retail outlets jumped from 720,000 to 4 million, rates of increase much greater than the three-fold growth in the U.S. population during the same years. While a growing proportion of America's selling establishments were large, many remained small stores. As late as 1929, 168,000 wholesalers employed 1.6 million people, for an average employment per establishment of fewer than ten people. Retailing remained even more the province of small businesses. In 1929, 1.5 million retail establishments employed 5.7 million people, for an average employment of just over three people per store.

The growth of big businesses in marketing assumed several forms. Large commodity dealers used the telegraph and the railroad to operate nationwide buying and selling networks for agricultural goods. By 1921, for example, just twenty-one firms marketed three-fifths of America's cotton. Full-line and full-service wholesalers and jobbers established nationwide organizations to move consumer products—dry goods, hardware, drugs, and groceries—from manufacturers to retailers. As early as 1870, Alexander T. Stewart, America's leading distributor of dry goods, boasted sales of $50 million and employed 2,000 people. And, as we have seen, many manufacturers set up their own sales outlets to reach customers across the United States. Soon, however, mass retailers challenged these marketers. Department stores—Macy's, Bloomingdale's, Lazarus, and a host of others—grew up in cities; and catalogue stores—Montgomery Ward and Sears, Roebuck—served rural and small-town America. Chain stores also got their start. The Great Atlantic and Pacific Tea Company (A&P) began operations in 1859 and had about 200 stores selling tea, coffee, and selected groceries by 1900. Beginning in 1879, F. W. Woolworth set up Five and Ten Cent Stores, which had a sales volume of more than $15 million by 1905. However, as late as World War I, most sales, especially at the retail level, continued to be made by small neighborhood stores in cities or by small general stores in the countryside. In 1890, only ten chains (each composed of at least two stores) existed in America; even by 1915, there were only 515. Such was the case in other lands, as well. While chain stores (called "multiples" in Great Britain) and department stores began operations in many industrialized nations, most retail sales were made by small, single-unit businesses.

If many of America's consumer goods still moved through long-established wholesale and retail channels at the time of the First World War, changes were occurring in those channels. The merchandising methods of the mass retailers had an impact on the independents. Mass marketers stressed high volumes of sales through quick stock turnovers and low unit costs as the paths to profits. Independents responded in several ways. Even more than in the antebellum years, urban retailers streamlined their operations by specializing in the goods they handled. Moreover, they often embraced new technologies as eagerly as their larger competitors. Cash registers made by the National Cash Register Company were, for example, cheap enough for even small retailers to purchase and came into common use throughout the nation by around 1900.

General country stores were less successful than independent urban retailers in their adaptations to the social and economic changes taking place in the United States. General store owners did make some alterations in their business methods. The coming of the railroad allowed them to order stock directly from representatives of manufacturers and wholesalers, known as "traveling men," rather than make tiresome month-long trips to eastern cities to purchase their supplies. The more progressive shopkeepers installed attractive showcases in which they grouped their goods by category or department and, like their urban brethren, began carrying more brand-name packaged goods, such as Ivory Soap, Uneeda Biscuit, and Quaker Oats. These moves were not enough. As they extended their reach, commodity dealers usurped the roles that country stores had played in purchasing and selling farm goods. Even more damaging was the adoption of the automobile by farmers, for automobiles allowed them to shop in nearby towns and cities. By the 1920s and 1930s, country stores were fast disappearing from the American scene, except in isolated rural areas. As historian Gerald Carson has observed, "So it was with the passing of the general store. It just slowly dried up, like a farm pond in the August heat, scarcely changing from one day to the next, until it was gone."

The development of an urbanized and industrialized society in America spurred the demand for the services of insurance companies, banks, and credit-rating agencies. Like firms in wholesaling and retailing, companies in the service industries felt the impact of the rise of big business. Some big businesses grew up in these fields. Two large companies dominated credit rating. By 1880, R. G. Dun had sixty-nine branch offices and employed 10,000 credit investigators, while its main rival, the Bradstreet Agency, also operated across the nation. Dun and Bradstreet was later formed from a merger of these two companies. However, while a few big businesses grew up in the service industries, it was mainly small firms that dominated them, just as in the antebellum years. Not even the Dun and Bradstreet agencies could avoid competition. With few barriers to entry, the credit-rating business was open to all, leading one Dun employee to lament in the late 1870s that other credit-reporting agencies were "getting as thick as blackberries."

The late nineteenth and early twentieth centuries witnessed a rapid expansion in the number of insurance companies in the United States. The growing impersonality of life in big cities led to a tremendous growth in the life insurance business, as families came to rely upon the companies to provide benefits they had once given their members. Some 59 companies had $1.5 billion worth of life insurance policies in force by 1880; forty years later 335 companies had $41 billion in force. The "Big Three" life insurance companies—New York Life, Equitable of New York, and Mutual Life of New York—dominated their industry for many years. Their dominance was broken, however, in the opening decades of the twentieth century, as government investigators revealed fraud in some of their practices and as new companies grew up to challenge them. Fire insurance also became necessary, as a growing proportion of people and businesses existed in crowded circumstances susceptible to conflagration (the fire following the 1906 earthquake in San Francisco laid waste to five square miles of the city's downtown district). In 1860, the country had 81 general insurance companies, most of which wrote fire insurance; just forty years later there were nearly 500.

Even more than the insurance industry, commercial banking remained a home for small businesses in the United States. Unlike many other industrialized or industrializing nations, the United States possessed no central bank, after the dissolution of the Second Bank of the United States in the late 1830s and the 1840s. Nothing resembling the Bank of England or the Bank of Japan lent coherence to commercial banking in the United States. Nor did there develop large city banks comparable to the "Big Five" in Great Britain, the large universal banks in Germany, or the big city banks in Japan. America's large geographic size and the suspicions that many Americans harbored of bigness militated against such developments. Instead, Americans depended upon a mixture of thousands of nationally or state-chartered banks to meet their commercial needs. In 1896, there were about 11,500 commercial banks with assets of roughly $6.2 billion in the United States; by 1920, there were some 30,300, possessing assets of $47.5

billion. Due to changes in federal banking laws in the mid-1860s, many commercial banks previously chartered by states chose to become nationally chartered institutions. Nonetheless, these institutions remained small and independently owned. As the members of the Indianapolis Monetary Commission, a body set up to examine the nation's banking system, observed in 1898, "Nowhere save in the United States is there such a multitude of small and unconnected institutions. There is perhaps no more striking characteristic of the banking system of the United States than the immense number of banks of low capitalization, and the absence of institutions of large capital with branches."

This financial system possessed both strengths and weaknesses. As in earlier times, commercial banks were owned by individuals or small groups who provided the original funding. These bankers served their local areas, giving loans to merchants, farmers, and manufacturers about whom they had personal knowledge. Living in their communities, the bankers were in close touch with the business needs of their neighborhoods, towns, and surrounding areas. Nonetheless, America's financial arrangements also possessed distinct weaknesses. Each bank operated to a considerable degree in isolation, having few outside resources upon which to rely during hard times. Some correspondent banking, in which small country banks deposited reserve funds in larger city banks, existed; but this system was unable to prevent bank runs and panics in 1873, 1884, 1893, 1903, and 1907. Branch banking might have provided some stability, but state and federal laws, inspired by a fear about the development of financial monopolies, placed so many restrictions on branch banking that as late as 1920 there were only twenty-one commercial branch-bank systems in the country (by way of comparison, forty-one British banks had 6,426 offices by 1913). Only with the establishment of the Federal Reserve System in 1913 did America begin moving toward the creation of a centralized banking system, and even then the steps were halting.

Small firms thrived in other types of banking as well. The 149 savings banks in existence in 1860 ballooned to almost 2,500 forty years later. Spurred especially by the voracious capital needs of America's railroads, investment banking houses developed out of mercantile establishments. While often large in terms of the funds they managed, most of the houses operated as if they were small businesses. Many investment bankers continued to think of themselves as merchants, and personal relations and trust pervaded the industry. While some investment banking houses became multiunit enterprises with branches in different cities, none were organized as corporations or had established elaborate managerial hierarchies.

In the early 1900s, the nation's and arguably the world's most important investment banking house, J. P. Morgan's House of Morgan, offered a good example of how investment banking houses continued to operate along personal lines. Morgan worked through four interlocking partnership arrangements—one each for New York (his headquarters), Philadelphia, London, and Paris. He and his ten or eleven partners handled most of the work of the firms by themselves, meeting as needs dictated rather than according to any set schedule. Morgan himself made the final decisions on all important pieces of business. The supporting staff was minimal. In 1903, the New York office had fewer than 150 employees, of whom only a half dozen were salaried associates. In the decade before World War I, the Paris house had about twenty employees, the London office fewer than fifty, and the Philadelphia office perhaps seventy-five. Personal relationships, rather than organized hierarchies, lay behind the work of the Morgan firms.

America's Businesses in a Dual Economy

The rise of big businesses combined with the persistence of small firms to begin creating a dual economy in the United States in the late nineteenth and early twentieth centuries. That is, America's economy began separating into two parts, with large and small businesses often found in different segments. As we have seen, the nation's largest companies developed primarily in manufacturing as vertically integrated enterprises. Benefiting from scale economies, they tended to be capital-intensive firms using large-batch or continuous-process manufacturing techniques. Sometimes called "center" or "core" companies by economists and historians, these large firms often came to exist in oligopolistic industries. By 1904, just a handful of companies controlled at least one-half of the output in seventy-eight different industries in the United States. In these industries, managers substantially determined the prices and outputs of the companies, as the "visible hand" of management replaced the "invisible hand" of the market. Small companies generally clustered in different segments of the economy: in labor-intensive manufacturing, in farming, and in sales and services, sectors where economies of scale were fewer. In manufacturing, for example, smaller firms were able to coexist with their larger counterparts in fields in which the flexible output of specialized items using relatively short production runs counted for more than the mass production of homogeneous goods in long production runs. As we have seen, this situation existed in the textile industry. Sometimes called "peripheral" companies by scholars, the smaller firms did not control their markets but instead were at their mercy.

The small business segment of the economy was much more volatile than the big business sector. Small businesses came and went with much greater frequency than big businesses. Of the 278 largest companies in the United States in 1917, 264 (94 percent) were still in operation fifty years later. Even in the fields in which they successfully competed or coexisted with big businesses, small firms formed and dissolved more often than that. The situation in Poughkeepsie, New York, may have been typical for businesses in the United States as a whole. Small firms did not last long there. Of some 1,530 businesses, most of them small companies, evaluated for credit there by R. G. Dun and Company and its predecessor agency between 1845 and 1880, some 32 percent lasted three years or less, and only 14 percent remained twenty years after their founding.

Women and Minorities in Small Business

Large and small firms also differed in the types of people they attracted as owners and managers. Almost without exception, big businesses were run by well-educated men who came from middle-class or upper-class backgrounds and who were native-born. No women or minorities and few immigrants rose to the top of large firms in the nation's emerging industrial economy. To the extent that they succeeded in business management and ownership, women, minorities, and immigrants moved ahead mainly in small firms.

The rise of big business did offer some opportunities for women, though few at high levels of management. Women secured white-collar positions as department store buyers, clerical workers, and saleswomen in large companies. Some women also found positions in advertising and marketing in large companies that were seeking to woo women consumers. Similarly, banks and insurance companies set up women's departments, staffed by women, to attract female customers; and some public utilities employed women as salespeople to sell electric appliances (then new devices) — such as stoves, irons, and refrigerators — to women. In a few new industries — such as movie making, the beauty industry, and professional rodeo — some women also found avenues for advancement. For the most part, however, distinct limitations were placed on how far women could travel up the corporate ladder, prefiguring what would be called the "glass ceiling" after World War II. No women made it into the upper echelons of big business management, except in the beauty industry.

Women remained very active in small businesses, however. The division of the lives of men and women into "separate spheres," public and private activities, if it ever really existed in the United States, did not extend far into small business ownership or management. As in earlier times, women played important roles in just about all sorts of small (often very small) firms, manufacturing being perhaps the one area in which they were not very significant. Nonetheless, women especially continued to operate small, family businesses, often in areas seen as "feminized": catering, confectionery shops, hairdressing, and boarding houses. In 1876, for example, 80 percent of the women listed in the pages of the *Boston Directory* (a business directory) prepared food, made clothing, or offered lodging; and more than half of these women entrepreneurs served other women.

For minorities, too, small firms offered opportunities not found in larger enterprises, but the participation of minorities in small businesses varied considerably by group and by type of business. Hindered by racism and by law from pursuing careers in manufacturing and farming, many Chinese and Japanese ended up in domestic service. Those who went into business on their own did so by running retail outlets, especially grocery stores, and service businesses, such as restaurants and laundries. In effect, the Chinese and Japanese succeeded by creating market niches for their small firms. Few white business people either wanted to go into their lines of work, as in laundries, or had the necessary knowledge to do so, as in the operation of stores and restaurants specializing in Asian food. As in the case of many small white businesses, these minority small business enterprises were predominantly family operations, in which the proprietor often employed unpaid family members. Some Chinese and Japanese also formed various sorts of insurance companies and banks to serve their compatriots. Here they were less successful. Hindered by hostile state legislation, none of the ten banks started by Japanese in California survived the 1920s.

Recent European immigrants to the United States also found small business activities attractive. Often drawing on kinship connections and networks of friends for capital and labor, immigrants formed many small enterprises. Immigrants from eastern and southern Europe (of whom about 2 million came to the United States between 1870 and 1910) established contracting companies for construction work, opened saloons, and started small shops selling food. Urban Jewish women were among the most active groups of all, opening many small shops, such as corner groceries. Although the ethnic makeup of the groups changed, immigrants continued to find small businesses an important economic opportunity throughout the twentieth century, as will be seen in later chapters.

Obstacles to black involvement in business in some ways resembled the barriers faced by Chinese and Japanese. In all three cases, racism and restrictive laws severely retarded full business development. Institutionalized in Jim Crow laws that segregated blacks from other groups (as in segregated eating establishments, transportation facilities, and restrooms), racism hurt. Racism cut off most blacks from the credit that they needed to form large manufacturing firms (one exception was the black hair-care and beauty aids industry, which offered a chance for a few black entrepreneurs, including women, to build regional and even national business empires) and made it difficult for black businesses to serve mixed communities. Consequently, most black businesses were small concerns, often family enterprises, designed to meet the needs of black communities. Within the limits set by the world of racism in America, blacks experienced what Juliet Walker, the leading historian of black businesses in America, has called "the golden age of black business" between 1900 and 1930. The number of black businesses in America increased from 4,000 in 1865 to 50,000 in 1914.

Black leaders encouraged business development. Booker T. Washington, arguably the most important African American leader of the late nineteenth and early twentieth centuries, cautioned blacks to be patient with their second-class social and political status in the United States while striving to get ahead economically. In 1900, Washington founded the National Negro Business League to stimulate the establishment of black businesses. Fifteen years later, the league had 600 chapters in thirty-four states. W. E. B. Du Bois, who is well-known for his role in helping start the National Association for the Advancement of Colored People and who rejected any acceptance by blacks of inferior social or political treatment, agreed with Washington, nonetheless, on the need for the formation of black businesses. At an important conference in 1898, he and other black leaders called upon blacks to become more involved in the business world by acquiring higher education, which would allow them to compete, and by patronizing black businesses.

Working within black communities, African American business people advanced at all levels, though not without difficulty. At the local level, blacks started grocery, dry cleaning, and personal service businesses.

Sometimes facing competition from knowledgeable white business owners eager to sell to them, blacks often proved less successful than Asian Americans in the operation of these businesses. In cities with sizable black populations, however, blacks did construct black hotels, recreation centers, and resorts (in 1910, some 10,000 black women ran boarding houses). At the regional and national levels, blacks, like Asian Americans, formed insurance companies and banks to serve their communities, and in this they proved relatively more successful. Between 1880 and 1910, for example, blacks established a host of fraternal insurance organizations. By 1927, the thirty-two largest black insurance companies, which accounted for 85 percent of all of the black-held insurance written by black-owned companies, had $316 million worth of policies in force. Nonetheless, these companies were relatively small firms. In the same year, a single white-owned company had $900 million worth of insurance in force on black policyholders, and in 1940 one large white company had a greater value of policies in force on blacks than did the top forty black companies combined. Small they might be when compared to their white counterparts, but the black insurance companies had a significance that cannot be judged by the size of their assets alone. They often involved their founders and investors in other business enterprises helpful to black communities: department stores, real estate developments, newspapers, and the like. Black banks — some 134 were founded between 1888 and 1934, though few survived the Great Depression of the 1930s — were also small, but they were significant as engines of advancement in some towns and cities.

As significant as small service and financial businesses were for blacks, farming was more important. In 1910, 73 percent of African American entrepreneurs were in agriculture (compared to less than 60 percent of white entrepreneurs). As a consequence, in that year the nonagricultural rate of entrepreneurship for blacks was just 6 percent, compared to 17 percent for whites.

Blurring and Cooperation between Big and Small Business
Although there were major differences between small and large firms and the two types of companies often existed in separate realms of business, there was also a considerable degree of interaction between them. To describe America's emerging modern business system simply in terms of center and peripheral firms misses some of the complexity of the situation. In fact, large and small firms grew up symbiotically, at least in some fields. While many large industrial businesses became vertically integrated

to some degree, few were totally integrated. Industrial districts often contained firms of many sizes, all dependent on each other. Small firms frequently acted as subcontractors for their larger brethren. As they expanded their output to meet the voracious demands of America's growing national market, some manufacturers, as we have seen, set up their own sales outlets. Others, however, came to rely upon franchised agents. Rather than possess their own sales outlets, a costly proposition, manufacturers depended upon agents closely tied to but still legally independent from their firms to make the sales. The I. M. Singer (Sewing Machine) Company and the McCormick Harvester Company employed primitive franchise sales systems in the nineteenth century, a practice that would be refined and become widespread in the twentieth century.

Small Business Thought

Small business owners — men and women, minority and nonminority alike — continued, as in the colonial and antebellum years, to value their small firms for nonpecuniary as well as monetary reasons. The psychic and social independence they derived from their businesses remained important for them. As we have seen, many of the owners of small manufacturing ventures continued to take pride in the quality of the products their shops turned out and continued to approach their work as craftsmen. Farmers like Lewis McMillen of Ohio identified with their land and their localities, even as they produced for America's expanding national market.

However, actual economic and social independence was becoming elusive by the turn of the century, as the United States was transformed from a land of isolated small farms, shops, and towns into a country in which more and more people lived in large cities and worked in the plants and offices of big businesses. In this situation, Americans formed organizations to mediate between themselves and the social and economic forces that were changing their country. Through organizational life they sought to achieve a new sense of order in the United States. Industrial workers formed nationwide labor unions; professionals founded professional societies, such as the American Medical Association and the American Bar Association; farmers formed buying and selling cooperatives; and large businessmen established trade associations and chambers of commerce. Small business owners were sometimes caught up in this organizational thrust of American society, and blacks and women set up their own nationwide business and professional associations, yet their continuing desire for independence meant that they would participate less fully in the organizational life of the United States than most other Americans, even when it might have been in their best economic interest to have done so.

Of those small business organizations that did develop, the most common were those that grew up at the local and state levels. Typical perhaps of local business organizations was the Manufacturer's Association of Montgomery County, Pennsylvania. Formed in 1908 by small industrialists worried about labor legislation then under consideration in their state, the body soon became more than a reactive organization. By the time of World War I, the association was offering a variety of services to its members, and the scope of these expanded still more in later years. By 1927, the organization had 212 members, by 1958 nearly 300, all served by a salaried staff in association headquarters. The state of California also provides examples of how business people running enterprises of all sizes established organizations during the Progressive era to advance their economic causes. Family farmers set up cooperatives, one of which became Sunkist; bankers joined the California Bankers' Association, whose officers worked through both voluntary methods and state legislation to upgrade banking practices; investment bankers formed their own associations for much the same reasons; and insurance agents established bodies to try to improve business practices and influence state legislation.

At the national level, small business organizations were less common, but two typify the varied approaches small business owners took to the problems they faced. In 1895, small and medium-sized industrialists, mainly in the Midwest, formed the National Association of Manufacturers (NAM) to press for federal government policies that would further the development of exports. Beginning in 1902, under the leadership of David M. Parry, NAM became an antiunion organization that rose to national prominence, boasting 3,500 member firms by 1914. Differing from this broad-based association was the industry-specific National Association of Retail Druggists (NARD). Established in 1898, NARD was powerful enough just eight years later to enforce a tripartite agreement among drug manufacturers, wholesalers, and retailers. This agreement set uniform prices through manufacturers' sales contracts that bound distributors to charge only agreed-upon resale prices. Declared to be in violation of the Sherman Act, this agreement was broken up in the Progressive era, whereupon NARD became a leading advocate of resale price maintenance legislation in the 1920s.

American Small Business at the Time of World War I

The rise of big business dramatically changed the world of small business in the late nineteenth and early twentieth centuries. In the colonial period and in the antebellum years, nearly all American businesses had been small firms, single-unit enterprises without managerial hierarchies. With the acceleration in industrialization that occurred after the Civil War, this situation changed. Especially in the field of manufacturing, large companies that benefited from economies of scale supplanted smaller ones in some lines of work. While continuing to grow in absolute numbers, small industrial firms became proportionally less important to the American economy.

Nonetheless, small business remained a significant part of that economy. In agriculture the family farm remained the norm, though the beginnings of agribusiness enterprises were visible. In the sales and service industries, too, small businesses continued as the dominant form of business organization; but in these realms as well they faced increasing competition from big businesses. Beginning a trend that would long continue, small manufacturers using flexible production methods and creating market niches for their products successfully coexisted with their larger counterparts in industry. They operated both as members of industrial districts, as in the case of the Philadelphia textile makers, and as independents. There existed no single path to success for small industrialists. Chapter 3 examines small and medium-sized manufacturers in one field, metal making, as a way of revealing how some small industrialists were able to coexist and prosper along with their larger brethren.

Additional Reading

Alfred D. Chandler Jr., *The Visible Hand: The Managerial Revolution in American Business* (Cambridge, Mass.: Harvard University Press, 1977), is the key work on the rise of big business in the United States. Naomi Lamoreaux, *The Great Merger Movement in American Business, 1895–1904* (Cambridge, Eng.: Cambridge University Press, 1995), is the best account of why mergers occurred at the turn of the twentieth century. Louis Galambos, *The Public Image of Big Business in America, 1880–1940* (Baltimore: Johns Hopkins University Press, 1975); Martin Sklar, *The Corporate Reorganization of American Capitalism, 1890–1916: The Market, Law, and Politics* (New York: Cambridge University Press, 1988); and Thomas McCraw, *Prophets of Regulation* (Cambridge, Mass.: Harvard University Press, 1984), are valuable sources on public attitudes and government actions with regard to business. David Hounshell, *From the American System to Mass Produc-*

tion, 1800–1932: The Development of Manufacturing Technology in the United States (Baltimore: Johns Hopkins University Press, 1984, provides a valuable look at industrialization in America. Mansel G. Blackford, *The Politics of Business in California, 1890–1920* (Columbus: Ohio State University Press, 1977), is a study in regional business and political change.

Philip Scranton has pioneered in the scholarly exploration of industrial districts in the United States. For information on Philadelphia's textile district, see his *Proprietary Capitalism: The Textile Manufacture at Philadelphia, 1800–1885* (Cambridge, Eng.: Cambridge University Press, 1983); and his *Figured Tapestry: Production, Markets, and Power in Philadelphia Textiles, 1885–1941* (Cambridge, Eng.: Cambridge University Press, 1989). For a broader study, see Scranton, *Endless Novelty: Specialty Production and American Industrialization, 1865–1925* (Princeton: Princeton University Press, 1997). See also Steven Fraser, "Combined and Uneven Development in the Men's Clothing Industry," *Business History Review* 57 (Winter 1983): 522–47. Charles Sabel and Jonathan Zeitlin, "Historical Alternatives to Mass Production: Politics, Markets, and Technology in Nineteenth-Century Industrialization," *Past and Present* 108 (August 1985): 131–76, examines flexible production methods in Europe; for more detail, see the eleven essays in Sabel and Zeitlin, eds., *World of Possibilities: Flexibility and Mass Production in Western Industrialization* (New York: Cambridge University Press, 1997). Five articles in *Enterprise & Society* 1 (March 2000), explore the importance of flexible production methods in industrialization worldwide. See also essays by Michel Lescure on France, Aurelio Alaimo on Italy, and Johzen Takeuchi and Takeshi Abe on Japan in Konosuke Odaka and Minoru Sawai, eds., *Small Firms, Large Concerns* (Oxford: Oxford University Press, 1999).

Fred Shannon, *The Farmer's Last Frontier: Agriculture, 1860–1897* (New York: Harper and Row, 1968); David Danbom, *Resisted Revolution: Urban America and the Industrialization of Agriculture, 1900–1930* (Ames: Iowa State University Press, 1979); and Earl Hayter, *The Troubled Farmer, 1850–1900: Rural Adjustment to Industrialism* (De Kalb: Northern Illinois University Press, 1968), remain valuable surveys of agricultural change. Wheeler McMillen, *Ohio Farm* (Columbus: Ohio State University Press, 1974), is a firsthand account. Regional studies include Daniel Nelson, *Farm and Factory: Workers in the Midwest, 1880–1990* (Bloomington: Indiana University Press, 1995); and David Vaught, *Cultivating California: Growers, Specialty Crops, and Labor, 1875–1920* (Baltimore: Johns Hopkins University Press, 1999).

H. Roger Grant, *Life Insurance Reform: Consumer Action in the Progressive Era* (Ames: Iowa State University Press, 1979); and Morton Keller, *The Life Insurance Enterprise, 1885–1910* (Cambridge, Mass.: Harvard University Press, 1964), are solid introductions to the structure and politics of America's insurance industry. Benjamin Klebaner, *American Commercial Banking* (Boston: Twayne, 1990); Vincent Carosso, *Investment Banking in America: A History* (Cambridge, Mass.: Harvard University Press, 1970); and Vincent Carosso, *The Morgans: Private International Bankers* (Cambridge, Mass.: Harvard University Press, 1987), are excellent introductions to the history of American banking in the late nineteenth and early twentieth centuries.

Essays by Frances Gregory, Irene Neu, and William Miller in William Miller, ed., *Men in Business* (New York: Harper and Row, 1952), explore the socioeconomic backgrounds of the leaders of large firms. Gillette Hutchinson, Arthur Hutchinson, and Mabel Newcomer, "A Study in Business Mortality: The Life of Business Enterprises in Poughkeepsie, New York, 1843–1936," *American Economic Review* 28 (September 1938): 497–514, is a valuable community study in business successes and failures. James Soltow, "Small City Industrialists in the Age of Organization," *Business History Review* 33 (Summer 1959), is one of the few works to examine the organizational activities of small business people. In addition to Angel Kwolek-Folland, *Incorporating Women* (New York: Twayne, 1998), the following studies examine women in business: Angel Kwolek-Folland, *Engendering Business: Men and Women in the Corporate Office, 1870–1930* (Baltimore: Johns Hopkins University Press, 1994); Margery Davies, *Woman's Place Is at the Typewriter: Office Work and Office Workers, 1870–1930* (Philadelphia: Temple University Press, 1982); and Susan Benson, *Counter Cultures: Saleswomen, Managers, and Customers in American Department Stores, 1890–1940* (Urbana: University of Illinois Press, 1986). On women in twentieth-century American business more generally, see Kathy Preiss, "'Vital Industry' and Women's Ventures: Conceptualizing Gender in Twentieth Century Business History," *Business History Review* 72 (Summer 1998): 219–242.

Scott Cummings, ed., *Self-Help in Urban America: Patterns of Minority Business Enterprise* (Port Washington, N.Y.: Kennikat, 1980); Ivan H. Light, *Ethnic Enterprise in America: Business and Welfare among Chinese, Japanese, and Blacks* (Berkeley: University of California Press, 1972): and Jan Rath, ed., *Immigrant Businesses: The Economic, Political and Social Environment* (New York: St. Martin's, 2000), are valuable introductions. In addition, Scranton surveys the historical importance of small businesses for immigrants in his essay, "Moving Outside Manufacturing: Research Perspectives on Small Business in Twentieth-Century America," in Odaka and Sawai, eds., *Small Firms, Large Concerns*. On blacks in business, see Juliet E. K. Walker, *History of Black Business in America* (New York: Twayne, 1998) and the following studies: Alexa Henderson, *Atlantic Life Insurance Company: Guardian of Black Economic Dignity* (Tuscaloosa: University of Alabama Press, 1990); John Ingham, "African American Business Leaders in the South, 1810–1945: Business Success, Community Leadership and Racial Protest," *Business and Economic History* 22 (Fall 1993): 262–72; Robert Kenzer, *Enterprising Southerners: Black Economic Success in North Carolina, 1865–1915* (Charlottesville: University Press of Virginia, 1997); Margaret Levenstein, "African American Entrepreneurship: The View from the 1910 Census," *Business and Economic History* 24 (Fall 1995): 106–22; and Loren Schweninger, *Black Property Owners in the South, 1790–1915* (Urbana: University of Illinois Press, 1990.

3

Industrial Districts and
Stand-Alone Companies

In *The Valley of Decision*, Marcia Davenport's moving novel about life in Pittsburgh in the late nineteenth and early twentieth centuries, the owner of a small steel mill explains how he competed successfully with the much larger Carnegie Steel Company. "'I could not compete with the steel rail production proposed for this Edgar Thompson Works [one of the Carnegie plants],' he said slowly. But he added, 'They cannot compete with me if I concentrate on special alloys for tools and farm machinery, that kind of thing. Nobody,' he said slowly, 'is opening up that kind of field much.'" Davenport's fiction described reality. By turning out specialty products and by creating market niches for themselves, small and medium-size iron and steel makers persisted and even prospered as viable concerns in the age of giant industrial enterprise. So did makers of nonferrous metals, such as zinc and brass goods. Small metal manufacturers often got ahead as members of industrial districts, much like the small firms composing Philadelphia's textile district; a major steel and iron district grew up in Pittsburgh, populated by scores of smaller concerns. Andrew Carnegie's Carnegie Steel (later United States Steel Corporation) was not the only game in town. In addition, in some areas small iron and steel companies developed on their own as independent firms. The Buckeye Steel Castings Company of Columbus, Ohio, was one such enterprise.

Large and Small Firms in Steel Districts

In America's iron and steel industries, large companies came to dominate important segments of their fields. By using new, large-batch production methods, they turned out vast quantities of homogeneous steel products, mainly railroad rails and structural steel, for America's expanding national market. Nonetheless, smaller iron and steel mills continued to thrive alongside the giants, even in Pittsburgh, the heart of the nation's iron and steel industry.

Pittsburgh's iron and steel industries took form, the historian John Ingham has shown, as collections of relatively small businesses. As late as 1870, the typical firm was capitalized at just $210,000, produced 3,000 tons of iron and steel annually, and employed only 119 workers. Like their counterparts elsewhere in America, Pittsburgh's iron and steel mills were unintegrated enterprises. They engaged in only one or two, not all, of the steps involved in turning out iron and steel products. The companies were, for the most part, family businesses, with about forty families dominating the industries. The owners lived in Pittsburgh or nearby areas and ran their businesses themselves, without the use of managerial hierarchies.

The switch from iron to steel, and with this change the use of the capital-intensive Bessemer and open-hearth methods, altered the situation in Pittsburgh, but only somewhat. Despite the expansion of new methods of steel making, iron production continued to grow as well; and older methods of steel making, such as the crucible process, continued to enjoy popularity. Many mills did become larger, but few approached the enormous size of the Carnegie operations. By the late 1880s, the average Pittsburgh iron and steel firm was capitalized at $805,000 and produced 14,000 tons of iron and steel with a workforce of 332. Many of these continued to be run by well-established Pittsburgh families (Carnegie was considered an outsider). The rise of a few giant firms, such as Carnegie Steel, should not obscure the continuing importance of the many other smaller companies, for there remained fifty-eight independent iron and steel mills in Pittsburgh in 1894.

The independent Pittsburgh mills (those not part of the expanding Carnegie empire) prospered by specializing. Rather than compete with Carnegie Steel in the large-batch production of rails and structural steel, most coexisted side-by-side with the Carnegie enterprises by producing specialized goods for niche markets. In pursuing this strategy Pittsburgh's independent iron and steel producers closely mirrored the approach to business taken by Philadelphia's textile makers in their competition with the larger companies of New England. Oliver & Phillips, the Sable Rolling Mill, Vesuvius Iron, Juniata Iron, Crescent Steel, Hussey Wells & Company, and LaBelle Steel were some of the firms that successfully specialized. Oliver & Phillips, for instance, went into the making of nuts and bolts, wagon hardware, and barbed wire, while Vesuvius engaged in the production of bar and sheet iron, rods, hoops, and nails.

The coexistence of many smaller iron and steel companies with a few giant ones continued well into the twentieth century. Not even the formation of United States Steel in 1901 radically altered the situation. Only a few of the old-line independents became part of United States Steel, and between 1898 and 1901 sixteen new iron and steel firms were set up in Pittsburgh. In 1901, the forty independent producers in Pittsburgh had a production capacity of 3.8 million tons of iron and steel, compared to the 2.6 million–ton capacity of United States Steel. In 1920, fully 78 percent of the independents in existence two decades before were still doing business, and even after America's second major merger movement, which occurred in the 1920s, about 50 percent were active. The Great Depression ended the existence of more, but on the eve of World War II 28 percent of the independents remained. The independents not only survived, but by 1938 had also increased their combined production capacity to 7.9 million tons.

Throughout the nineteenth and into the twentieth century, the independent mill owners composed much of the social elite of Pittsburgh, in marked contrast to the lesser social role played by the textile makers in Philadelphia. From the 1840s through the 1890s, 141 families owned and operated iron or steel mills in Pittsburgh. About one-half of these were considered to be among the city's upper class. This situation continued into the mid-twentieth century, as many iron and steel families branched out into banking. It was this social elite — based upon iron, steel, and finance — that largely controlled Pittsburgh's political and cultural life for many years, losing its hegemony only after the Second World War.

Their positions as leaders in their community influenced how the independent iron and steel mill owners dealt with their labor forces. Perhaps both because they were close to their workers in relatively small plants and because they cared deeply for the welfare of Pittsburgh, most tended toward a grudging acceptance of unions and a pragmatic willingness to try to work with them. More than the operators of the much larger Carnegie mills, the owner-operators of the small independent facilities sought to achieve a harmonious relationship with their workers, especially in the 1870s and 1880s. In the 1890s and later, following the lead of the larger firms, the independent mill owners became less tolerant of labor. As they adopted more capital-intensive equipment and were influenced by the examples of violence against labor at Carnegie Steel, they turned more of their attention to breaking unions.

In Europe, too, steel districts composed of small producers arose. One of the most well-known steel districts lay in the Sheffield area of England. Small quantities of iron and steel had been made in Sheffield since the 1400s, but in the 1700s and 1800s the Sheffield district emerged as a center for the production of crucible steel in Europe. In crucible steel making, which is sometimes called "cast" steel, clay pots contained the iron bars and alloys melted by charcoal (and later by coking coal) to become steel. Long an art more than a science, these melts were small, often less than 100 pounds per crucible.

Several factors led to Sheffield's emergence as a crucible-steel center. The region possessed a skilled, intelligent workforce, a legacy of its many centuries of experience in making iron and steel. A tremendous diversity of skills was present, with many of the skilled workers, using funds from family and friends (not a lot of capital was needed in the early days), becoming "little masters" who ran their own crucible steel firms. In addition, Sheffield had rivers to provide waterpower for the forging, grinding, and rolling operations needed to produce cutlery (knives) and other finished products. Charcoal, clay, and bar iron were also available. Finally there was rising demand for the crucible steel, which was very hard and which could thus be used for the cutting edges of cutlery and all sorts of tools. By 1856, Sheffield had 124 crucible steel makers. Most of these were small, specialized family firms engaged in one or two types of operations, such as grinding or hardening steel. The many firms competed with each other, but they also complemented each other. That is, they depended on each other to make finished products; few of the companies performed all the steps needed to turn out a final product. Their factories composed a definite cluster or district several miles long; and this clustering fostered innovation, adaptability, and a quest for quality, as people and ideas moved fairly freely from firm to firm. Altogether, they made 90 percent of Britain's steel and 50 percent of the world's steel.

Sheffield continued to develop as a steel district between 1850 and 1920. Eschewing the Bessemer and open-hearth processes by which mass-produced steel was made, most of Sheffield's steelmakers stayed with the crucible method. They turned out specialty-steel products for niche markets — steel projectiles for cannons and steel plating for ships, for example. They produced ever more sophisticated cutting tools, and they used chemical processes to make more alloyed steels (using elements such as manganese and tungsten), which went into bicycles, automobiles, machine tools, and the like. Many of the firms contributed to funding for the Sheffield

Technical School (later part of Sheffield University), established in 1884. Research from the school, in turn, helped the companies in their quest for new processes and products. One breakthrough was stainless steel. Most of Sheffield's steel companies remained small or medium-sized enterprises. There were about 150 steelmakers in the Sheffield district at the time of World War I, along with hundreds of toolmakers. Most were run as family-owned, personally managed firms.

Stand-Alone Companies in Steel and Other Metals

The success of small firms in the iron and steel industries was not limited to the Pittsburgh region or to other steel districts. The growth of the Buckeye Steel Castings Company of Columbus, Ohio, suggests the continuing importance of stand-alone small businesses in manufacturing across the nation. Formed as a partnership in 1881, Buckeye Steel initially was simply one of some twenty companies producing a variety of cast-iron goods for the local market in central Ohio. Buckeye lacked a specialty product or any other advantage over its competitors and came very close to failing during the hard times of the mid-1880s. However, through personal ties, the founders of the company were able to attract new investors, most importantly Wilbur Goodspeed. Hailing from Cleveland, Goodspeed moved to Columbus in 1886, assumed the presidency of Buckeye Steel, and reorganized the company as a corporation.

Goodspeed saved Buckeye Steel, and how he did so illustrates some of the ways by which small firms were able to coexist with their larger counterparts. Like many of the independent Pittsburgh steel companies, Buckeye Steel developed a specialty product for a niche market: an automatic railroad car coupler. Made out of cast iron in the 1890s, but out of stronger cast steel in the twentieth century, this technologically sophisticated coupler gave Buckeye an edge over its competitors and allowed the company to break into the national market. In entering this market, Buckeye Steel's executives relied heavily upon their personal connections with other business people. While in business in Cleveland, Goodspeed had come to know high-ranking executives at the Standard Oil Company, which was headquartered in that city. The men all belonged to the Cleveland Gatling Gun Regiment, a private group of businessmen (there were no women members) who purchased several Gatling guns in the wake of a nationwide railroad strike. Their intention was to be prepared to meet with force any future labor disturbances. Soon after he took over at Buckeye Steel, Goodspeed negotiated an arrangement favorable to both parties.

In return for receiving a large block of common stock in Buckeye Steel for free, the Standard Oil executives agreed to use their influence to persuade all of the railroads that shipped Standard's petroleum products to market (few long-distance pipelines existed then) to purchase their couplers solely from Buckeye Steel.

Railroad orders soared. As had been hoped, railroads carrying Standard's oil bought almost exclusively from Buckeye Steel. Buckeye Steel emerged as a very successful business. Personal connections continued to play a substantial role in Buckeye Steel's growth. Almost every officer in the company had ties to railroads and used those connections to help sell Buckeye Steel's couplers. Beyond this fortunate circumstance, other factors contributed to Buckeye's rise. The firm's owner-managers reinvested the company's earnings in their corporation, building what became in the first decade of the twentieth century the most up-to-date steel mill of its type in the United States. Imbued with the principles of scientific management, they designed and operated an ultra-efficient steel mill. That was not all. Like the independent iron and steel mill owners in Pittsburgh, Buckeye Steel's officers were deeply interested in the progress of their community and closely involved in community affairs. This concern, combined with a desire to lessen the turnover rate of workers in their steel foundry, led Buckeye's officers to institute a broad range of corporate welfare activities for their workers. Largely successful in achieving a sense of harmony with their workforce, Buckeye's owner-managers kept their plant free of labor strife. In addition, from the early 1910s well into the 1940s Buckeye's officers, in violation of America's antitrust laws, met with their competitors each year to set prices and divide markets. The result was that by the onset of World War I Buckeye Steel Castings had become a medium-size and quite profitable company.

In brass making, another example of small business success in metal making, the competitive situation differed from that in the production of iron and steel. Because of the small size of the total market for brass products, no truly large companies emerged. Rather, a host of small firms composed the brass-making industry. The development of the Smith & Griggs Company of Waterbury, Connecticut, was typical of that of the many small firms in the brass industry. Founded as a partnership in 1865, the company was incorporated a few years later but continued to be run as a family business into the twentieth century. Smith & Griggs moved ahead by devising technical innovations in the manufacturing of specialty products for a distinct market niche (mainly buckles and buttons) and through the maintenance of close personal ties between its owner-managers and the wholesalers purchasing its goods. In 1900, the company earned $47,000 on sales of $220,000 (85 percent of these sales were made to just ten customers, underlining the necessity of maintaining good relations with the wholesalers).

Successful in its nineteenth-century operations, Smith & Griggs went into decline in the twentieth century. A new president, a person still related to the founding families of the company, assumed power in 1908 but failed to meet several pressing challenges. In particular, many former customers were integrating backward, setting up their own production facilities as the availability of new types of machinery made this step feasible. At the same time, deterioration in its service cost Smith & Griggs orders from many of its largest and oldest wholesalers. Strapped for funds, the company engaged in less research and development than before and failed to develop a new market niche to compensate for the one it was rapidly losing. As was occurring in many of Philadelphia's textile companies at about the same time, flexibility was replaced by inflexibility at Smith & Griggs. Faced with mounting losses during the Great Depression, the firm went out of existence in 1936. A possible lesson to be drawn from the experiences of Smith & Griggs is that small firms survive only if new technology does not preempt their "niche" status.

Something of the same story developed with regard to the Platt Brothers, a small metals manufacturer in Connecticut's Naugatuck Valley. Formed in 1847 as a processor of zinc and later becoming a manufacturer of zinc and brass buttons, the company succeeded through five generations of owner-managers well into the twentieth century, by which time the firm had become a maker of zinc fuses. By using and often developing the most current technologies (Platt Brothers' owner-managers loved to get their hands dirty, often working on the factory floor themselves) and by rapidly adapting to changing market demands, Platt Brothers generally enjoyed handsome profits. Platt Brothers succeeded in part by intentionally staying small and avoiding head-to-head competition with larger firms. Family considerations always played important roles in the development of the business. So did community ties. Treating its workers well, Platt Brothers generally paid high wages and enjoyed the services of a well-trained and highly motivated labor force.

Successful Small Metal Manufacturers

Common themes run through the successes of those small companies that proved capable of coexisting with big businesses in metals. Consciously or unconsciously, the small manufacturers adopted a growth strategy that would remain one of the keys to success in small business into the late twentieth century: they developed specialty products which they then sold in niche markets, thereby often avoiding direct competition with their larger counterparts. To make this growth strategy work, the firms usually adopted (or developed themselves) the most advanced production technologies available. These small companies were not backward workshops using obsolete equipment but were instead among the most advanced industrial establishments of their day.

Running the companies were managers deeply committed to their success. Most of the companies, even those organized as corporations, continued to be operated as family enterprises. The businesses remained single-unit enterprises, devoid, for the most part, of managerial hierarchies (though some of the independent Pittsburgh mills developed simple hierarchies in the late nineteenth century). More than a quest for profits animated their owners. A sense of personal satisfaction, almost a sense of craftsmanship, remained an important motivating factor for their executives and workers. Writing his wife about business affairs in 1908, the president of Buckeye Steel captured this feeling when he observed, "We have had hard times to bear, but surely we should not care to have our lives easy, for there would be no accomplishment, no development." Not surprisingly, personal connections and informal ways of conducting business continued to be important in the daily operations of the firms.

Nonetheless, new management techniques crept into the world of small business manufacturing. As small manufacturing companies became more capital-intensive, some emulated their larger counterparts in instituting new accounting practices. The adoption of innovations especially in cost and capital accounting helped them compete with larger companies. For instance, some firms in the cut nail industry of the Ohio Valley, small businesses all, developed new cost accounting methods as early as the 1850s and 1860s. In the decades after the Civil War the nail companies improved their systems of inventory control, and by the 1870s and 1880s the most successful of the firms were using cost accounting as a diagnostic tool in their planning processes, one of the first group of American companies to do so.

At Buckeye Steel, as well, both cost and capital accounting were well advanced as early as 1903, when the company was still a small firm. In his approach to cost accounting, Buckeye's plant superintendent was among the most sophisticated managers of his day, pioneering in the inclusion of indirect and overhead expenses as part of his costs of production, at a time when many manufacturers, large and small, simply ignored them. In capital accounting, the superintendent carefully figured monthly charges for furnace, building, and machinery repairs, together with depreciation charges — again at a time when many industrialists failed to account for such expenses.

Perhaps because of their continuing personal involvement in their businesses, small-scale industrialists were often more concerned about the welfare of their labor forces than their larger counterparts. Many of the smaller, more profitable manufacturers were both more receptive to unions and more willing to engage in welfare capitalism. This situation was most apparent in Pittsburgh's iron and steel industries, at least into the 1890s. Despite its reputation of being antilabor, small business was, as these cases show, often receptive to the needs of workers. Not all small business owners adopted a benevolent attitude, however. The picture of small business response to labor was a complex one. In 1895, owners of small and medium-size firms formed the National Association of Manufacturers, which soon grew to become a national trade association and which became virulently antiunion in the twentieth century.

Factors external to their companies also prepared the way to success. In some instances government aid helped. Such was the case with Buckeye Steel. In 1893, Congress passed legislation requiring that all railroad cars be equipped with automatic couplers within five years. (This act was a piece of safety legislation designed to protect trainmen, who were often injured while joining cars together with the old-style manual couplers.) This law helped create a national market for Buckeye Steel's main product. In other cases, a favorable local environment proved valuable.

Along with their larger brethren, small and medium-size manufacturers, including metal-making companies, faced new challenges during the 1920s, 1930s, and 1940s, as described in Chapter 4. Two world wars and a time of prosperity followed by the worst economic depression in America's history all created an unstable, very fluid business situation. Small firms had to adjust to these changing circumstances and to the continued development of big business. How they did so (and failed to do so) would help shape the nation's business system to the present day.

Additional Reading

John Ingham, *Making Iron and Steel: Independent Mills in the Pittsburgh Area, 1820–1920* (Columbus: Ohio State University Press, 1991), is a path-breaking account dealing with small and medium-sized iron and steel firms. Geoffrey Tweedale, *Steel City: Entrepreneurship, Strategy, and Technology in Sheffield, 1743–1993* (Oxford, Eng.: Clarendon, 1995), examines developments in Sheffield. Studies of individual companies include Mansel G. Blackford, *A Portrait Cast in Steel: Buckeye International and Columbus, Ohio, 1881–1980* (Westport, Conn.: Greenwood, 1982); Theodore Marburg, *Small Business in Brass Fabricating: The Smith and Griggs Manufacturing Co. of Waterbury* (New York: New York University Press, 1956); and Matthew W. Roth, *Platt Brothers and Company: Small Business in American Manufacturing* (Hanover, N.H.: University Press of New England, 1994). Amos J. Loveday Jr., *The Rise and Decline of the American Cut Nail Industry: A Study of the Relationships of Technology, Business Organization, and Management Techniques* (Westport, Conn.: Greenwood, 1983), is a valuable industry study. For a fictional account, see Marcia Davenport, *The Valley of Decision* (New York: Scribner's, 1942).

4

Small Business in Boom and Bust, 1921–1945

In 1938, at the suggestion of his secretary of commerce, President Franklin D. Roosevelt invited 1,000 small business people from around the nation to a conference in Washington, D.C. Roosevelt hoped to show that small business people, as opposed to their big business counterparts, supported the New Deal. Convened on February 3, the Small Business Conference achieved no such consensus. From beginning to end, the meeting was in almost constant turmoil, as the delegates divided by region, type of industry, and the sizes of their businesses (some small businesses were larger than others). At the start of the first afternoon session, a typical disagreement surfaced. Seventeen New York business people seized the front of the Department of Commerce auditorium demanding to be heard on behalf of the millions they said they represented, whereupon non–New Yorkers broke into the raucous chant of "New York sit down! New York sit down!" Lasting for several more days, the conference accomplished little except to show disunity among small business people. No more than in the past did small businesses compose a monolithic group.

At times throughout the mid-twentieth century, as in 1938, it seemed that there were as many types of small businesses—each with its own agenda—as there existed small business firms. Yet, all operated in a similar environment. The two and a half decades after 1921 witnessed a marked decline in the importance of small firms relative to larger companies. During the mid-twentieth century, American business people, building upon the accomplishments of their predecessors, brought their nation's economy to a new level of maturity through the completion of a national market for their goods. As America's national economy matured, small businesses in many fields found their roles shrinking relative to big businesses. As we have seen, public attitudes and governmental actions have helped shape the external environment of business in the United States, thus partially determining what firms can and cannot do. In the mid-twentieth century, as the American economy went through cycles of boom and bust, government policies became increasingly important in influencing business decisions. The 1920s, 1930s, and 1940s were unstable times for all American businesses, as the decades were punctuated by wars, bursts of prosperity, and years of depression. In addition to the secular, long-term rise of big business in many fields, small and medium-size firms had, thus, to adjust to very unsettled economic circumstances between 1921 and 1945.

American Attitudes toward Small Business

The mixed emotions that Americans had long held toward big business continued into the 1940s. As in earlier years, Americans harbored fears about the threats that big businesses might pose to economic opportunities and, though to a much lesser degree, to political democracy in their land. As the second and third generations of Americans exposed to big business, however, citizens after 1920 showed a greater degree of acceptance of it. Criticism became muted. Not even the Great Depression shook the faith of most middle-class Americans in their nation's business system. Yet, at the same time—especially from the 1930s on—a growing number viewed small firms and their owners in a more positive light. Small businesses came to be seen as institutions that, by their very nature, could make valuable contributions to the development of America's business system.

Many of the attitudes established by the turn of the century continued to hold sway into the 1920s and 1930s. During the 1920s, most professionals, landowning farmers, and skilled workers admired big businesses for the prosperity, job security, and material goods they seemed to provide. Rising incomes, the fact that many were themselves now members of large organized groups—cooperatives, labor unions, and professional associations—and the fact that big business had been part of the American scene for forty years led most Americans to accept its permanence. The Depression decade sorely tried the faith of Americans in big businesses, as many blamed them for the coming of hard times. Yet, this break with big business was remarkably brief. By the close of the 1930s, as some prosperity returned, most Americans had reaffirmed their acceptance of the large corporation. The boom times of World War II sealed the pact, and there existed little active opposition to big business in the first quarter century after the war.

Surveying the nation's graduating college class of 1949, the editors of *Fortune* found that the typical graduate "wants to work for somebody else — preferably somebody big." "No longer," they concluded, "is small business the promised land." By the same token, an extensive public opinion poll taken by the Institute of Social Research of the University of Michigan in 1951 revealed that old suspicions of big business were fading fast. Asked to assess the general social effects of big business, most Americans responded in a favorable vein — "The good things outweigh the bad things: 76 percent; the bad things outweigh the good things: 10 percent; they seem about equal: 2 percent; confused: 12 percent."

Their acceptance of big business did not, however, preclude Americans from liking the small business person and small business. To the contrary, many continued to admire small business owners and, as time passed, to see a growing role for small business in the American economy. As in earlier times, some Americans who worked for large corporations hoped, upon retiring, to start their own independent small businesses. Reflecting public attitudes, popular magazines sometimes glorified the small business person as a staunch individualist but portrayed small businesses in the 1920s as part of a vanishing breed — as retail concerns in small towns, enterprises without much of a future in the face of growing competition from chain stores. However, writers for business journals adopted a more positive point of view. They perceived small businesses as serving useful roles in an economy dominated by big businesses. Small businesses could fill market niches ignored by larger concerns and, by using flexible management and manufacturing methods, might even compete with large industrial enterprises. Marking a reversal from their earlier stances, popular magazines in the 1930s picked up this trend and began picturing small businesses as vibrant parts of the nation's economic system. By the close of the decade, popular magazine articles were promulgating the notion that small and large firms could coexist and that small firms were not necessarily doomed by the rise of big business.

From the 1920s into the 1940s, the policies of the federal government toward business in general and small business in particular followed a labyrinth of twists and turns. Astute politicians and governmental officials sought to balance an appreciation for the economic benefits of big business with sensitivity to the ideological needs of Americans. A perceptive editorial published in *Collier's* in 1938 observed the ambivalent feelings of Americans toward small business and the varied policies taken by the government with regard to them:

The record is that for a hundred years and longer we have been building our business big and at the same time cheering patriots who advocated laws commanding our business to stay small. We built business big because we craved the fruits of large-scale production. . . . Surely the time is ripe for common sense and plain speech on this vital issue. Business is going to be big and small, too, for that matter, and it should not be beyond the wisdom of statesmen to contrive policies and laws which will preserve the obvious advantages of the industrial system which is so distinctly American.

Government Policies during the Interwar Years

During World War I, business leaders who cooperated with the federal government benefited from increased outputs, higher profits, and a growth in industrial efficiency. In 1917, to coordinate the output of war goods, President Woodrow Wilson established the War Industries Board (WIB). This federal agency was given the power to set uniform prices that all government organizations, including the army and navy, would pay for war materials produced by private industry. The WIB also established production quotas for different industries and set priorities for the distribution of scarce raw materials between different industries and between individual companies within industries. Directed by Bernard Baruch, a former Wall Street whiz, the WIB operated through committees, one for each major industry. The committees were composed of government officials and representatives from private industry, usually big businessmen who headed industry-specific trade associations.

To encourage maximum production of war materials, the WIB set the prices to be paid by the government considerably above prevailing market prices. An unexpected result was that larger, more efficient firms made greater profits than most small companies. For instance, in the steel industry the four largest and most highly integrated producers earned an average 31 percent return on their capital, while smaller firms earned an average of 16 percent. Small businesses sometimes fell behind in other ways. When raw materials were in short supply, they usually went to big businesses, not small companies. The federal government found, not for the last time, that working with a handful of big businesses to boost output quickly was far easier than trying to coordinate the work of thousands of smaller enterprises. Nonetheless, some small firms benefited as subcontractors for larger companies, and still others won prime defense contracts. The Buckeye Steel

Castings Company of Columbus, Ohio, earned rich profits turning out gun casings and other products.

Many business leaders wanted collaboration with the federal government to continue after World War I. Business and government leaders had worked together in a wide variety of industries—including the railroads, shipbuilding, and food production—as well as those producing materials needed directly for fighting on the front lines. After the war, some big business executives hoped to work with federal government officials in smoothing out the ups and downs of the business cycle to achieve steady economic growth. In Herbert Hoover, secretary of commerce under Presidents Warren Harding and Calvin Coolidge, they found a ready ally; Hoover wanted government and business to work together voluntarily to bolster the economic strength of the nation. Although it was largely unable to moderate swings in the business cycle, as the economic collapse in the early 1930s graphically demonstrated, such government-business cooperation—which scholars have labeled "associationalism"—reached a new high point in the mid- and late 1920s.

The impact of associationalism upon small business was mixed. Hoover and other federal government officials worked closely with trade association officers, who were usually the heads of big businesses; and many of the resulting policies favored large businesses more than small ones. At the same time, U.S. Supreme Court decisions, based upon the "rule of reason," first enunciated in 1911, continued to favor the development of big businesses. The Supreme Court also permitted trade associations to engage in many cooperative activities that previously had been forbidden. Not surprisingly, given these favorable political policies, concentration proceeded in the American business system. The United States experienced its second major merger movement between 1925 and 1931, as 5,846 mergers occurred. Yet, Hoover's policies also strengthened small businesses in some fields. Over the course of the 1920s, the proportion of gainfully employed Americans who were self-employed nonfarm business people remained steady, rising slightly from 6.5 percent to 6.6 percent. In the lumber, movie, and aviation industries, conferences for business people, many of them small business owners, sponsored by the Department of Commerce led to the adoption of more efficient production methods and more cooperation among firms. For instance, conferences in 1922, 1923, and 1925 led lumber company owners to adopt standard sizes and grades for their boards and, in general, to reduce waste in their mills.

Much of the cooperation between government and business begun during World War I and the 1920s continued into the early years of President Franklin D. Roosevelt's New Deal. Only the situation had changed: by the time Roosevelt took office in 1933, the economic growth of the 1920s had vanished, replaced by the hard times of the Great Depression. By 1932, industrial production had fallen to one-half of what it had been just four years earlier, and at least one-quarter of the nation's workforce was unemployed. In the four years following the stock market crash of 1929, some 110,000 businesses failed.

Black-owned and women-owned businesses were especially hurt. The "golden age" of black business ended abruptly. The high unemployment rate of blacks, about twice that of whites, bit into the sales of black stores. Between 1929 and 1935, the number of black retail businesses declined by 10 percent, and their sales plummeted by more than half. Sales by black-owned stores remained small by national standards. In 1939, black retail sales amounted to less than 0.2 percent of the national total. In some service businesses the story was even grimmer. Only 12 of the 134 banks formed by blacks between 1884 and 1935 remained in operation in 1936, leading scholar Abram Harris to observe at the time, "Notwithstanding the public assertions of many Negro leaders to the contrary, the conviction is growing among them that the future of Negro finance and business is dismal." Most companies owned by women were, we have seen, like black businesses, small and clustered in sales and services. They, too, faced very hard times during the Great Depression. As explained by the historian Angel Kwolek-Folland, "The years of the mid-twentieth century marked time for women in business, riding out the storms of economic and diplomatic collapse while witnessing incremental change in the number of women workers, managers, and entrepreneurs."

Initially, Roosevelt's main engine for pulling the economy out of the Great Depression was the National Recovery Administration (NRA), a federal government agency modeled partly upon the WIB. Established by the passage of the National Industrial Recovery Act in the summer of 1933, the NRA was intended to mobilize the economy for recovery. As had the WIB, the NRA set up committees organized by industry and staffed by government officials and business executives, usually big businessmen who were officers in trade associations. The goal of the NRA was to raise business profits and thereby, its proponents hoped, bring about a return of prosperity. To do so, the industry committees of the NRA adopted codes of fair business practices. Under these codes, businesses limited competition with each other by cutting back production and raising their prices (the nation's antitrust laws were suspended to allow these actions). As had happened in the operations of the WIB, big business generally benefited more than small business from the work of the NRA, for big business officers called the shots in the operations of the agency. Declared unconstitutional by the Supreme Court, the NRA went out of existence in 1935.

Roosevelt also sought to bring about recovery by having the government make loans directly to businesses; here, too, large firms generally benefited more than small ones. Established in 1932 under President Herbert Hoover, the Reconstruction Finance Corporation (RFC), a federal agency, was empowered in 1934 to make loans to industrial and commercial businesses. By the end of 1946, the agency had made 35,000 loans totaling $3.3 billion. Most of the money went to big businesses. Just 298 transactions of more than $1 million apiece accounted for 55 percent of the agency's loans by value. By way of contrast, 11,000 loans of $5,000 or less composed 1 percent of the total value of the loans granted. In 1934, legislation also empowered the Federal Reserve System to grant direct loans to private businesses under certain conditions. Again, big businesses received most of the loans. During the first three years of this program, for example, only 564 of the 2,406 loans approved were for $5,000 or less, only about 1 percent of the total value of all loans. After analyzing the capital needs of small businesses, a federal government investigatory body concluded in 1941 that the RFC and the Federal Reserve banks "have contributed only slightly to the alleviation of this difficulty" and "cannot be considered important factors in this area."

Even as some programs of the New Deal sought economic recovery by offering aid to big business, other programs tried to help small firms. Far from being a carefully thought-out blueprint for the redesigning of the American economy, the New Deal was composed of a series of ad hoc measures hastily thrown together to stimulate recovery from the worst economic crisis in America's history. As such, the New Deal contained many anomalies and inconsistencies.

At the same time that Roosevelt and Congress worked with big business leaders through the NRA, politicians sought to protect small businesses from competition with some of those same large firms. In the 1920s, chain store operations developed to challenge smaller "mom-and-pop" stores in the grocery and drug trades. Some state legislatures passed protective laws, and Congress followed suit. Between 1933 and 1942, Congress considered 390 bills designed to protect small businesses and enacted 26, most of which dealt with retailing. Two pieces of legislation were of most importance. The Robinson-Patman Act of 1936 restricted volume discounts often given by manufacturers and wholesalers to their largest retail customers, and the Miller-Tydings Act passed a year later sought in a variety of ways to protect small retailers from the competition of the chains.

As time passed, Roosevelt soured in his views on big business leaders. Failing to win their support for many of his New Deal measures, Roosevelt increasingly turned to other groups, especially labor, for backing. Coming to believe that the nation's economic recovery was being retarded by the monopoly power of big businesses, Roosevelt in 1938 asked Congress to fund an examination of competitive conditions in American business. Congress responded by establishing the Temporary National Economic Committee (TNEC), which carried out a series of economic investigations. At the same time, Roosevelt appointed a new attorney general, Thurmond Arnold, and, reversing his earlier stance, instructed him to enforce the nation's antitrust laws. Bolstered by the findings of the TNEC, Arnold prosecuted a number of companies and won several convictions. His efforts did little, however, to change the economic structure of the United States and were, in any event, soon cut short by World War II. With the coming of war, the federal government shifted its emphasis to insuring the production of war materials by private industry. A chagrined Arnold shelved his antitrust actions, as wartime demands once again took precedence over other concerns.

Just as the New Deal was ending, however, the federal government took several actions to help small businesses, steps that paved the way for additional aid in the postwar years. Congress set up committees to look after the needs of small businesses, the Senate Committee on Small Business in 1940 and the House Committee on Small Business a year later. At about the same time, a Small Business Division was established within the Department of Commerce, charged with the goal of "re-inforcing the position of small enterprise and retarding the trend toward concentration."

What impact did these mixed, and at times contradictory, actions have on small business? The Depression decade witnessed a surge in the ranks of small business. The proportion of gainfully employed who were nonfarm self-employed business people rose from 6.6 percent to 8.0 percent during the 1930s. This rise in the share of Americans engaged in small business did not, however, indicate a revival in the health of small firms, but resulted from a lack of other employment options. Laid off by large firms, some Americans tried to survive by setting up their own small businesses. There

TABLE THREE. The United States Business Population, 1900–1938 (in thousands of firms)

Year	Total Listed Concerns[a]	New Enterprises	Discontinued Firms
1900	1,174	272	248
1910	1,515	358	348
1920	1,821	459	353
1925	2,113	496	451
1930	2,183	423	481
1932	2,077	338	454
1935	1,983	392	385
1938	2,102	388	365

Source: U.S. Temporary National Economic Committee, "Problems of Small Business," Monograph No. 17 (Washington, D.C.: U.S. Government Printing Office, 1941), 66.
[a] Total listed concerns means the total of all industrial and commercial names in the July issue of the Dun & Bradstreet Reference Book. This listing does not include most banks, railroads, professionals, and farmers.

was an especially large increase, for instance, in the number of small retail outlets between 1929 and 1933—grocery stores, restaurants, and gasoline stations—constituting what scholar Joseph Phillips has called a "flight into independence." The number of gasoline filling stations, for example, rose from 98,976 in 1929 to 156,538 just four years later, not because the American economy required such an expansion, but because the jobless sought employment through opening them (the financing came from oil companies eager for their own reasons to expand their retail operations). To some extent, the same phenomenon developed in manufacturing. Unemployed cigar makers became "buckeyes," self-employed cigar makers with few or no employees; in part of the silk-weaving industry, unemployed workers became owners of petty "cockroach" shops. However, despite the formation of these new small businesses, more businesses discontinued operations between 1929 and 1932 than began them. The depression years were hard times indeed, for small as well as large businesses. This reversed the past trend, for in every year since 1900, except 1917, more businesses had been formed than discontinued (see Table 3).

New small enterprises led tenuous lives. A comprehensive survey of corporations engaged in manufacturing, mining, and trade between 1931 and 1936 revealed a direct relationship between size and profitability: the smaller the firm, the lower the profit margins. As noted in Chapter 2, only a few small businesses lasted very long during the years 1880 through 1920. During the Great Depression the situation probably worsened. Generalizing from dozens of separate business mortality studies, TNEC officers concluded, "To the extent that local studies in scattered communities of the United States represent the general experience, approximately 30 percent of retail firms discontinue business within the first year. An additional 14 percent dissolve before reaching their second anniversary." Manufacturers and wholesalers, the TNEC report showed, performed slightly better, but most went out of existence fairly quickly. After surveying mortality studies for all types of firms, the head of the TNEC concluded that small businesses led very perilous lives, "The material makes it very clear that business mortality is a problem of major proportions. In study after study, in industry after industry, in area after area, the record is the same. The chance of a newcomer becoming an established member of the business community is sadly slight. He carries on until his funds are exhausted, and then he disappears from the scene."

Small Business and Government during World War II

World War II brought a return of prosperity to the United States, but small businesses did not benefit from it as much as their larger counterparts. As during World War I, the federal government's main concern was to increase the output of war materials as rapidly as possible, and governmental officials paid scant attention to insuring that defense contracts went to small firms. Army and navy procurement officers found it easier and faster to work with big businesses than to encourage the participation of small companies in production for the war effort. A Senate committee reported in February 1942 that just 56 of the nation's 184,000 manufacturing establishments had received 75 percent of the value of the army and navy contracts awarded up to that time. Small companies often suffered as well when they tried to maintain their production of civilian goods, because scarce raw materials were often allocated to big businesses. With so much government spending going to large firms and so little to smaller concerns, it became a bittersweet joke that a small business was "any business that is unable to maintain a staff in Washington to represent its interest."

Congress took actions to try to correct this situation with the passage of the Small Business Act in June 1942. This law sought to increase small business participation in the war effort by setting up a Smaller War Plants Division (SWPD) within the War Production Board, the federal agency coordinating the production of war materials. The SWPD was charged with seeing that a greater share of defense contracts went to small businesses. The act also established the Smaller War Plants Corporation (SWPC) to make loans to small firms that needed them to enter into defense businesses. Hindered by poor leadership, lacking strong support from small businesses (which remained, as at the 1938 meeting, quite divided), and inadequately funded by Congress, the SWPD and the SWPC were only partially successful in achieving their goals. Most of the defense contracts continued to flow to big businesses. Officers in the army and navy continued to argue that only large companies were "equipped with the plant and machinery, specially skilled workers, managerial know-how, financial stability, and established contracts with a wide variety of suppliers" needed to produce vast quantities of goods on time.

Big businesses received the lion's share of governmental wartime spending. Of the $175 billion worth of prime defense contracts awarded between June 1940 and September 1944, over one-half went to just thirty-three companies. Nor was the picture for small businesses much brighter with regard to subcontracts. A survey completed by the SWPC in 1943 revealed that, while a group of 252 of the largest prime contracting companies did subcontract about one-third of the value of their prime contracts, three-fourths of the subcontracts went to businesses with over 500 employees, not to smaller firms. A Senate committee concluded in 1945 that "in the period in which the greatest effort was presumably being made to speed contracts to small business, nothing was actually accomplished."

During the postwar reconversion to civilian production, big businesses continued to win more from government actions than did small firms. Large firms were in a better financial position than small firms to purchase production facilities built by the government during the war, and they did so. Two-thirds of government plants and equipment sold at war's end went to only eighty-seven big businesses.

What was the case for the war years was true for the entire period from 1921 through 1946: small businesses fell behind larger firms in their participation in the nation's economic development. Beginning with the merger movement of the late 1920s, many fields of business became increasingly concentrated. This was particularly true of manufacturing. Establishments with more than 250 workers employed 46 percent of the wage earners in American industry in 1914, and that proportion rose to 56 percent in 1937.

The movement toward bigness accelerated during World War II. Between 1939 and 1944, firms with 100 or fewer employees saw their share of industrial employment drop from 26 percent to 19 percent. By way of contrast, firms with 10,000 or more employees increased their share from 13 percent to 30 percent during the same period. Industrial concentration continued with postwar reconversion. Despite increasing their numbers from 206,000 to 255,000 between 1947 and 1954, single-plant firms saw their share of the nation's value added by manufacturing drop from 41 percent to 32 percent. Multiplant businesses, in spite of experiencing a decrease in numbers from 35,000 to 32,000, increased their share of value added by manufacturing from 59 percent to 68 percent.

Both women and black business owners benefited somewhat from World War II. (They benefited much more as workers, especially in manufacturing fields, as production for defense ended the Great Depression.) Only a few black businesses, mainly those in shirt manufacturing and in general construction work, received defense contracts. Nonetheless, war-induced prosperity helped black-owned retail and service companies. A survey of 3,866 black businesses in eleven major American cities showed that 74 percent experienced an increase in sales between 1941 and 1944; another 19 percent reported no change, and 7 percent had a decline. Even so, white-owned businesses continued to capture the dollars of black consumers. "Black business statistics," writes the historian Juliet Walker, "provide compelling evidence" that black businesses lacked "the capacity to sustain a separate black economy." The impacts of World War II on women in business were, Kwolek-Folland has concluded, "mixed." On the one hand, she writes, the war "surely accelerated the long-term trend toward women's paid employment"; on the other hand, the conflict "strengthened many people's desire for domesticity" and retarded some aspects of women's participation in business.

Small and Large Business in Manufacturing

During the 1920s, 1930s, and 1940s, more than in earlier times, America became a consumer society. That is, business sold an ever wider range of goods — automobiles, electric stoves, radios, and the like — to the public. In doing so, the companies at first found a vast virgin market, continental in scope, for their products. Ford Motors sold 15 million Model Ts between 1908 and 1927, the last year in which the car was produced. Advertising firms, many of which grew to become big businesses during the 1920s, stimulated demand for these consumer durables, products designed to last for more than just a year or two. Often paid for on time, a practice called "installment buying," consumer durables changed the nature of American culture; Americans came increasingly to value themselves and their neighbors in terms of the goods they possessed rather than intrinsic character traits.

As consumers bought a wider array of goods, large manufacturers entered new fields and developed new management methods. The DuPont Company went from making munitions into the production of paint and nylon. In the automobile industry, too, important changes occurred. By the mid-1920s, the virgin market for cars was filled, and buyers wanted a greater variety of automobiles. General Motors supplied that variety of automobile lines, with models ranging from Chevrolet to Buick and Cadillac; in doing so, General Motors overtook Ford Motors and became America's and the world's largest automobile producer.

As they made a greater variety of products for a wider variety of markets (a concept often called "market segmentation"), large manufacturers found that they needed to devise new organizational structures and management methods to handle the growing complexities of their businesses. Led by General Motors, they developed decentralized management for their diversified operations. The head office (or corporate office) oversaw grand strategy for the company and coordinated its operations, but it left the details of those operations to managers in charge of divisions, which were often based on product lines (such as the Chevrolet division at General Motors). Greatly improved accounting methods and information flow held together the many layers of management — top, middle, and lower — that developed in these new large firms, as did numerous committees made up of executives from the head office and the divisions. More and more important in the industrial sector of the American economy between the mid-1920s and the early 1970s (and in some other nations, such as Great Britain, in the 1960s and 1970s), large, decentralized, multidivisional firms took market share away from their smaller brethren.

Interestingly, in light of the recent debate on the importance of research and development in America's reindustrialization in the 1990s and on the roles of large and small firms in it, it was not a lack of involvement in industrial research that hurt small firms. In fact, smaller companies appear to have participated in industrial research nearly as much as the nation's industrial giants. Between 1921 and 1946, the rates of participation of the largest 200 manufacturers and smaller companies were about the same. Except in chemicals, in which large companies dominated research efforts, smaller firms held their own. Moreover, as time progressed, small and medium-size firms increased their relative importance in the research being done. The relative decline of small business in manufacturing was due more to the continued existence and exploitation of economies of scale in manufacturing by the larger firms, furthering a trend begun shortly after the Civil War.

However, not all small and medium-size manufacturers were hurt by the rise of large multidivisional enterprises. In some cases they could coexist with them by serving targeted markets particularly well. In short, they could occasionally outplay their larger competitors in segmenting markets. Asked about how his small firm competed with larger companies in the late 1920s, the president of a New England concern specializing in the production of air valves captured the essence of how some small businesses succeeded. "A small company must have a product with a limited market potential," he observed. "If the potential of a product developed by a small company is too big," he continued, "a large corporation will take it away." Like the maker of air valves, a growing number of small manufacturers tailored their products and services to very specific niche markets.

The metal-fabricating and machinery-making industry of New England provides an instructive example of the success of small business in America from 1890 to 1960. The historian James Soltow has shown that small and medium-sized companies dominated this industry. Of the eighty firms composing the industry, all but eighteen employed fewer than 100 workers, only fifteen possessed assets exceeding $500,000, and only ten had a net worth of more than $500,000. These companies shared common patterns of development, management, and success.

Like those starting small manufacturing enterprises in earlier times — the Philadelphia textile makers and Pittsburgh's independent iron and steel makers, for example — the entrepreneurs setting up the metal-fabricating and machinery-making shops usually had prior knowledge of the business. Often the necessary technical knowledge was gained through experiences on the shop floor as skilled workers, although some of those entering the industry had graduated in engineering from Massachusetts Institute of Technology (MIT) and similar institutions. Most established their ventures because of a strong desire to control an independent business of their own, a desire that often extended back into their childhood. These entrepreneurs were far from the "organization men" so typical of American businesses in the 1950s and 1960s. One explained that he liked being "a lone operator," able "to make decisions instantly and to carry them out." Or, as another put it, "I can do what I want, and I don't have to take any bull from anyone." A desire for freedom more than a quest for large profits provided their motivation. Still, a desire for self-preservation also played a role in the founding of the companies. More were started during the trough of the business cycle than during any other of its stages, suggesting again that many Americans go into small businesses when they find other employment options cut off.

Growth and success most frequently came through the development of specialty products for niche markets, a strategy that offered some hope of insulation from competition with other, often larger, firms. Some entrepreneurs, like the owner of the company making air valves, specialized in products with only a limited demand, thus avoiding competition with big businesses disdaining to enter such unappealing fields. Others engaged in just one process: metal stamping, heat-treating, or electroplating. By performing custom work, they secured nonstandardized orders overlooked by larger mass-production firms. Still others differentiated their products by providing extraordinary service and by building up reputations for dependability. For example, a manufacturer of screw-machine products honed its competitive edge through its ability to make an item "in a hurry" for its customers "when it has to be right."

Personal ties held these small businesses together. Most of the founders, like those in small businesses in other industries and in other times, began their enterprises as partnerships or single-owner proprietorships, though all except six eventually reorganized their businesses as corporations. Whatever legal forms they assumed, nearly all of the businesses were directly run by their owner-founders. One-man shows, characterized by hands-on, seat-of-pants administration were common. Except in the largest of the firms, little delegation of authority occurred and no managerial hierarchies came into being. Family enterprises in which fathers and sons or brothers jointly handled affairs frequently existed; sometimes wives also participated, usually looking after the finances of the operations.

This personal approach to business carried over into financing and labor relations. Personal savings — supplemented by family funds, funds from local business acquaintances, and, to a much lesser extent, bank borrowing — provided most of the initial capital. Almost no use was made of borrowing from federal government agencies. Capital used to finance expansion came mainly from retained earnings and debt financing. Few of the entrepreneurs had access to equity markets. Even if they had possessed such access, few would have made use of it, for most were not willing to dilute their ownership and managerial control over their companies. Over one-half of the companies began with five or fewer employees. As the firms developed, they were able to acquire and keep their growing number of employees through a combination of monetary and nonmonetary incentives. Some paid more than the prevailing wage rate. Others provided chances for rapid advancement and opportunities to learn new skills, and, in all, the owner-managers continued to know their workers individually.

Small Business in Japanese Manufacturing

Small businesses were dominant in Japanese manufacturing during the interwar years, and their successes provide a valuable comparison to the fortunes of small businesses in American manufacturing. As industrialization in Japan came to emphasize heavy industry (steel, chemicals, shipbuilding, and the like) over light industry (cotton, silk, and tea) during the 1930s and 1940s, large business combines called "zaibatsu," which had begun developing in the late 1800s, grew in importance. The zaibatsu (those formed in the interwar years are often called "new zaibatsu") were business empires that contained banks, trading companies, and mining concerns, in addition to industrial companies. Few of the industrial ventures in the zaibatsu (or in nonzaibatsu firms) were vertically integrated, however. Instead, in contrast to the situation in the United States, large manufacturers relied heavily on smaller manufacturers as subcontractors. In fact, despite efforts made by the Japanese government to consolidate firms in many branches of industry, the importance of small subcontractors actually increased. By the mid-1930s, at least 20 percent of the manufacturing value of products in Japan's automobile, textile weaving, and electrical equipment industry came from subcontractors.

In addition, small manufacturers remained important as independent producers not tied to larger industrialists. The machine tool industry, for example, despite concerted government efforts to force mergers and cooperation, remained home to many small and fiercely independent firms. In 1938, the industry was composed of 1,978 companies (up from 397 firms in 1932), of which only 93 had more than 100 workers (1,531 had fewer than 30). Not even the exigencies of World War II, including renewed government efforts to make their industry more efficient, succeeded in forcing the toolmakers to combine. Small manufacturers using flexible production methods remained the norm in this industry after World War II. Many clustered in industrial districts, such as Sakaki in the Nagano Prefecture on the main Japanese island of Honshu, where they could benefit from the presence of similar firms—borrowing workers, and even machinery from each other from time to time, and cooperating in the establishment of marketing institutions.

The establishment of Osaka as an industrial district also illustrates well the importance of small firms in Japanese manufacturing. Throughout the 1920s, 1930s, and 1940s, Osaka was the nation's leading industrial district, with textiles, metals, machinery, ceramics, and chemicals as its leading products. In 1935, Osaka's 12,580 industrial firms employed 327,000 workers and turned out 17 percent of Japan's industrial goods. Most of the Osaka firms were small, independent businesses. Less than 1 percent of the factories employed as many as 500 workers, and only 2.5 percent employed more than 100. Firms with no more than 100 workers apiece employed 60 percent of Osaka's workers. The most common career path for owners of metals and machinery factories and shops—there were 11,847 such entrepreneurs in Osaka in 1937—led from a job as a worker following graduation from a school, through upgrading skills, the accumulation of start-up funds from family and friends, and the expansion of networks needed for the opening of business. This was a career path strikingly similar to that for owners of metalworking and machinery-fabricating firms in New England. Universities, secondary schools, vocational schools, and research institutes provided skilled workers and the information needed for the Osaka district to grow and prosper. As late as 1985, the district's 76,367 industrial firms employed 964,000 workers and made 8.4 percent of Japan's industrial products.

Thus, industrial districts in America and around the world continued to provide alternatives to large, vertically integrated manufacturing concerns. Aggregations of many small and medium-sized companies in a region could, in fact, act as functional equivalents to their larger brethren. While often competing furiously with each other, the small companies also frequently shared workers, ideas, and institutions. Nor did this end with World War II. After the conflict, industrial districts, usually building on prewar foundations, continued to develop. In the machine tool and machinery-making industries, vibrant industrial districts grew up in parts of northern Italy, especially around Bologna; in Birmingham, England; and in Tokyo's Ota Ward. Sometimes operating as subcontractors, but also often as completely independent firms, members of these districts, mainly small and medium-sized firms, used flexible production techniques to turn out a broad range of goods. Often bound together through various types of horizontal webs and informal ties, the firms composing the districts were important for national well-being. In the early 1990s, for example, the 40,000 businesses in Tokyo's Ota Ward (an area of fifty-four square kilometers) employed 350,000 people.

Small Business in Retailing

Writing in 1931, retailing expert Malcolm P. McNair correctly observed, "In the United States the major scene of the industrial revolution has definitely shifted from production to distribution." The most notable change lay in the rapid increase in the importance of chain stores. The number of chains in the United States (groups consisting of two or more stores) rose from 905 in 1921 up to 1,718 just seven years later. By 1929, the Great Atlantic and Pacific Tea Company (A&P) was operating 15,418 stores, Woolworth 1,825, and J. C. Penney 1,395. In 1929, chains accounted for 10 percent of all retail stores in the United States and did 20 percent of the nation's retail business. The expansion of chain stores slowed during the Great Depression and the immediate postwar years, but chains remained an important part of the nation's retailing structure. By 1935, chains controlled 8 percent of the nation's retail outlets but had increased their share of sales to 23 percent, a proportion that dropped, however, to 22 percent in 1939 and to 20 percent a decade later.

The spread of chain stores was part of a more general trend in distribution: the growth in the importance of large-scale stores. By 1949, in addition to the 20 percent of the nation's retail sales made by chain stores, department stores accounted for 8 percent, supermarkets 7 percent, and mail-order houses 1 percent. Independent retailers, who as late as 1890 had handled nearly all retail sales, accounted for only two-thirds of the sales by the time of the Korean War. Most of the chain outlets were considerably larger than those of independent retailers. By 1939, for example, the average chain store had annual sales of $75,000, roughly four times the volume of the typical independent.

Developments in grocery sales demonstrate well the changing relationships between chain stores and independents. In 1900, only twenty-one chains existed in the grocery trade. By 1920, the number had risen to 180, and by 1929 to 807. In the latter year, grocery chains operated 54,000 stores, one-third of all of the chain units in the nation, and accounted for over one-third of grocery sales in the United States. By 1931, the five largest chains alone—A&P, Kroger, American Stores, Safeway, and First National

Stores—made up 29 percent of America's grocery sales, up from just 6 percent ten years before.

What accounted for this dramatic rise in the chains and the equally precipitous decline of the independents? Chain stores possessed numerous advantages. Most importantly, chain stores offered lower prices to consumers—prices the business historian Richard Tedlow has concluded were "never less than 3 percent and often as much as 10 or 11 percent lower" than those of independents. Chains could offer lower prices and still earn substantial profits. They provided customers fewer personal services than did independents, made no deliveries, dealt strictly in cash, and dispensed fewer premiums and trading stamps. More frequently than independents, chains engaged in the most up-to-date business practices: new accounting methods to keep track of inventories, new store layouts, and new forms of advertising. Their scale of operations allowed the chains to pass on savings in costs to their customers. Many chains cut out middlemen in distribution, dealing instead directly with the growers and producers of goods. By 1936, A&P had eliminated many wholesalers through the ownership of 111 warehouses. Chains also engaged in extensive backward vertical integration. A&P possessed subsidiaries that controlled many of its sources of milk, cheese, coffee, canned salmon, and bread. While chain stores still depended upon outside providers for most of their goods, by the mid-1930s 12 percent of their sales came from goods they manufactured themselves.

While the development of chain stores presented the first challenge to independents in the grocery industry, the growth of supermarkets offered a second one from the 1930s onward, a challenge that chains such as A&P also had to meet. Much larger in floor space than the outlets of established chains, the supermarkets, like the chains before them, built up their trade on the basis of low prices. Supermarkets provided even less personal service than most chains. For the first time, customers were expected to pick their goods off shelves throughout the stores rather than have them gathered by clerks. Two factors explain the timing of the supermarket challenge. The widespread adoption of automobiles by Americans meant that supermarkets could locate on the outskirts of town where land was cheap, allowing the construction of large stores with extensive parking lots. In addition, supermarkets emphasized sales of nationally known, brand-name goods advertised on the radio—something most Americans wanted, but something the established chains, tied to private in-house labels, failed to provide. About 300 supermarkets were in operation in 1935, and within a year 900 more had opened their doors.

A&P and most of the other national chains that had come into prominence during the 1920s successfully adjusted to the development of supermarkets by closing their small outlets and opening their own supermarkets. A&P, for example, operated 14,926 grocery stores in 1935, but just six years later the number was down to 6,170, of which 1,594 were supermarkets. This transformation made A&P the largest retailer in the world. In 1951, the company boasted sales of nearly $3.2 billion and profits of $32 million, $5 million more than the combined profits of its two nearest rivals, Safeway and Kroger.

Independent retailers responded politically to the chain store and supermarket challenges. Independent retailers sought the passage of legislation at both the state and national levels to slow or halt the growth of the chains. The political campaign against the chains began at the local and state levels, with efforts to slow their expansion through taxation. As early as 1923, a tax measure received serious consideration, though not passage, from the Missouri state legislature. Four years later, thirteen such bills were introduced into state legislatures, with four securing approval. As the Great Depression hurt independents, the movement to limit chains quickened. Between 1930 and 1935, more than 800 chain store taxation measures were considered. By 1941, twenty-seven states had passed anti–chain store taxes; and, despite the repeal of many of these laws, nine remained effective. Except in a few localities, such as Portland, Oregon, it was less the opposition of independent retailers (who, like most small business people, remained less well organized than their larger counterparts) and more the spontaneous crusades of politicians that led to the passage of laws taxing the chains. Especially in the South and West the chains were seen as outside, "foreign" interests dominated by Wall Street, which were sapping local enterprise and initiative. The chains also appeared as handy targets for state legislatures strapped for tax revenues during the hard times of the 1930s.

Even as they tried to restrain chains through political action, independents also formed their own voluntary chains, such as the Independent Grocers Association (IGA). Designed to bring the benefits of mass purchasing to the smaller stores, while maintaining their independence, the voluntary associations spread rapidly. By 1930, there were thirty-three voluntary chains composed of 40,000 stores in the United States. Ten years later, the number of participating stores had mushroomed to 110,000 in grocery chains alone. By 1974, 57 percent of America's supermarkets operated as members of cooperatives or voluntary chains.

The political campaign against the chains soon shifted to the national level, where it focused upon two measures. The first was the Robinson-Patman Act, a modification of the Clayton Act of 1914. The Robinson-Patman Act ostensibly sought to protect independent retailers from chain store incursions in a number of ways, most importantly by prohibiting growers, manufacturers, and wholesalers from giving chains discounts for large-quantity purchases, even though those savings were often passed on to consumers in the form of lower prices. Although originally written by officials of the U.S. Wholesale Grocers' Association, whose members disliked giving discounts to the chains, the bill was nonetheless characterized as an aid to small retailers. In a highly charged debate on the bill, the goals of preserving economic opportunity and protecting small business people were presented as more important than economic efficiency and lower prices for consumers. As Wright Patman, who sponsored the bill in the House, put it, "There are a great many people who feel that if we are to preserve democracy in government, in America, we have got to preserve a democracy in business operation." Facing little organized opposition — the chains had not yet mastered the art of political lobbying — the bill became law in 1936.

The second national measure to win approval was the Miller-Tydings Act, an amendment to the Sherman Act of 1890, passed by Congress in 1937. Pushed especially hard by the powerful National Association of Retail Druggists, this act sought to standardize prices charged consumers for goods sold at retail. A retail price maintenance measure, the proposal forbade chain stores from selling their goods at prices below those set by manufacturers. Like the Robinson-Patman Act approved the previous year, the Miller-Tydings Act placed the interests of small business people above those of consumers. And, as in the debate on the Robinson-Patman Act, supporters of the Miller-Tydings bill appealed to emotions more than to economics. The measure was needed, its proponents testified, to keep alive an American way of life based upon business opportunities for everyone. As the secretary of the American Pharmaceutical Association argued, "These small businesses have been and are the backbone of the communities of this country. . . . If we ask ourselves honestly, whether we want this country to become a nation of clerks or to remain a nation of opportunity for individual enterprise, there can be only one answer consistent with American ideals."

From these efforts to restrain chains through alterations in the nation's antitrust laws, the antichain movement shifted back to an attempt to limit chain growth through taxation. In 1938, Representative Patman introduced a measure in the House to impose a heavy federal tax on all chains conducting business in more than one state. Quickly dubbed the "Death Sentence Tax" by its opponents, Wright's measure would have created a tax steeply graduated by the number of units a chain owned. In 1938, for example, the tax on A&P alone would have come to $472 million. Never reported outside of committee, this measure failed to win serious consideration after 1940.

The demise of Wright's tax proposal reveals a great deal about the increasing political sophistication of the chains and their growing acceptance by Americans. The chains, especially A&P, became more adept in mustering support for their side of political issues. In 1936 and 1937, representatives of the chains had been ineffective in their opposition to the congressional antichain measures, but they learned from these experiences. In 1938 and 1939, A&P placed advertisements in 1,300 newspapers, stressing their low prices and denouncing the proposed tax, and chain spokesmen talked to thousands of women's clubs about Wright's measure. Few consumer groups testified on behalf of the tax. Probably most important in explaining the defeat of Wright's measure, however, was the fact that chains were more fully accepted by most Americans than had been the case just a few years before. A&P's recognition of unions and its entrance into collective bargaining did much to defuse earlier labor hostility against the chains, and a host of American Federation of Labor (AFL) unions testified against Wright's proposal. Similarly, farm organizations, led by the American Farm Bureau Federation, recognized the importance of chains as purchasers of their products and spoke out against the tax proposal. Then, too, with economic recovery beginning and the growth of the chains at least temporarily slowing in the late 1930s, much of the urgency went out of the antichain campaign.

It is doubtful that any of these laws had much impact on the chains. Few of the state tax laws remained on the books for very long, and the Robinson-Patman and Miller-Tydings Acts contained numerous loopholes, which allowed chains to continue conducting business with few changes. For instance, the Robinson-Patman Act declared it "unlawful for any person engaged in commerce . . . to discriminate in price between different purchasers of commodities of like grade and quality." Since it was often possible to demonstrate that the goods involved in sales to different purchasers varied somewhat, the law was rendered ineffective. Then, too, the act never applied to services, only to the sales of goods.

Small Businesses in Retailing in Other Countries

Retailing in some foreign nations underwent changes similar to those going on in the United States. In Great Britain, chain stores (multiples), department stores, and cooperatives challenged independent retailers. Nonetheless, well over two-thirds of Britain's retail sales continued to be handled by single-outlet retailers, a higher proportion than in the United States. British families often did not want to build enterprises to a size larger than they could easily oversee, a circumstance that limited department stores and multiples to growth in single regions. In addition, it proved easier to legally enforce retail price maintenance agreements in Great Britain, which undercut advantages that large retailers might have obtained by purchasing and selling goods in bulk. The fragmented nature of British markets and tastes further delayed the spread of national retailers. In Japan, as well, small retailers remained more important than in the United States. The political strength of small retailers led the Japanese Diet in 1937 to enact a Department Store Law that limited store sizes; and legislation of this type remained on the books into the 1980s.

Small Business in Farming

Of all of the business fields under consideration in this study—manufacturing, sales, services, and agriculture—farming witnessed the most precipitous decline of small business in the years after 1920. Long-term economic trends combined with short-term emergencies to favor larger, more mechanized farms over smaller family holdings. Yet, some family farmers continued to do reasonably well—many of them, as in other types of businesses, by specializing.

Small and medium-sized farms suffered more than larger units during the 1920s and 1930s. Many American farmers had expanded operations as demand for foodstuffs skyrocketed during the First World War, often using loans backed by mortgages on their farms. When European demand collapsed in the 1920s, many found themselves unable to pay back those loans, went into bankruptcy, and lost their farms. For many farmers, hard times began well before the 1930s. The Great Depression led to a further drop in farm prices and an increase in farm distress across the nation. Most of the New Deal farm programs put funds in the hands of landowners, who often did not pass any of the aid on to their tenants. In the South, units farmed by sharecroppers fell from 776,278 to 541,291 during the Depression decade. Black tenants and sharecroppers often found themselves evicted from the lands they had worked. Despite a recommendation from the TNEC that more action was needed to help the sharecroppers, little was forthcoming. In the postwar period, as before, most federal aid went to sustain landowning farmers.

A major response of many small farmers to the problems they faced was to leave agriculture. Between 1920 and 1945, about 3 million more Americans left farming than entered it. In 1920, about 27 percent of all working Americans were engaged in agriculture, but by 1945 the proportion was only 14 percent. In general, farming became increasingly concentrated. Smaller farms, those of fewer than 259 acres, fell in number between 1920 and 1940; and so did those that were medium-sized, those comprising 260 to 500 acres. Only farms greater than 500 acres in size grew in number, with by far the greatest growth occurring in the number of those with more than 1,000 acres. By 1948, the largest 10 percent of America's farms produced 24 percent of the nation's farm output.

Even so, family farms were important into the mid-twentieth century. The scholar Mary Neth has shown, for example, that family farms long remained significant in the Midwest. Using the unpaid labor of children and women, the farms still depended partly on kinship and neighborhood values in their economic transactions; they were not completely integrated into a market economy. Community events such as threshing loomed large in rural life. According to Neth, rituals like threshing continued to lend some coherence to rural life; far from everything changed overnight on the farms.

Some family farmers prospered by specializing in the crops they grew. Such was the case with fruit growers in California and throughout the Pacific Northwest. Farm specialization increasingly spread throughout the nation. One success story was the Riggin family, the owners of a dairy near Muncie, Indiana. Rea Riggin, who founded the dairy in 1911, had gained previous experience in specialty garden and flower operations—raising vegetables for sale in the local market and growing roses, carnations, and chrysanthemums for a larger regional market. Riggin also owned a small dairy herd. During the 1920s, the Riggins expanded their dairy operations dramatically by specializing in the home delivery of high-quality dairy products. Like most farmers, the Riggins suffered from the Great Depression. By emphasizing their dairy work still more—building new modern facilities and adding to their line of dairy goods—the Riggins were, however, able to recover and expand after World War II. By the 1970s, their business was operating in four counties. By specializing in one line of goods, for they dropped vegetables and flowers, the Riggins were able to succeed in agriculture.

Small Business at Mid-Century

Not all small business people were as successful as the Riggins, however. At mid-century, small firms seemed to be in decline relative to their larger brethren in many fields. True, small businesses could survive and even prosper in some fields by providing special products or services for niche markets; New England's metalworking and machinery-making companies showed that that strategy remained a viable option in some circumstances. Overall, however, possibilities for small business advances seemed to shrink. The rise of chain stores and other large retail outlets cut into the sales and profits of mom-and-pop groceries and retail shops. In farming, the picture seemed particularly bleak, as large corporate farms increasingly supplanted smaller family operations. Federal government policies seemed unable to reverse these trends. A pessimistic verdict put forward by the TNEC in 1941 concluded that, unless the federal government intervened more forcefully than it had so far, the future of small business was dim. "There can be no denying the fact that the long-run trend of the competitive battle in most lines has been against small business," a report of the agency observed. "The small businessman has been displaced from entire industries."

One possible way to succeed as a small business continued to be by providing a specialty product or service for a niche market. The next chapter examines one such situation by looking at how Wakefield Seafoods put Alaskan king crab meat on the plates of American diners. Born of the turmoil of World War II, the company almost failed during the first few years of its existence, only to succeed and grow as a food specialist during the 1950s and 1960s. By developing a new product for a new market, Wakefield Seafoods showed how some smaller firms could survive and prosper during decades when big businesses seemed to reign supreme in the United States.

Additional Reading

David M. Kennedy, *Freedom from Fear: The American People in Depression and War, 1929–1945* (New York: Oxford University Press, 1999), is a masterly overview of social, economic, and political change in the United States. See also Alan Brinkley, *The End of Reform: New Deal Liberalism in Recession and War* (New York: Random House, 1996); Steve Fraser and Gary Gerstle, eds., *The Rise and Fall of the New Deal Order, 1930–1980* (Princeton: Princeton University Press, 1989); Colin Gordon, *New Deals: Business, Labor, and Politics in America, 1920–1935* (Cambridge, Eng.: Cambridge University Press, 1994); Ellis Hawley, *The New Deal and the Problem of Monopoly* (Princeton: Princeton University Press, 1966); and Patrick D. Reagan, *Designing a New America: The Origins of New Deal Planning, 1890–1943* (Amherst: University of Massachusetts Press, 1999). On changes in business, see Alfred D. Chandler Jr., *Strategy and Structure: Chapters in the History of American Industrial Enterprise* (Cambridge, Mass.: MIT Press, 1962).

On the politics of small business, see especially Jonathan J. Bean, *Beyond the Broker State: Federal Policies Toward Small Business, 1936–1961* (Chapel Hill: University of North Carolina Press, 1996). See also John H. Bunzel, *The American Small Businessman* (New York: Knopf, 1962); Joseph D. Phillips, *Little Business in the American Economy* (Urbana: University of Illinois Press, 1958); and Harmon Zeigler, *The Politics of Small Business* (Washington, D.C.: Public Affairs Press, 1961). On small businesses during World War II, see especially Harold Vatter, *The U.S. Economy in World War II* (New York: Columbia University Press, 1985), ch. 3; Jim Heath, "American Mobilization and the Use of Small Manufacturers, 1939–1943," *Business History Review* 46 (Autumn 1972): 295–319; and Otto Reichhardt, "Industrial Concentration and World War II: A Note on the Aircraft Industry," *Business History Review* 49 (Winter 1975): 498–503.

James H. Soltow, "Origins of Small Business: Metal Fabricators and Machinery Makers in New England, 1890–1957," *Transactions of the American Philosophical Society* 55 (1965): 1–58, is a pioneering study of small business manufacturing. See also Wayne G. Broehl Jr., *Precision Valley: The Machine Tool Companies of Springfield, Vermont* (Englewood Cliffs, N.J.: Prentice Hall, 1959). David Mowery, "Industrial Research and Firm Size, Survival, and Growth in Manufacturing, 1921–1946: An Assessment," *Journal of Economic History* 43 (December 1983): 953–80, is valuable. Two important case studies of small business success in manufacturing are Paula Petrik, "The House That Parcheesi Built: Selchow and Righter Company," *Business History Review* 60 (Autumn 1986): 410–38; and Michael Santos, "Laboring on the Periphery: Managers and Workers at the A. M. Byers Company, 1900–1956," *Business History Review* 61 (Spring 1987): 113–33. On industrial districts in Japan, see the essay by Minoru Sawai in Konosuke Odaka and Minoru Sawai, eds., *Small Firms, Large Concerns* (Oxford: Oxford University Press, 1999); David Friedman, *The Misunderstood Miracle: Industrial Development and Political Change in Japan* (Ithaca: Cornell University Press, 1988); and D. H. Whittaker, *Small Firms in the Japanese Economy* (Cambridge, Eng.: Cambridge University Press, 1997). On industrial districts in Italy, start with the essay by Aurelio Alaimo in Odaka and Sawai, eds. *Small Firms, Large Concerns*, and the essay by Vittorio Capecchi in Charles Sabel and Jonathan Zeitlin, eds., *World of Possibilities* (New York: Cambridge University Press, 1997).

Nonmanufacturing fields have also attracted scholarly attention. Much has been written about the fight against chain stores and, more generally, about small firms in sales. Richard Tedlow, *New and Improved: The Story of Mass Marketing in America* (New York: Basic, 1990), ch. 4, provides a valuable survey. See also David Horowitz, "The Crusade against Chain Stores: Portland's Independent Merchants, 1928–1935," *Oregon Historical Quarterly* 89 (Winter 1988): 341–68; Carl Ryant, "The South and the Movement against Chain Stores," *Journal of Southern History* 39 (May 1973): 207–22; and Joseph Palamountain Jr., *The Politics of Distribution* (Cambridge, Mass.: Harvard University Press, 1955). David Vaught, "State of the Art— Rural History, or Why Is There No Rural History of California?" *Agricultural History* 74, no. 4 (2000): 759–74, is an insightful survey of recent studies in agricultural history. On farming in the Midwest, see Mary Neth, *Preserving the Family Farm: Women, Community, and the Foundations of Agribusiness in the Midwest, 1900–1940* (Baltimore: Johns Hopkins University Press, 1995). For the story of a successful family farm, see E. Bruce Geelhoeld, "Business and the Family: A Local View," *Indiana Social Studies Quarterly* 33 (Autumn 1980): 58–67.

On the involvement of minorities and women in business during this period, Juliet E. K. Walker, *History of Black Business Enterprise* (New York: Twayne, 1998) and Angel Kwoleck-Folland, *Incorporating Women* (New York: Twayne, 1998), are key accounts. For contemporary studies, see Abraham L. Harris, *The Negro as Capitalist: Banking and Business among American Negroes* (New York: Negro Universities Press, 1936); and J. H. Harmon Jr., Arnett G. Lindsay, and Carter Woodson, *The Negro as Businessman* (College Park, Md.: McGrath, 1929).

CHAPTER 5

Specialty Products and
Niche Markets

Niche markets and innovative management continued to be keys to the success of small firms after World War II. Occasionally, small businesses could get ahead as specialized vertically integrated companies. A prime example lies in the success of Wakefield Seafoods as a food producer, processor, and marketer. Formed right after World War II to catch, process, and sell Alaskan king crab meat to Americans—an enterprise no other U.S. company was involved in—Wakefield Seafoods both pioneered in the development of a new industry and illustrated how small firms could succeed in modern America. The advance of the company also illustrates the importance of military spin-offs from World War II for commercial enterprises. Wakefield's ships made effective use of radar, sonar, and other high-technology devices first developed during the war.

The Formation of the Company

Lowell Wakefield spearheaded the venture, which took his name. Like many people starting small firms, Wakefield had previous experience with related businesses. He came from a family with a very extensive background in Alaska's salmon and herring fisheries; in fact, his father was one of the territory's leading cannery owners. Wakefield became acquainted with king crabs through exploratory efforts made by the federal government in the early and mid-1940s. Searching for new sources of protein for the American public and the armed forces, the government sponsored fishing expeditions along parts of the Alaskan coast, and these ventures suggested that king crabs could become a significant food source. Part of the federal government's survey was conducted right in front of a Wakefield cannery and revealed plentiful supplies of crab in the water. When the survey was completed, much of the gear was left behind with the Wakefield family, and Lowell Wakefield completed additional, promising fishing expeditions. (Even earlier, in the 1920s and 1930s, a few Russian and Japanese companies harvested king crabs and sold them in the American market as canned crabmeat.) The success of his fishing surveys and those of the federal government, his feeling that Alaska's herring and salmon industries were in decline, and a desire to strike out on his own led Lowell Wakefield to decide to break away from his family's business and set up his own company.

From these very experimental beginnings, Lowell Wakefield decided to start full-scale operations immediately after World War II. To put his ideas into practice, he spearheaded the formation of a new enterprise, Deep Sea Trawlers (soon renamed Wakefield Seafoods), incorporated under the laws of the state of Washington in October 1945. His concept for the work of his company was new to the American fishing industry. Breaking with past experience, he intended to have a single ship catch, process, and freeze king crabs and bottom fish. Previous operations had employed small ships to catch crabs and fish, which they then transferred to shore plants or large mother ships for processing and canning. Processing on board the catching vessel appealed to Wakefield as highly efficient. He expected to greatly reduce costs by decreasing spoilage and by integrating previously separated stages of fish processing into one continuous-flow operation. Freezing, which came into use for food processing in America only in the 1930s and 1940s, appealed to him as ultramodern and as a way to differentiate his crab from the canned crab of competitors. After processing, the crab and fish would be stored on board the ship in refrigerated holds until they could be packaged and sent to market.

Funding was the new company's first concern. Wakefield Seafoods' budget called for two blocks of funds, $400,000 for the construction of a ship, christened the *Deep Sea*, and $50,000 for the first year's operating expenses. Unable to secure funding for his speculative venture from commercial banks, Wakefield turned to the federal government. The Reconstruction Finance Corporation (RFC), the federal agency set up in 1931 to help businesses during the Great Depression, agreed to loan Wakefield $243,000, with the Seattle First National Bank participating to the extent of another $27,000. Private shareholders provided the rest of the funding needed to get the company going. Lowell Wakefield and his wife were the largest investors, owning 12 percent of the company's stock in the early days. Wakefield also persuaded friends and business acquaintances in Alaska's herring and salmon industries to subscribe to an additional 10 percent of the stock. The Seattle First National Bank put Wakefield in contact with another group that was considering entering the king crab industry, whereupon that group gave up its independent efforts and joined forces with Wakefield, taking up 25 percent of the stock. A group of Seattle investors, who had heard of Wakefield's fledgling firm from neighbors who were in the salmon business, subscribed to another 20 percent. A Chicago group entered the fold to take 8 percent of the stock, through connections to one of their members who had learned of Lowell Wakefield's plans while serving in the navy in Alaska during World War II.

By 1950, 126 individuals had purchased stock in Wakefield Seafoods, completing the roster of those willing to gamble on the company's future. As in most small businesses at mid-century, personal connections were of utmost importance in raising equity capital for Wakefield Seafoods. Family and business ties brought in the needed funds. The company's founders relied on themselves and a growing number of new stockholders to sell the stock. No salesmen, brokers, or public flotations were involved.

The founders and investors shared certain characteristics. They were young men on the make in their twenties or thirties. World War II had disrupted their lives, and they found themselves at loose ends at the conclusion of the conflict. Many had become water-oriented by service in the navy, often in Alaska, during the war. All were well educated and possessed funds to invest in the company. All were extremely optimistic; founders of new, small firms have to be, or the companies would never be started. They all expected that their new company would be returning hefty profits within two or three years of starting operations. More than simply money, they were looking for adventure in setting up their business venture. As one explained, Wakefield's proposal had "a lot of glamour and excitement," and by joining the venture he would be "trying something that had never been done." Or, as another put it, "When you are going to the moon, everyone wants to crowd on board."

Despite the federal loan and the private investment, Wakefield Seafoods began its existence on shaky feet. Like most people starting small businesses, those setting up Wakefield Seafoods were overly optimistic about their company's future, expecting to earn large profits quickly. Such was not to be, for the company encountered unexpected difficulties in every stage of its operations. At first, the crabs proved elusive and difficult to catch; the continuous-process cooking and freezing equipment often broke down, and markets for the frozen crab were hard to open. Within a few years, the problems were solved, but in the meantime they nearly brought Wakefield Seafoods to its knees. Like most small American businesses, Wakefield Seafoods was underfunded and lacked the financial resources to deal with difficulties. By the middle of 1948, the company had accumulated liabilities of $400,000 against assets of only $140,000 (and those consisted mainly of an unsold inventory of crab meat). Wakefield Seafoods was in default of its RFC loan and loans from commercial banks. It could pay neither its fishing crews nor its suppliers of fishing gear. Its officer-investors could take no money out of the company to live on. The company's cash on hand had dwindled to a paltry $14!

At this point, the firm's officers voted to disband and liquidate their company. They hoped to sell their one ship for a good price, pay off their many debts, and voluntarily go out of business. Had Wakefield Seafoods disbanded, it would have been typical of postwar small firms. About one-third of all new small businesses disband within one year of their formation, two-thirds within five years. However, unable to find a buyer for its specialized vessel, Wakefield Seafoods continued operations. A loan from Lowell Wakefield's father and a charter of their vessel for work for the federal government temporarily saved the situation. Even so, survival was a near thing. Learning from a friend with the Standard Oil Company that the fuel provider, which was owed thousands of dollars by Wakefield Seafoods, was about to place a lien on his ship, the captain on the firm's vessel quickly fueled up in Seattle, rounded up a scratch crew, and motored north to Alaska literally in the dead of night. Additional crew members were later flown in for the 1948–49 fishing season.

Work and Life in Alaska

The daily operations of Wakefield Seafoods inevitably revolved around the fishing expeditions of the company's one ship, the *Deep Sea*. Revolutionary in design, the vessel carried highly sophisticated electronics gear. Yet for all of the technological advances, fishing in Alaskan waters remained a rigorous and sometimes dangerous occupation.

From the outset, the *Deep Sea* pioneered in applying military electronics gear to commercial fishing. Loran, a navigational aid developed by Sperry Gyroscope, helped the vessel's officers fix the *Deep Sea*'s location. The ship's loran set picked up radio impulses transmitted from Coast Guard stations, and from these signals the officers could pinpoint their location. Loran proved especially useful in the Bering Sea north of the Aleutian Islands, where stormy skies hindered celestial navigation and where a lack of distinguishing features on the ocean floor restricted the use of depthfinders as navigational aids. The *Deep Sea*'s crew discovered that crabs could frequently be found at certain spots at particular times, and soon learned that the ability to return to those precise areas could greatly boost their catches. Loran presented problems in northern waters, however. Not until the 1950s did the Coast Guard place enough transmission stations in Alaska for fishermen to place full reliance on the system.

To augment loran, the officers of the *Deep Sea* devised what they labeled "radar fishing." In 1950, the vessel was fitted with a Sperry radar system, which, in addition to helping with navigation, was soon applied in a novel way to fishing. In catching crabs, the *Deep Sea* worked as a trawler, dragging a net along the ocean floor to scoop up crabs, and encountered difficulties remaining on top of migrating schools of crabs. In haphazard trawling operations, the schools were easily lost. To avoid this fate, the ship's officers constructed radar-reflecting buoys, made from fifty-gallon oil drums and stainless steel mesh, that projected ten feet above water. When they located a "hot spot" in trawling, they dropped off a buoy to mark it. If fishing continued to be good a considerable distance from the buoy, they would set a second buoy at the limit of the radar range. Radar could pick up images of these buoys in any weather, allowing the *Deep Sea* to thoroughly work over a promising area. The equipment needed for this type of fishing was expensive but soon proved its value. The loran set cost $3,000, the radar $15,000. These purchases were possible only because Sperry Gyroscope was willing to defer payments for them, probably due to the fact that several of Sperry Gyroscope's officers had invested heavily in the stock of Wakefield Seafoods. By the early 1950s, the use of loran and radar had, officers on the *Deep Sea* believed, boosted their crab catch by about half.

The *Deep Sea* carried a complement of about twenty-five men to work the ship and process the crab. Thoroughly unionized, they worked on a share basis. At the start of each fishing season, company and union officers agreed on the value of a packed case of crab. Each crew member received an equal share of the voyage's proceeds, computed on the basis of the value of the completed crab pack minus the company's fishing expenses. That is, each crew member shared in the profits of the company, as was common in Pacific Coast fishing. In lean years, crew members could end the season with little to show for their efforts, especially since they paid for their own meals and ship's stores, such as cigarettes and liquor, while at sea. After one trip in 1947, for example, crew members received only $169 each for three months of hard work; the voyage was, one company officer, who worked aboard the *Deep Sea* as a deckhand, ruefully noted, "a real stinker." In good years, on the other hand, crew members took home about $10,000 apiece for a fishing season of eight or nine months, considerably more than they could earn in the salmon or herring fisheries. About half of the proceeds of the sale of each year's catch went to the ship's officers (who also worked on a share basis) and crew, with the other half reserved for the company.

In the Bering Sea the daily shipboard routine varied little. The men worked alternating twelve-hour shifts, with several short breaks for coffee and food. Card games, dominoes, and drinking enlivened the end of the working day. Occasional movies, delivered by ship from the Alaska Movie Exchange, helped break the monotony.

So did physical dangers. Hoisting the heavy net and radar buoys on board in heavy seas could be hazardous. As the *Deep Sea*'s captain later recalled, "the men became adept at not getting killed," but bruises and lacerations were common. Weather was the number-one enemy, as the *Deep Sea* conducted fishing expeditions in near-arctic conditions. Only one man was lost at sea in the 1940s and 1950s, but the circumstances of his death suggest the savage conditions in which the *Deep Sea* carried on fishing. "We have been through one of the worst storms I have ever experienced at sea," the ship's captain wrote to Lowell Wakefield in April 1950. "The night Andy Peterson was lost was a nightmare," he continued, "A two-hour search was conducted using radar ranges and bearings on Amak Island, search being abandoned at darkness. The sea was 30–40 feet, wind NW 60–70 [knots, about 80 miles per hour], and it was snowing hard." In a public statement a little later, the captain, who was also a founder and investor in Wakefield Seafoods, summed up the working situation well. It was "a hard, strenuous life" in which the "hours are long, the weather bad, and the men away from home and their families for months at a time." In the winter of 1961–62 alone, thirteen king crab boats were lost at sea in storms whose winds exceeded 137 knots—a disaster that led Wakefield to lament that, while risks had always been "the lot of those who follow the sea," the "final reckoning is never easy."

A Successful Small Business

Wakefield Seafoods thus barely remained in operation, a fortunate occurrence that allowed the company to emerge as a very successful enterprise in the 1950s. By 1952, the firm had paid off its most pressing debts, and within just four more years was paying handsome dividends. No single factor made possible the firm's step back from the brink of bankruptcy; instead, several related elements accounted for the success of Wakefield Seafoods. In fact, a confluence of several factors is often needed for small firms to succeed.

First, as we have seen, the company's officers eagerly embraced technological advances, many of them spin-offs from World War II. Their ship, the *Deep Sea*, was the first to use radar, sonar, and loran in fishing and, similarly, to develop new methods to process, cook, and freeze the crabs it caught. Captain of a minesweeper in the Aleutian Islands and later captain of a destroyer escort in the North Atlantic during World War II, the skipper of the *Deep Sea* was well versed in the most advanced nautical technologies.

Second, those starting the company were persistent, willing to endure hard times to get their company moving. They refused to give up. When unable to attract fishing and processing crews, the owner-managers manned the nets and processing lines themselves. (Due to low profit shares, there was a lot of turnover among members of fishing crews for the *Deep Sea* in the early years. Under such circumstances, Wakefield Seafoods had great difficulty recruiting men to man its ship.)

Third, the personal ties that had been so important in starting Wakefield Seafoods also helped account for the firm's survival. Personal friendships between the founders of the company and the heads of the Seattle branch of the RFC, Seattle's commercial banks, and the suppliers of fishing gear were especially important in helping secure extensions on the company's loans. For instance, the head of the Seattle branch of the RFC had been a fraternity brother of Lowell Wakefield in college and was also a friend and neighbor of one of the Seattle founders of the company. These connections proved crucial in getting the RFC to allow delayed repayment of the loan made to Wakefield Seafoods. More than that, the head of the Seattle branch of the RFC intervened to convince secondary lenders to delay in the collection of their loans.

If internal factors help explain the success of Wakefield Seafoods, so do external elements, factors outside the control of the firm. The supporting role of the federal government was important in many ways, from the initial fishing surveys that suggested the possibility of a new industry to the provision of the RFC loan. Finally, pure, blind luck—an element often underrated by scholars assessing the success and failure of small businesses—helped save Wakefield Seafoods. In 1949, for no particular reason, the *Deep Sea*'s officers found twice as many king crabs as in the previous year. Coming at a crucial juncture in their company's development—at a time right after company officers had voted to disband their enterprise—this event was of great importance. In 1948, Wakefield Seafoods packed 160,000 pounds of crab, but in 1949 the firm put up over 400,000 pounds. This good fortune was a turning point in the company's struggle for survival. Without this bit of luck, the *Deep Sea* could not have gone fishing again. As Lowell Wakefield later mused, "I don't know what we'd have done."

In their scramble to survive, the owner-managers of Wakefield Seafoods paid scant attention to establishing a formal management structure for their firm. In the early years, as one founder recalled, the company was simply "a gang" of friends fighting for their lives. There was little distinction between owners and managers, for all in the company's management owned considerable blocks of stock. Many of the investors took an active part in running the company. Lowell Wakefield, a real bundle of energy, was everywhere at once, trying to sort out his firm's manifold problems. Other investor-managers took charge of various parts of the company's activities and, as we have seen, even manned the *Deep Sea*'s nets and lines. Still, despite some reliance on others, Lowell Wakefield remained firmly in charge. "We were just a heap of five guys led by Lowell," remembered one early-day officer. This setup worked in the opening years of the development of Wakefield Seafoods. Operations were relatively simple, despite the many challenges, and the scope of the work relatively small—when compared to what would soon develop with the expansion of the company. "When an operation is small, one guy can do an awful lot," Lowell Wakefield observed. No managerial hierarchies or organizational charts were needed or used at Wakefield Seafoods.

Expansion and Merger

From these beginnings, Wakefield Seafoods grew rapidly in the 1950s and 1960s to become a large company by Alaskan standards. Yet, with sales of less than $10 million even in 1967—the year before Norton Simon, a Los Angeles-based conglomerate, acquired it in a friendly takeover—the firm remained small, or at most medium-size, by national standards. As in earlier years, its success derived from numerous factors, but two were basic. Perhaps most fundamental was the initial decision to engage in all of the steps necessary to bring a new type of food to the attention of the American public, with much of the profit coming from processing and marketing. Moreover, like so many other successful small businesses in modern America, Wakefield Seafoods moved ahead as a niche marketer:

its founders saw an opportunity ignored by larger businesses and took advantage of it. Wakefield Seafoods was fortunate in coming of age at a time of general prosperity for many Americans. Possessing more disposable income than ever before, Americans could afford to purchase frozen king crab meat. Placing tremendous emphasis on quality control as a way of differentiating its crab from that of its competitors, Wakefield Seafoods developed a reputation nationwide as having a very high-quality "Tiffany" product, capable of commanding a premium market price.

Expansion led to management problems, very typical of those that occur in successful, growing businesses. It became impossible for one person, even someone as energetic and determined as Lowell Wakefield, to run the company single-handedly. Between 1953 and 1964, Wakefield Seafoods placed several more processing vessels in service and constructed three major shore plants to cook and freeze crab purchased from independent fishermen. Dispersed over a large area of Alaska with poor communications, the plants and ships proved difficult to supervise from company headquarters in Seattle. In addition, the firm took tentative steps to develop other seafood products, which further complicated operations. Management problems surfaced. In 1960, the company's treasurer and second-in-command left Wakefield Seafoods because of "policy differences" with Lowell Wakefield and others. A year later, the manager of the firm's most important processing plant in Alaska was fired for unexpectedly losing $300,000. Those at Wakefield Seafoods successfully addressed managerial challenges in two ways. They recruited new people from outside the company to assist Lowell Wakefield in running the firm, and they greatly improved information flow between the head office and the ships and plants, in part by moving the company headquarters to Alaska. In taking these steps, they found a workable balance between centralized and decentralized management methods for their firm. Lowell Wakefield remained in overall charge, but there was a lot of consultation with others in making decisions.

No sooner had Wakefield Seafoods been reorganized, than it faced additional challenges. In 1964, a major earthquake led to land subsidence along the Alaskan coast, leaving the company's shore plants under water and out of operation. This problem proved to be only temporary. Wakefield Seafoods secured a disaster relief loan from the Small Business Administration and rebuilt the plants on higher ground. More serious was a decline in the king crab catch, brought on by overfishing. The American king crab catch rose from a scant 23,000 pounds in 1946 to 1.5 million pounds in 1950 and

160 million pounds in 1966. Then the catch plummeted to just 50 million pounds in 1969. Well aware of this decline, those at Wakefield Seafoods sought relief by trying to diversify their company's product line beyond king crab meat and by trying to have conservation measures put in place. Nothing worked, however.

In the end, Wakefield Seafoods merged with a much larger company and went out of existence as an independent enterprise. By the mid-1960s, many of those owning stock in Wakefield Seafoods, including many of the firm's founders, were becoming interested in the prospect of a merger, for they were ready to retire from business. The problem was that there existed no real market for their stock in Wakefield Seafoods. They hoped that by merging with another, better-known firm they could acquire more marketable stock (for in a merger they would give up their stock in Wakefield Seafoods for stock in the larger company), which they could then sell. Then, too, they were alarmed by the fall in the crab catch and feared for the future of Wakefield Seafoods. At the same time, Wakefield Seafoods looked attractive to potential purchasers. Larger companies admired the success Wakefield Seafoods had had in creating a "Tiffany" reputation for its products. They noted that Wakefield Seafoods was quite profitable, and they knew little about the falloff in the king crab catch.

The result was the acquisition in 1968 of Wakefield Seafoods by the Norton Simon Company, a very large, very diversified company headquartered in Los Angeles. In selling their firm, those at Wakefield Seafoods did well financially. Many, in fact, quickly sold the Norton Simon stock they received for their shares in Wakefield Seafoods and retired as wealthy individuals. Those at Norton Simon were burned by their acquisition of Wakefield Seafoods, for the company, now operating as part of a division within Norton Simon, never again made a profit, as problems with the king crab catch continued into the 1970s.

Wakefield Seafoods and American Small Business

The Wakefield Seafoods story highlights many of the elements often present in the success of small firms in modern America. It shows, first of all, that success cannot usually be attributed to a single factor; to the contrary, a constellation of reasons usually lies behind the success of small companies—some internal to and some external to the firms. Still, as has often been the case in successful small firms that we have examined in this book, one major factor was the production of a specialty product for a niche market. The Wakefield Seafoods saga also demonstrates just how difficult it is to succeed in business and how important luck can be. Finally, the history of Wakefield Seafoods shows how patient stockholders of small businesses need to be. Major profits came only a decade after the founding of Wakefield Seafoods. Real gains for stockholders came only by selling their firm to another company, a strategy that became increasingly common in the 1970s, 1980s, and 1990s.

Even as America's economy boomed during the three decades following World War II, opportunities for smaller firms seemed to narrow. As the story of Wakefield Seafoods shows, it remained possible for small and medium-size companies to succeed, but the odds against such success were long. Between 1946 and 1971, as Chapter 6 describes, larger companies came increasingly to dominate many fields of enterprise in America, making success elusive for many small businesses.

Additional Reading

This chapter is based on Mansel G. Blackford, *Pioneering a Modern Small Business: Wakefield Seafoods and the Alaskan Frontier* (Greenwich, Conn.: JAI, 1979). On life and work in the king crab industry during the 1970s, 1980s, and 1990s, see Patrick Dillon, *Lost at Sea: An American Tragedy* (New York: Dial, 1998); and Spike Walker, *Working on the Edge* (New York: St. Martin's, 1991). For a fictional account, see William B. McCloskey Jr., *Highliners* (New York: McGraw-Hill, 1979). My father, William Blackford, now deceased, was captain of Wakefield Seafoods' ship, the *Deep Sea,* for a decade, and I want to thank him for sharing with me his experiences in Alaska.

CHAPTER 6

Small Business in an Expanding
Economy, 1946–1971

With the end of World War II and increased consumer spending that came with it, the United States boomed economically, to the extent that some pundits claimed the beginning of an "American Century." The full development of a consumer society at home, combined with increased exports to foreign markets, brought tremendous prosperity to many American firms. Small businesses, however, shared only partially in this economic upsurge, which came to a temporary end in the early 1970s. As in previous times, public attitudes and governmental actions helped shape the external environment of business in the United States, thus partly determining what firms could and could not do. This chapter begins by surveying public attitudes and governmental actions in the context of overall economic growth for the American economy, but relative decline for small businesses in many sectors, between 1946 and 1971. The chapter then proceeds to examine, field by field, the fates of small businesses during this period and concludes by looking at the nature of small business people during the first two or three decades after World War II.

Public Attitudes toward Business

Cold War concerns in the 1950s and 1960s sparked a revival of interest in small businesses, which came to be seen by many Americans as bastions of individualism and democracy against the threats of totalitarianism and communism. The 1950s were years in which many middle-class men aspired to be "organization men." (At this time there were almost no women in the top, or even the middle, ranges of management in big business.) Far from being innovative risk-takers, organization men were primarily interested in security, which they increasingly sought in the embrace of the large corporation. Of course, not all business people were of this ilk; those who founded Wakefield Seafoods were definitely taking risks. Yet, even as Americans embraced big business, they deepened their admiration of the small business person. John Bunzel, a perceptive political scientist writing in 1962, observed that most citizens viewed small business owners favorably, "as a kind of modern-day American underdog." He concluded, "The small businessman has always been identified with all of the homely virtues of Main Street America and thus is in something of a charmed if not sacred category along with Motherhood and the American Flag." Especially in the Cold War atmosphere of the 1950s and 1960s, small business came to be seen as "a cornerstone of American democracy" and as part of the American way of doing things.

American attitudes toward small business were clearly complex. As in the late nineteenth century, Americans continued to favor big businesses for the rising standard of living they were perceived as creating. Yet, small business as a way of life still tugged at the heartstrings of Americans, who longed for independence from concentrated economic power. As in earlier times, these attitudes helped shape public policies toward business, policies every bit as tangled as the attitudes themselves.

Postwar Government Policies for Small Business

America experienced great economic growth during the first twenty-five years following the Second World War. A postwar recession feared by some political and business leaders failed to materialize, as Americans rushed to spend income saved during the war years. Big-ticket consumer durables, largely unavailable during the war years—cars, electrical appliances, televisions—sold especially well as Americans embraced consumerism whole-heartedly, even more than they had in the 1920s. Between 1945 and 1960, the nation's real GNP rose by 52 percent, with per capita GNP increasing 19 percent; in the 1960s, real GNP climbed an additional 46 percent and per capita GNP rose by 29 percent.

Numerous factors accounted for this economic explosion. Above all, the very dynamic domestic market for consumer goods pushed the American economy ahead. Made in great numbers by mass-production techniques in large factories, these products stimulated economic growth and spurred the continuing development of big businesses in the United States. In addition, through its support of two international agreements—the Bretton Woods Agreement in 1944, which stabilized currency exchange rates worldwide, and the General Agreement on Tariffs and Trade (the GATT Agreement) three years later, which lowered barriers to trade across the globe—the federal government spurred the opening of international markets for American goods. Moreover, most advanced industrial nations other than the United States had had their factories destroyed or run down by wartime demands and ravages. The world was, for a time, America's oyster. In 1950, American firms sold 9 percent of their output abroad, twenty years later 13 percent, and foreign markets would become still more important for Americans in the 1970s and 1980s. The federal government was important in other ways. Some industries received direct help. The building of an interstate highway system, authorized by Congress in 1956, aided the trucking industry, and federal funding for airports helped commercial airlines. With the advent of the Cold War, defense spending grew in importance, accounting for between 4 and 8 percent of the nation's GNP in the 1950s and 1960s.

While not specifically designed to spur the development of big business, many of the federal government's policies had that effect. Big businesses benefited more than smaller concerns from the opening of world markets to American goods. Not until the 1980s did small companies begin exporting their products in appreciable volume. Nor did small businesses benefit as much as their larger counterparts from defense spending. In 1964, for example, just ten big businesses accounted for $3 billion of the $5.1 billion the Department of Defense awarded in research and development funds. Similarly, the construction of highways and airports helped large companies operating on a national scale more than it helped smaller local and regional firms.

Even as many of their actions continued to aid big business development in America, however, federal government officials took steps to help small businesses. As in the interwar years, the federal government's business policies remained complex and often confused. Reflecting the existence of contradictory public attitudes, no single, unified government policy existed.

Antitrust matters were a case in point. As we have seen, public attitudes favored big business development after World War II, and no public clamor arose to revive antitrust actions in the postwar years. As historian Richard Hofstadter noted in the mid-1960s, "The antitrust movement is one of the faded passions of American reform." Nonetheless, despite the decline in public interest, the federal government revived prosecutions. In 1950, Congress passed the Cellar-Kefauver Act, which allowed the Justice Department to use market share as proof of practices in restraint of trade. The administration of President Dwight D. Eisenhower established an Attorney General's National Committee to Study the Antitrust Laws in 1955, and this body reported favorably upon keeping the nation's antitrust legislation intact. By 1962, the Antitrust Division of the Justice Department had a budget of $6.6 million, employed 300 lawyers, and was prosecuting ninety-two cases. Judicial decisions forced some large firms to divest themselves of parts of their operations, as in cases involving Alcoa and DuPont, and, less frequently, punished price-fixing arrangements, as in a case decided against General Electric and other large firms in the electrical manufacturing business.

The Small Business Administration

At about the same time that the federal government was mounting its antitrust actions, it established the Small Business Administration (SBA). In part, the SBA grew out of federal agencies set up earlier to help small businesses—the RFC, SWPD, and the SWPC. In addition, after World War II some of the RFC's programs for small business were delegated to the Commerce Department, which set up an Office of Small Business. Moreover, in 1951 Congress established the Small Defense Plants Administration (SDPA) to help small firms win defense contracts during the Korean War. Throughout these years, the RFC continued to offer funding and other forms of assistance to some small firms—as we have seen in the case of Wakefield Seafoods. During the early 1950s, however, RFC officials became involved in a series of well-publicized scandals involving favoritism in granting loans. It was out of these scandals that the SBA was born.

Coming to power in 1953, President Eisenhower and many other Republicans wanted to abolish the RFC, which they viewed as a holdover from the Democratic New Deal and as a symbol of political corruption. However, they realized that they needed to insure the continuation of the aid given by the agency to small business. Even if the actual amount of aid was not great, its symbolic value was. From these concerns came new legislation that ended the RFC and created the SBA. Both bills worked their ways through the House and Senate with relatively little debate. Support came from several small business groups that had been formed in the wake of the Small Business Conference in 1938 and from the National Federation of Independent Business and the American Association of Small Business. Small business people remained divided, however, and other small business organizations—including the National Small Business Men's Association and the Conference of American Small Business Organizations — opposed the creation of the SBA, preferring that government get out of business affairs altogether. Opposition also came from some big business groups, whose members argued that small firms needed no special aid. However, most politicians agreed with Secretary of Commerce George M. Humphrey, who asserted that while he thought that "in theory there should be no difference between lending money to a large business or lending money to a small business. . . . in practice, in just good common sense, I think, there should be some additional body arranged to assist small business." As signed into law by President Eisenhower in July 1953, the legislation set up the SBA as a temporary agency.

As political scientist Sandra Anglund has recently shown, "traditional interest group and institutional approaches to explaining policy do not provide a full understanding of small business aid." In Anglund's words, "a cluster of core values often referred to as the American Creed must also be taken into account." There were, in fact, few well-organized small business constituencies. Instead, in trying to protect small businesses, members of Congress reacted on the basis of values they thought Americans shared. Anglund identifies those core values as individualism, freedom, equality, and democracy. Congressional action was also based on the assumption that small business had been hurt by events beyond its control, that it was a victim. Congress thus established the SBA out of concern that small firms were suffering from conditions beyond their control and from a desire to ensure economic democracy in America as the Cold War began. President Eisenhower reluctantly accepted the creation of the SBA as a way of showing that his Republican Party was not simply a pawn of big business.

Made permanent in 1958, the SBA was charged by Congress to "aid, counsel, assist, and protect, insofar as is possible, the interests of small-business concerns in order to preserve free competitive enterprise . . . to maintain and strengthen the overall economy of the nation." But what were small firms? This was the first question SBA officials had to answer. The enabling legislation establishing the SBA was intentionally vague on this matter: "For the purposes of this Act, a small-business concern shall be deemed to be one which is independently owned and operated and which is not dominant in its field of operations." SBA administrators soon found it necessary to devise size categories based upon the type of industry in which a firm operated. Small businesses in manufacturing came to be defined as firms with no more than 500 employees, those in wholesaling as companies with no more than $5 million in annual sales or receipts, and those in retail-

DuPont products. The Justice Department took few actions against a new type of merger that developed in the 1960s, conglomerate mergers. Conglomerates were companies that had operations in many unrelated fields, and business executives often formed conglomerates by merging previously independent companies.

Throughout the 1950s and well into the 1960s, the Justice Department looked favorably upon the formation of conglomerates, as a means of bringing new competition into established fields of business. Asked in 1966 whether he was worried about possible antitrust actions against his firm, the president of Litton Industries, one of the nation's fastest growing conglomerates, replied that he was not. "I think we've generally been on the side of the Justice Department because we've so often been the challenger in a field where someone else had a dominant position." The permissive attitude of the Justice Department set the stage for America's third major merger movement, which took place in the 1960s. This movement peaked in 1968; in that year 2,500 mergers of manufacturing and mining companies occurred, including 715 conglomerate-type mergers.

The companies resulting from these mergers and the businesses that continued to develop through internal growth were large indeed. By 1962, the top 5 industrial companies in the United States controlled 12 percent of all of the nation's manufacturing assets, the 50 largest accounted for one-third, and the largest 500 had over two-thirds. By 1965, General Motors, Standard Oil of New Jersey (later Exxon), and Ford had a combined gross income greater than that of all the farms in the United States. In 1963, General Motors possessed revenues over eight times as great as those of the state of New York and almost one-fifth those of the federal government.

In these circumstances, it is not surprising to find that the erosion of the position of small business relative to big business continued. Scholar Kurt Mayer, in examining the social roles of small businesses in America, observed in 1947, "The feeling that all is not well with small business has been growing." In his 1962 book, *The American Small Businessman*, the most thorough study of small business in the United States published up to that time, political scientist John Bunzel noted, "Despite its numerical preponderance from the Bronx to Chula Vista, small business is not looking particularly healthy these days." Small business, the book concluded, "is weak, though not abysmally so; essentially it seems to be hanging on." Statistics bore out the general validity of these gloomy assessments. The total number of self-employed nonfarm business people in America declined steadily from 1950 to 1972, reversing the earlier upward trend. While the total share of employment held by small firms (those with 500 or fewer workers) declined only slightly, from 41 percent in 1958 to 40 percent in 1977, the share of business receipts received by those small companies plummeted from 52 percent to a scant 29 percent of the total for all American firms during those same years.

Small Business in Manufacturing

The decline of small manufacturing firms relative to their larger brethren continued in the 1950s and 1960s. Single-plant companies (a good proxy for smaller firms) decreased slightly in absolute numbers from 255,000 in 1954 to 251,000 by 1972, while their share of America's industrial employment fell from 39 percent to just 25 percent. Continuing a trend from the nineteenth century, larger multiplant establishments rose in number from 32,000 to 70,000 and increased their share of industrial employment from 61 percent to 75 percent. These trends led economist Harold Vatter, who was investigating the changing relationships between large and small industrial firms, to conclude, "Relative crowding out of individual, small entrepreneurship from manufacturing was the apparent record of the U.S. economy in the quarter century after World War II."

Not all small manufacturers suffered, however. In a perceptive essay in the *Harvard Business Review* in 1957, Arnold Hosmer showed that some small companies continued to succeed. Foreshadowing many of the findings of scholars twenty to thirty years later, Hosmer summarized well how some small firms (companies employing no more than 100 workers), admittedly a distinct minority of the nation's small businesses, had managed to prosper. Some served national markets whose total demand was too small to attract large firms. Others operated in areas that required "special knowledge and background, special methods and skills in manufacture, and contact with customers by men with particular backgrounds." Still others manufactured products for regional markets in which service and speed of delivery were of utmost importance. Finally, small businesses succeeded in fields in which flexibility, especially the capability to turn out rapidly small batches of goods in short production runs, was the highest priority. Like the Philadelphia textile-makers of the nineteenth century, these small firms got ahead by differentiating their products from larger manufacturers that relied on long runs in mass-production industries.

The history of Burg Tool of Los Angeles, written by historian Max Holland, illustrates how small industrial firms could prosper in America after World War II. Founded in 1946 by an inventive machinist, Fred Burg, the company enjoyed great success as a personal, family business producing high-tech products for niche markets. Only after its acquisition by a conglomerate and the subsequent introduction of new management goals and methods in the mid-1960s did Burg Tool falter.

Fred Burg had successfully operated a department store in Cicero, Illinois, but his first love had always been for things mechanical. Burg had been a skilled machinist before family concerns led him into the department store business, but in 1943, at the age of forty-seven, he sold his store and moved to Los Angeles, ostensibly to retire. Once there, however, Burg found life more expensive than he had expected, and within four months he was working as a tool-and-die maker for a defense contractor in the region's booming wartime economy. Always an innovator, Burg devised a new sort of machine tool, which he was soon producing in his garage in his spare time. In 1945, Burg struck out on his own, leaving his salaried job and forming his own firm, Burg Tool.

Set up as a partnership in 1946, Burg Tool was family owned and operated. Fred Burg recruited his son Joe and his son-in-law Norm Ginsburg to join him in the business (incorporation came only in 1951). Using their own money and $5,000 borrowed from a sister, they entered the machine tool industry with the production of a turret drill, which they dubbed the "Burgmaster." In the late 1940s and early 1950s, Burg Tool successfully broke into established markets with this product. Innovative in design, the Burgmaster was backed up by dependable, rapid service. Fred Burg himself traveled to the factories using the tool to make repairs, if necessary. If innovation, service, and the possession of a specialty product contributed to Burg Tool's initial success, so did the existence of a favorable external environment, for defense spending on the Korean War boosted Burg Tool's sales. In 1954, the company earned a net income of $35,000 on net sales of $574,000 and employed sixty-two people.

Burg Tool's emergence as a machine tool builder of national repute during the Korean War marked the beginning of a decade of rapid growth. In 1964, the company's net sales reached $7.4 million and the firm employed 275 people. Several factors lay behind this success. First, Fred Burg and the others running the company remained innovative. Trained in machine tool building themselves, they spent a lot of time on the factory floor getting their hands dirty in devising new processes and new machines. Burg Tool was one of the first companies, for instance, to produce numerically controlled machine tools, tools that could be programmed by early-day computers. (The advantage of such tools was that they could be quickly and cheaply reprogrammed for new tasks.) Second, as a consequence of this approach, they worked very closely with their employees in formulating new ways of doing things, encouraging and then using suggestions put forward by their machinists. The relationship between management and labor was paternal, complete with summer picnics, Thanksgiving turkeys, and Christmas dinners. Unionization did occur in the 1960s, but relations between the Burgs and their workers nonetheless remained cordial and mutually supportive. Third, Burg Tool provided its customers with state-of-the-art machines backed up by high quality service. Finally, a continued favorable economic environment helped Burg Tool move ahead. Government spending on aerospace and defense and the expansion of the American automobile industry bolstered machine tool sales in the late 1950s and the early 1960s.

Burg Tool's rise attracted national attention, and the company found itself being wooed as a takeover target by a conglomerate, Houdaille. Running a company based on automobile parts, construction materials, industrial and engineering services, and machine tools, Houdaille's officers saw in Burg Tool a vehicle by which to continue a diversification drive they had begun several years earlier. The Burgs were willing to sell out, for by this time Fred Burg was beginning to think again of retirement, and even Joe Burg and Norm Ginsburg were aging. In the short run, the Burgs desperately needed funds to expand their factory to keep up with an exploding demand for their tools, funds that Houdaille agreed to provide. Moreover, the Burgs thought they received verbal assurances that their ways of conducting business would be preserved. The result, after lengthy negotiations, was a friendly takeover in 1965.

That year marked a turning point in Burg Tool's fortunes: from 1965 the company's course was nearly all downhill. The most basic change was managerial, for over time the Burgs were forced out of management. The Houdaille executives who replaced them knew little about the machine tool industry. Taking a short-term approach to business, they insisted upon milking the company for profits at the expense of long-term investments in research and development. As a consequence, Burg Tool gradually lost its innovative edge and its reputation for high quality production and service. Labor relations also soured. As the company, now a division within Houdaille, came to be run by executives trained in finance and marketing rather than in production, a split developed between labor and management. Cooperation disappeared and strikes occurred. These developments, in turn, left Burg Tool ill prepared to meet the growing competition of machine tool imports from Japan. Unable to cope with competition from American and foreign firms, Burg Tool went out of existence in 1986.

The rise and fall of Burg Tool illustrates some of the factors needed to successfully operate small businesses in modern American industry. The Burg family succeeded in large part through constant innovation in their company's specialty products — innovation made possible, as in the case of many of the New England metal fabricators and machinery makers, by their direct involvement in management. They got their hands dirty on the shop floor, with no managerial hierarchies separating them from their employees. After Houdaille acquired Burg Tool, this approach to business changed. Immediate profits took precedence over other goals, managers untrained in and unmindful of production methods took charge, and rifts increasingly separated labor from management. A favorable external environment, especially government purchases, aided the development of the machine tool industry in general and Burg Tool in particular in the 1950s and 1960s, but this environment turned more hostile with the growth of foreign and especially Japanese competition in the 1970s and 1980s, competition that Burg Tool and many other American machine tool makers were poorly prepared to meet.

Despite the temporary success of Burg Tool, small manufacturers on the whole lost out relative to larger ones in the United States; nor was that trend limited to America. In many economically advanced nations, large mass-production companies met the needs of people eager for consumer goods, as those countries recovered from World War II. In Great Britain, manufacturing establishments with 200 or fewer employees dropped in number from 103,000 in 1948 to just 70,000 by 1971. By the mid-1970s, small industrial firms accounted for only a quarter of Great Britain's industrial output. In Germany and Japan, small industrialists often lost their independence as they became more and more closely tied to larger manufacturers as subcontractors. By 1971, for example, 59 percent of Japan's small industrial companies were acting as subcontractors for larger manufacturers, a figure that rose to 66 percent ten years later. The story in France was mixed. The number of French manufacturing firms dropped by 80,000 between 1951 and 1963, with most of that decline occurring among very small firms. Medium-sized ventures increased in importance. In 1962, France had 61 percent of its industrial workforce in companies employing fewer than 500 workers — compared to 54 percent for Germany and just 33 percent for Great Britain. Of course, this relative decline of small manufacturers was far from universal. Industrial districts continued to flourish in some fields of production in all industrial nations—perhaps nowhere more so than in Italy—and, as we shall see, these districts increased in importance during the 1980s and 1990s.

Sales and Services

In the postwar years, small retailers mounted partially successful responses to the inroads of larger competitors. Like successful small manufacturers, some adopted the strategy of specialization. Mom-and-pop grocery stores continued to attract patronage by offering services, such as home delivery, that were no longer provided by the chains and supermarkets, or they specialized in terms of the types of goods they carried. In field after field, small retailers also banded together in associations to secure some of the benefits, especially the discounts won through high-volume purchases, obtained by large-scale enterprises. In the grocery industry, for example, independent retailers established voluntary groups, such as the Independent Grocers' Association (IGA), and retailer-owned cooperative warehouses. By the 1940s, over one-third of all grocery wholesale sales passed through these institutions. Through them, retail grocers sought to cut their costs of doing business, and they were partially successful.

Changes taking place in hardware retailing demonstrate well the changes that were occurring in retailing throughout the nation. Like some grocers, some hardware retailers specialized in the goods they handled, and in the postwar years still more joined retailer-owned cooperatives.

Kirk's, a hardware retailer in Muncie, Indiana, typifies how some independents successfully altered their marketing practices. Founded in 1865, Kirk's originally sold hardware, toys, and many other products. As Muncie grew, the store prospered, earning a reputation for reliable goods and services. A major turning point in the store's development occurred in the late 1880s and early 1890s, when Kirk's began to sell and repair bicycles because the store's owner, Charles B. Kirk, and his wife were cycling enthusiasts. Kirk met Ignatzs Schwinn in Chicago in 1909 and adopted the Schwinn brand as the only make of bicycle his store would carry. In the mid-twentieth century, Kirk's continued to grow as a family-owned and -operated store, with Charles's three sons and later several grandchildren going into the business. While never abandoning other lines of stock completely, Kirk's placed an increasing emphasis on bicycle and sporting goods sales. These specializations served Kirk's well. Having weathered the Great Depression, the firm expanded in the postwar years. Still a family business, Kirk's moved to two new locations in the Muncie area in the 1970s.

Like grocers, many hardware retailers also entered into cooperative arrangements to win some of the rewards of large-scale operations. John Cotter put together one such cooperative as "True Value" hardware stores. Brought up in the hardware business, Cotter founded True Value in 1948, by which time independent hardware retailers were facing severe competition from chain stores and discount outlets. In this system, hundreds of independent retailers came to own Cotter & Company, which in turn acted as their wholesaler. Profits earned at the middleman's sales level were rebated every year to the retailers, which remained independently owned. By the mid-1980s, True Value had 7,000 member stores and fourteen major distribution centers, making it the largest hardware distributor in the United States.

The effectiveness of small retailers in blunting the encroachments of their larger competitors varied considerably by field. Most small independent retailers failed to adjust to the new way of selling groceries. In this field, in which low prices were of utmost significance, the chains and supermarkets ruled supreme. By 1971, five large supermarket chains dominated food retailing in the United States by emphasizing rapid turnover of stock, high sales per employee, and large store size. Similarly, the rise of discount stores suggested a limited future for small-scale retailers. Between 1960 and 1966, the number of discount stores increased from 1,329 to 3,503, and by 1966 discounting was well established in the East and Midwest for the sale of toys, children's clothing, sporting goods, housewares, and automobile accessories. Wal-Mart, just beginning operations in the 1960s, took discounting to new heights over the next three decades, becoming the world's largest retailer in the 1990s. On the other hand, despite the rise of fast-food restaurants, independents held their own into the 1970s. In 1933, chains had just 15 percent of sales in America's restaurant and drinking industry, and forty years later still held only 21 percent. In hardware, a field in which customer service remained important, independents working through groups like True Value also did well. The number of retail hardware outlets in the United States declined from 35,000 in 1954 to 26,000 in 1972 but then stabilized and even rose a bit in the mid- and late 1970s.

The provision of services remained the home of small businesses even more than retailing. Possessing fewer economies of scale than stores selling goods, service industries were inherently less conducive to the spread of large firms. For example, as scholar Marc Weis noted in 1989, real estate agencies continued to be mainly "project based, small scale, and noninstitutional." Most real estate firms were closely tied to their local communities. Only with the development of new communication and computer technologies in the late 1970s, 1980s, and 1990s did local and regional companies like Century 21 and Coldwell Banker grow to become national giants. Small local businesses also dominated the field of law. As in real estate, the development of new media and communications techniques were required for some law firms to grow large, as did Hyatt Legal Services in the 1980s. However, in some service industries the power of small companies was eroded. With the continued growth of the United States as an urban nation, insurance and banking companies expanded their reach. Although small firms continued to thrive in both of these fields, their status was less secure than in earlier times.

Rapid growth characterized the life insurance industry, as the increase in the number of companies greatly outpaced the nation's rise in population. In 1920, 335 companies served 106 million Americans, but by 1957 some 1,271 firms sold policies to a population of 171 million. The average size of life insurance companies increased. In 1920, life insurance companies had an average of $121 million of policies in force, by 1957 an average of $360 million. Nonetheless, even after World War II there was plenty of room for new small companies and independent agents. New types of insurance developed, most notably medical insurance. In 1940, only 9 percent of Americans had hospitalization insurance, but by 1957 some 72 percent did. While Blue Cross dominated hospitalization insurance, its share of the coverage in this field dropped from about 50 percent in 1940 to 43 percent seventeen years later. Not all fields of medical insurance witnessed a broadening of opportunities for new plans and companies, however. Blue Shield increased its share of surgical insurance from 12 percent in 1941 to 36 percent by 1957.

Banking remained a realm dominated by small businesses. The number of commercial banks in the United States fell by one-half during the Great Depression of the 1930s but then stabilized at around 15,000 through the 1980s. The average assets of American banks rose substantially. In 1920, average bank assets stood at just $1.7 million; by 1957 the average had risen tenfold, to $17 million, with only one-quarter of the gain due to inflation. In the 1920s and 1930s, branch banking came to the United States in a major way. In 1920, less than 5 percent of banking offices were branches. Only twenty-one states permitted branch banking at that date, and until the passage of the McFadden Act by Congress in 1927, branch banking was forbidden at the national level. With liberalization of the laws by the McFadden Act and later legislation, banks with branches came to compose one-fifth of the total by 1935, and in 1957 over one-half of the 13,617 commercial banks had branches. Chain and group banking also developed in the 1920s, only to fall into disrepute because of numerous failures during the depression decade. The coming of federal deposit insurance in 1933 enhanced the safety of small banks and gave them a new lease on life.

While the closing of very small units was the norm in commercial banking, some small investment banking firms remained prosperous into the postwar years—as shown by the experiences of K. J. Brown, formed in Muncie, Indiana, in 1931 at the nadir of the Great Depression. Run as a family partnership by Kenneth J. Brown and later by his son, the business made money in good times and bad by staying close to its customers through the provision of personal services in its local and later regional market. By 1981, through what historian Bruce Geelhoeld calls "a combination of good management, sound planning, hard work, and maybe even a measure of luck," K. J. Brown grew to become a regional power in investment banking, with branches in Marion, Kokomo, and Richmond, Indiana; Ottawa, Illinois; and Lexington, Kentucky.

With regard to small firms in sales and services, Great Britain and Japan offer valuable contrasts to each other and to the United States. In Great Britain the repeal of retail price maintenance laws in the 1950s and 1960s contributed to a trend toward concentration in retailing, which was already underway, much like that which was occurring in America. By the mid-1980s, small shops made only about one-third of the retail sales in Britain. Multiples (chain stores) were the big winners, especially in consumer durables, clothing, grocery, and alcohol sales. Long more centralized than America's banking system, Britain's financial system was dominated by just a handful of banks, known as the "Big Four," which by the mid-1970s held 92 percent of the nation's banking deposits. In Japan, the political clout of small retailers, who were very important to the nation's dominant political party, the Liberal Democratic Party (LDP), led to an outcome somewhat different from the concentration that occurred in Britain and America. In 1956, the Japanese Diet passed legislation that made it difficult for large retailers such as department stores to move into fields that already had small mom-and-pop retailers. As a result, as late as 1976, 1.6 million retail outlets employed 5.6 million workers to serve Japan's population of 112 million— a much higher density of retailers than that found in any other economically advanced nation. Only later, with revisions to this law, would discount houses develop into a really major force in Japan, mainly in the 1980s and 1990s.

Farming and Small Business

The ending of the farm crises of the 1930s did not bring much relief to family farmers, for they faced long-term problems and, except for relatively brief periods, were rarely prosperous. The basic difficulty was that, as a technological revolution swept through agriculture, farming became increasingly capital-intensive. As relatively small businesses, family farms found it ever harder to raise the funds necessary to grow and prosper. Larger tractors and mechanized equipment, artificial fertilizer (whose use climbed tenfold between 1940 and 1970), and hybrid seeds all cost money. Moreover, as agricultural machinery came into increasing use, the minimum profitable size of farms grew larger.

Most of the profits in the farm sector came less from producing foodstuffs than from processing and marketing them, and in the postwar years large vertically integrated agribusinesses came to control certain segments of the food industry, from growing to marketing. By 1972, such companies accounted for 97 percent of broiler chicken production, 95 percent of vegetable processing, 85 percent of the trade in citrus fruits, 70 percent of potatoes marketed, 54 percent of the production of turkeys, and 51 percent of the fresh vegetables grown in the United States. Writing in 1960, the well-known rural sociologist Everett M. Rogers summarized the changes occurring in agriculture:

1. American farms are increasingly specialized.
2. American farming is . . . also becoming more capitalized.
3. It is characterized by greater efficiency and productivity.
4. American farms are increasing in size. . . .
7. Interdependence between industrial employment and farming is increasing; there is a marked increase in part-time farming. . . .
8. One of the most important changes in the nature of farming is the increasing interdependence of farmers upon agriculture-related industry. . . . A new term — agribusiness — is now applied to the total agricultural economy.

The response of many small farmers was to leave agriculture. Begun earlier, the exodus continued in the postwar years; between 1945 and 1974 4.2 million more Americans quit farming than began it. In the 1960s alone, some 600,000 independent family farms disappeared. A smaller proportion of Americans was choosing farming as a livelihood. In 1920, about 27 percent of all working Americans were engaged in agriculture, but by 1945 only 14 percent were; by 1973, it was down to just 4.5 percent. As more

TABLE FOUR. Farms by Size in America, 1920–1954 (in thousands of farms)

Year	Acreage				
	1–49	50–259	260–499	500–999	1,000+
1920	2,300	3,455	476	150	67
1930	2,358	3,239	451	160	81
1940	2,286	3,389	473	167	89
1954	1,696	2,281	482	192	131

Source: U.S. Bureau of the Census, *Historical Statistics of the United States, Colonial Times to 1957* (Washington D.C.: U.S. Government Printing Office, 1960), 279.

families left agriculture, farming became more concentrated in the hands of agribusiness. In 1948, the largest 10 percent of America's farms produced 24 percent of the nation's farm output, but by 1968 they accounted for 48 percent. Many small farmers could no longer make a living exclusively by farming, so they also worked at jobs in nearby towns. By 1960, farms with annual sales of $20,000 or more, just 24 percent of the nation's farms, accounted for 70 percent of net farm income. The postwar decline of small-scale farming had its greatest impact on farms of fewer than 260 acres. From 1950 to 1983, average farm size more than doubled, from 200 acres to 450 acres.

The Small Business Person

Small business owners differed from the salaried managers of big businesses in the mid-twentieth century. Those who formed and ran small businesses differed in motivation from the typical managers of large corporations. Owning their businesses, small business people identified very closely with their enterprises. Far from being organization men, small business owners were interested in more than making money and finding a comfortable plateau or niche within a big business. In background, too, small business people were different from their counterparts in larger firms. In Lexington, Kentucky, in the 1950s, for example, small business people were generally younger and less well educated than their counterparts in big businesses across the nation, and a higher proportion of small business people came from families with nonbusiness backgrounds. The first regular job of a small business owner was often that of an unskilled or semiskilled worker or clerical worker. For those who were successful, always a minority of the total who entered small business, involvement in small business ventures offered some chance for upward social and economic mobility. As sociologist Gordon Lewis, who studied the situation in Lexington, observed, "While in small business younger men can achieve headship of a firm, the leadership of big business is becoming increasingly age-graded."

For some minority groups, small businesses offered opportunities not found in larger enterprises; however, as in earlier times, those opportunities varied considerably by group and type of enterprise. Black businesses remained concentrated in services and sales. In 1969, nearly 60 percent of minority-owned businesses (with blacks composing 90 percent of the minority owners) were found in personal services and the retail trades. As before, few black businesses were found in manufacturing. Most black businesses remained small businesses. Only 5 percent of minority-owned businesses employed ten or more people, compared to 20 percent for white-owned businesses; and only one-third of the minority-owned businesses enjoyed gross receipts of at least $50,000 per year, while one-half of the white-owned businesses did so. Small businesses did not bring economic advancement to blacks commensurate to their numbers in America's population. In 1969, when they constituted 11 percent of the nation's population, blacks owned just over 2 percent of the country's businesses (see Table 5).

The civil rights movement brought major changes to black business. From the 1910s, black businesses had served primarily black consumers. Before the flowering of the civil rights movement in the 1950s and 1960s, segregation had meant, for example, that blacks had to stay in black hotels, eat at segregated restaurants, and patronize segregated resorts—all of which, ironically, had opened up opportunities for black entrepreneurs. With the development of the civil rights movement, those opportunities faded, as blacks increasingly patronized integrated establishments. From the 1960s on, health and beauty aids and publishing were about the only two major industries left in which black-owned businesses almost exclusively served blacks. However, opportunities opened for blacks to begin advancing in white-owned businesses, especially from the 1970s on; and black-owned businesses in a few fields, such as entertainment, found new opportunities in selling to white consumers. Thus, Motown Records reached well beyond a black consumer base and found white consumers eager to buy its recordings of top black musicians. Even so, racism, the historian Juliet Walker reminds us, remained a continuing problem for black businesses. "The reality, which cannot be ignored," she writes, "is

TABLE FIVE. Size Distribution of Minority-Owned Businesses, 1969

Size Measure	Minority-Owned (%)	Other (%)
Number of paid employees		
0	31	26
1–9	64	55
10–49	4	13
50–99	1	3
100+	0	3
Gross receipts (in thousands of $)		
0–9.9	33	19
10–19.9	15	12
20–49.9	19	19
50–99.9	14	15
100–999.9	17	26
1,000–4,999.9	2	9
5,000+	0	9

Source: U.S. Small Business Administration, *Annual Report, 1969* (Washington, D.C.: U.S. Government Printing Office, 1970).

that black economic advancement continues to be hindered by racism." As we shall see, blacks remained underrepresented as business owners in the United States into the twenty-first century.

As before World War II, other minorities, especially groups of Asian Americans in large cities, found small business development more appealing than blacks did. Like Chinese and Japanese immigrants before them, Koreans coming to America found in small business one viable road for personal advancement. Moving into Los Angeles in significant numbers during the 1960s and 1970s, many went into service and retail ventures — restaurants, grocery stores, and the like. In part, the Koreans formed small businesses to compensate for the lack of job opportunities with larger enterprises. Racism combined with a lack of language skills and an attachment to Asian customs to prevent their rapid movement into established large businesses. More positively, the possession of enough education and wealth to start new businesses also led them in this direction, as did the existence of support groups such as clubs and voluntary associations. Many Korean firms even ventured into black neighborhoods that lacked business services.

Few changes took place in the roles women played in business in the decades right after World War II. America's postwar conversion stressed domesticity and familial roles for women, as did the national security needs of the Cold War; and women's roles as consumers were heightened. Still, small business offered some place for women, if a fairly traditional one. A survey undertaken in 1954 by the Business and Professional Women's Association revealed that women-owned firms remained concentrated in just a few fields: general retailing (33 percent of the total of women-owned businesses); personal service (11 percent); real estate, insurance, and finance (11 percent); education (10 percent); and hotels and restaurants (6 percent), figures that closely resembled those of black business ownership. Most women-owned businesses were small, with owners typically deriving incomes of between $2,000 and $5,000 from their companies. "The years of mid-century essentially marked time for women in business," concludes Angel Kwolek-Folland, a leading historian of women in American business.

Small business owners continued to differ from the executives of large companies in their propensity to join business organizations, especially at the national level. Prizing their independence, small business people were reluctant participants in America's growing organizational culture. Although small business owners were active in local service clubs such as the Lions and the Rotary, they paid much less attention to organizational developments at the national level. It required an external event — President Franklin D. Roosevelt's convocation of small business people in Washington, D.C. in 1938, described in Chapter 4 — to bring about the creation of the National Advisory Council of Independent Small Businesses, the first organization claiming to speak for all types of small business people across the nation. Other national organizations of small business owners developed in the postwar years: the National Federation of Independent Business (NFIB), the National Small Business Men's Association, and the Conference of American Small Business Organizations. However, these organizations did not fully represent small businesses. For one thing, they had relatively few members, at most 100,000 to 200,000 of the millions of owners in the United States. Nor did they accomplish much for their members. Some did engage in lobbying activities, but most were simply fund-raising vehicles for their founders, who ran them as their own private enterprises. Far from being grassroots groups set up by local small business owners, the groups were highly centralized organizations supported by very active membership recruiters in the field. (This situation changed a bit in later decades. The NFIB grew to have 600,000 members by 1980, leading one scholar to call its expansion one of the most significant developments in interest-group politics in modern America.)

In one area small business owners were quite similar to most other Americans: in their political views and stances. No distinctly small business attitude toward politics existed in America after World War II. Small business owners were no more likely to be Republican or conservative than, for example, salaried Americans who worked as middle-level managers in large firms. In the 1964 presidential election, which pitted a conservative Republican, Barry Goldwater, against a liberal Democrat, Lyndon Johnson, a majority of small business owners voted Democratic. Nor were small business people more likely than others to be opposed to government aid and welfare programs. By the 1960s, for example, a majority favored a federal government role in guaranteeing medical aid for Americans, since in competitive sectors they needed government compulsion to keep the playing field level. Nor, finally, were they necessarily antilabor in their political and cultural outlooks, unless their firms were actually threatened.

Small Business by the 1970s

During the twenty-five years after World War II, as had been true since the Civil War era, America's business system continued to divide into two segments. Large capital-intensive "center" firms came to dominate key segments of American industry, crowding out smaller enterprises, especially in manufacturing. Yet, smaller firms, sometimes labeled "peripheral" businesses, that were able to develop special products and niche markets continued to thrive, even in manufacturing. In other parts of the economy—sales and distribution, and personal and business services—small firms also lost ground to their larger counterparts but generally fared better than in industry. In farming, the decline in small business was precipitous. Nonetheless, it is a bit simplistic to view the growth of America's business system in strictly dualistic terms—that is, as the development of a system consisting of big business in one sector and small business in the other. In fact, there was a considerable blurring of the line between large and small firms, a blurring that would intensify in the 1970s and 1980s.

A noteworthy example of such blurring was franchising, as historian Thomas Dicke has shown. A few industrial companies used franchising to extend their sales across America during the late nineteenth and early twentieth centuries, but franchising grew in popularity in the 1920s and 1930s as oil companies, automobile manufacturers, and restaurants set up nationwide systems of franchised dealers and outlets. Franchising expanded still more rapidly after World War II, until by 1967, sales made through franchised outlets accounted for about 10 percent of GNP. In franchising, the franchisee remained a legally independent business, most often a small business, separate from the parent company, the franchiser. Many commentators in the 1950s and 1960s praised franchising as a middle way in business, a means by which large companies (the franchisers) and small businesses (the franchisees) could cooperate to their mutual advantage.

To some extent their observations were true. Both could benefit: the franchiser from the rapid development of a national marketing system with relatively little capital investment, the franchisee from the national advertising and business advice provided by the franchiser. Here, it seemed, was an arrangement by which small businesses could maintain their independence while reaping the benefits of belonging to large umbrella organizations. Frequently, however, those hopes proved chimerical. Too often it was the franchiser who gained the most, through various fees and (as in the case of many fast-food operations) the sale of raw materials to its franchisees. It often required hotly contested legal battles for local franchisees to win even a modicum of rights from the dictates of their powerful franchisers. In franchising, as in so many other fields, the independence of small business was often more apparent than real.

Despite some efforts at cooperation, tension continued to characterize relations between large and small firms in postwar America. On that score, not much had changed since the rise of big business in the late nineteenth century. Friction would continue into the twenty-first century, but new developments in an increasingly global economy were destined to shift the balance of power a bit more in favor of small firms, particularly those in manufacturing, a field under attack by foreign competitors. In fact, an economic era ended for American firms in the early 1970s. The "American Century," it turned out, was remarkably short-lived. The recovery of other industrial nations, such as Japan and West Germany, from the ravages of World War II led to rapidly increasing competition for the products of American factories by the late 1960s; and the demise of the Bretton Woods Agreement and temporary movement by some nations away from GATT

(General Agreement on Tariffs and Trade) increased the instability of the global market for American goods in the early 1970s. A major recession in the early 1970s seemed to underline for many Americans a need for basic changes in their nation's business system.

Even earlier, developments in California's Silicon Valley—described in Chapter 7—showed the continuing importance of small firms to parts of the American economy. In the 1950s and 1960s, dozens of small high-tech companies in this region of northern California illustrated just how important entrepreneurship remained to the United States. Grouped together in one area, reminiscent of the nineteenth-century textile makers in Philadelphia, these high-tech firms were among the most dynamic enterprises in the world. Whether or not the business situation that developed in Silicon Valley could be replicated elsewhere long puzzled policy makers.

Additional Reading

On business developments in postwar America, see especially Alfred D. Chandler Jr., "The Competitive Performance of U.S. Industrial Enterprises since the Second World War," *Business History Review* 68 (Spring 1994): 1–72; Jon Didrichsen, "The Development of Diversified and Conglomerate Firms in the United States, 1920–1970," *Business History Review* 46 (Summer 1972): 202–19; Michael French, *US Economic History since 1945* (Manchester: Manchester University Press, 1997); and Harold Vatter and John Walker, eds., *History of the U.S. Economy since World War II* (Armonk, N.Y.: Sharp, 1996). The roles the federal government played in small business development, especially through the Small Business Administration, are covered well in Sandra Anglund, *Small Business Policy and the American Creed* (Westport, Conn.: Praeger, 2000); and Jonathan Bean, *Big Government and Affirmative Action: The Scandalous History of the Small Business Administration* (Lexington: University Press of Kentucky, 2001). Addison Parris, *The Small Business Administration* (New York: Praeger, 1968), remains a valuable contemporary account. For international comparisons of the roles small businesses played in economic developments in different nations, see the essays in Konosuke Odaka and Minoru Sawai, eds., *Small Firms, Large Concerns* (Oxford: Oxford University Press, 1999); and David Storey, ed., *The Small Firm: An International Survey* (New York: St. Martin's, 1983).

W. Arnold Hosmer, "Small Manufacturing Enterprises," *Harvard Business Review* 35 (November–December 1957): 111–22, is a valuable overview; Max Holland, *When the Machine Stopped: A Cautionary Tale from Indus-*

trial America (Boston: Harvard Business School Press, 1989), is a history of Burg Tool. Edward Kantowicz, *John Cotter: 70 Years of Hardware* (Chicago: Regenery, 1986); Sandra Vance and Roy Scott, *Wal-Mart: A History of Sam Walton's Retail Phenomenon* (New York: Twayne, 1994); Marc Weis, "Real Estate History: An Overview and Research Agenda," *Business History Review* 62 (Summer 1989): 241–82; Nancy Lisagor and Frank Lipsius, *A Law Unto Itself: The Untold Story of the Law Firm Sullivan and Cromwell* (New York: Morrow, 1988); Gerald Fischer, *American Banking Structure* (New York: Columbia University Press, 1968); Bruce Geelhoeld, *Bringing Wall Street to Main Street: The Story of K. J. Brown and Company, Inc., 1931–1981* (Muncie, Ind.: Ball State University Business History Series, 1981), provide insights into small businesses in services and sales. On the history of franchising, see Thomas Dicke, *Franchising in America: The Development of a Business Method* (Chapel Hill: University of North Carolina Press, 1992).

Much has been written about America's farm crisis. Particularly valuable accounts include John Shover, *First Majority—Last Minority: The Transforming of Rural Life In America* (De Kalb: Northern Illinois University Press, 1976), which reprints the conclusions of Everett M. Rogers; Jay Staten, *The Embattled Farmer* (Golden, Colo.: Fulcrum, 1987); Richard Rhodes, *Farm: A Year in the Life of An American Farmer* (Lincoln: University of Nebraska Press, 1989); and Jon Lauck, *American Agriculture and the Problem of Monopoly: The Political Economy of Grain Belt Farming, 1953–1980* (Lincoln: University of Nebraska Press, 2000).

Gordon Lewis, "A Comparison of Some Aspects of the Backgrounds and Careers of Small Businessmen and American Business Leaders," *American Journal of Sociology* 65 (January 1960): 348–55, looks at small business people in Lexington. For a solid introduction to the changing nature of black businesses, see Juliet E. K. Walker, *The History of Black Business in America* (New York: Twayne, 1998), chs. 8–11. See also Ronald Bailey, ed., *Black Business Enterprise: Historical and Contemporary Perspectives* (New York: Basic, 1971). Scott Cummings, ed., *Self-Help in Urban America: Patterns of Minority Enterprise* (Port Washington, N.Y.: Kennikat, 1980) is a valuable overview; and Ivan Light and Edna Bonachich, *Immigrant Entrepreneurs: Koreans in Los Angeles, 1965–1982* (Berkeley: University of California Press, 1988), is a useful case study. On the roles women played in business development, see Angel Kwolek-Folland, *Incorporating Women* (New York: Twayne, 1998), ch. 5.

7

Small Firms in
the Silicon Valley

Small and medium-size firms were — and, to a great extent, still are — the lifeblood of California's Silicon Valley. Nimble, ever changing, and amorphous, these companies made the region the foremost high technology center in the world after World War II. In a 1991 interview, the founder of MasPar Computer Technology captured well the nature of the firms and Silicon Valley. "The Valley is fast-moving," he explained, "and start-ups have to move fast." He continued, "You have this culture of rapid decisions, rapid movement, rapid changes, which is exactly the environment that you find yourself in as a start-up." As it developed in the postwar decades, Silicon Valley assumed many of the characteristics of industrial districts of earlier times in the United States and abroad. First and foremost was the importance of small, very flexible companies at its core. As the scholar Annalee Saxenian has explained, these companies formed "a regional network-based industrial system that promotes collective learning and flexible adjustment among specialist producers of a complex of related technologies."

How Silicon Valley developed is the topic of this chapter. While interactions among many small firms were of prime importance, many other factors were involved. The roles of educational institutions, the federal government, individual entrepreneurs, and larger companies were also significant. Together, the people and their companies produced many new jobs. Silicon Valley firms employed about 115,000 high technology workers in 1975, and over the next fifteen years the district generated an additional 150,000 high technology positions. Understandably, many other regions in and beyond the United States sought to replicate the Silicon Valley experience, but with only limited success. This chapter closes by examining several of the efforts to recreate Silicon Valley elsewhere. Small high technology firms, these experiences showed, could not always be relied upon to become engines of economic growth.

The Origins of Silicon Valley

"If anyone deserved to be called the 'father of Silicon Valley,'" historians Stuart Leslie and Robert Kargon have written, "it was Frederick Terman." As a faculty member in engineering, later as the dean of engineering, and finally as the provost of Stanford University, Terman pioneered in establishing and nurturing connections between academia and industry, trained students in high technology fields, and helped those students get started in business. Two of his best known graduate students, William Hewlett and David Packard, formed Hewlett-Packard in 1937, using a personal loan of $538 from Terman to get started. Other start-ups, often associated in one way or the other with Terman, were also important in the prewar years. Charles Litton established Litton Industries in 1932, and Sigurd and Russell Varian started Varian Associates a few years later.

Federal government spending boomed these firms during World War II, and their growth attracted additional enterprises to what became known by the 1970s as Silicon Valley, named after the main ingredient in semiconductors. Military spending remained important for the companies during the Cold War, especially during the 1950s and 1960s. So did Stanford University. Prodded by Terman, the university established the Stanford Research Institute (SRI) and the Stanford Industrial Park (SIP), which accepted Varian Associates as its first tenant. Both of these entities brought together academic researchers and business people. Nor did it stop there. As some of the high technology firms developed, they "hived off" many new, smaller companies. A case in point was Fairchild Semiconductor, founded in 1957 by Robert Noyce and other scientists who broke away from Shockley Transistor Laboratories, a company that had been established in the SIP by William Shockley, the coinventor of the transistor. During the 1960s, employees who left Fairchild to try to capitalize on their specialized knowledge founded over two dozen semiconductor-related companies, the historian Leslie Berlin has explained. Called "Fairchildren," these small firms added greatly to the vibrancy of Silicon Valley. Noyce himself later left Fairchild to help start the firm that became Intel in 1968.

What had been a small cluster of companies expanded into a full-fledged high technology district. At first, the firms located near Stanford University, but they soon spread southward down the San Francisco Peninsula. Hemmed in by natural boundaries of mountains and ocean, the companies quickly formed a very dense network of enterprises. Proximity encouraged communications among the firms and stimulated their continued growth, much as had occurred earlier in the Philadelphia textile district and the Sheffield steel district in the nineteenth century. Bars, restaurants, and other institutions such as professional and business associations, where scientists and entrepreneurs could meet informally, also encouraged the spread of information among the firms.

Few of the resulting firms were large, vertically integrated companies. To the contrary, most of Silicon Valley's makers of computer hardware and software, producers of communications equipment, and manufacturers of defense products were smaller firms that consciously avoided vertical integration. Instead of trying to internalize all facets of their companies' work in single firms, Silicon Valley entrepreneurs got ahead by forming a large, informal, flexible network of linked, but independent, companies. The companies worked very closely with specialized venture capitalists, suppliers of components, and legal and marketing consultants. Workers moving from job to job — and job-hopping was very common — spread information across firm boundaries. Located in one region, this agglomeration of many mainly small businesses allowed producers to benefit from economies of scale without forming big businesses. Even large firms tended to operate like smaller companies. Hewlett-Packard, which came to employ tens of thousands of workers, was known for its informal management style and work practices.

By the late 1970s, Silicon Valley possessed nearly 3,000 electronics firms, 70 percent of which had fewer than ten employees and 85 percent of which had fewer than 100. These firms faced a major crisis in the mid-1980s, when they lost the market for semiconductor memories to Japanese companies, and in 1985–86 about 20 percent of the semiconductor employees in Silicon Valley lost their jobs. However, as a mark of their flexibility and reliance, most of the Silicon Valley firms recovered later in the decade as producers of specialized, complex, high-value-added electronics goods. Developments around Boston — especially in a complex of firms located near Interstate Highway 128, known as Route 128 firms — offered an instructive contrast. Generally larger and more hide-bound than the smaller, more nimble companies in Silicon Valley, the Route 128 businesses did not respond as adequately to the Japanese challenge; and, over time, Route 128 declined relative to some other regions as a high technology area.

Efforts to Replicate Silicon Valley

Silicon Valley's success in job generation led to efforts to replicate the high technology district elsewhere. Terman was sometimes involved in these actions. In New Jersey he worked with Bell Labs, other high technology firms, and educational institutions to try to establish a "Silicon Valley East." The venture failed when the companies and the educational facilities proved unable to cooperate. New Jersey's high technology firms developed, as a consequence, as individual companies, not as part of an industrial district. In the Dallas–Fort Worth area, Terman's work with high technology companies, such as Texas Instruments, and Southern Methodist University was cut short by a recession, which dried up funding. Terman had much more success in Korea, where the national government succeeded in getting major companies to cooperate with the Korea Advanced Institute of Science in a broad range of high technology ventures.

High Technology Efforts in the Hawaiian Islands

Among the many regions of the world to embrace high technology business as its economic savior were the Hawaiian Islands, especially the island of Maui. Hard-hit by declines in the plantation-agriculture crops of sugar cane and pineapple, Maui's residents turned to other avenues of economic advance in the 1970s, 1980s, and 1990s. Some sought salvation in tourism, but that industry proved fickle, experiencing lots of ups and downs with fluctuations in the global economy. For a time, high technology businesses seemed to offer solutions to Maui's economic difficulties. However, an investigation of the history of high technology efforts on Maui reveals problems that often arise in trying to turn high technology dreams into realities. In the end, high technology businesses did not solve Maui's problems.

Well aware of their island's economic difficulties, Maui's political and business leaders formed the Maui Economic Development Board (MEDB) in 1982 to try to diversify their island's economy, especially by nurturing high technology ventures through the creation of a high technology park. Colin Cameron, whose family had long been on Maui and who was taking the family business from plantation agriculture into tourism, and Donald Malcolm, an engineer and newcomer to the island, were especially important. When Malcolm moved to Maui in the early 1980s, Cameron convinced him to become president of the MEDB. For the next decade, Cameron and Malcolm worked closely together to develop what became known as the Maui Research and Technology Park (MRTP). Those forming the MEDB and its child, the MRTP, believed that high technology businesses could become a "third leg" of Maui's economy, along with agriculture and tourism.

Those hoping to create a high technology park on Maui first of all had to establish an organizational structure. They set up the MEDB as a non-profit "public-private partnership," composed of a who's who of Maui's business and political leaders: land developers, bankers, and members of the county and state governments. The initial plan was for the MEDB to find a mainland developer who had the capital and resources needed to construct the MRTP and then step into the background. As events soon showed, that relatively low-key approach proved unworkable.

Mainland developers did not prove up to the tasks at hand. In 1984, the MEDB selected a California developer who had built a research and development park in Santa Clara County (part of Silicon Valley) to build the MRTP. With the California economy faltering, the savings and loan that had been financing that developer's Santa Clara work failed, his business empire collapsed, and he withdrew from the Maui project. The MEDB then picked a Phoenix development company to develop the park, but within a year that firm, concerned about environmental problems in preparing the site for the MRTP, withdrew from the undertaking. Forced back on their own resources, Maui's leaders formed the Maui R and T Partners to develop the high technology park, with the MEDB acting as the managing partner for the development—a major enhancement of the board's role. The MEDB, in turn, entered into agreements with the State of Hawaii, the University of Hawaii, Maui County, and the federal government to try to make the MRTP a reality.

State and federal funding helped. Malcolm traveled to Honolulu, where, with the strong support of State Senator Mamoru Yamasaki, he persuaded the state government to finance the first major building, to serve as an incubator for newly formed high technology companies. The state's agreement to participate in the MRTP broke the impasse. Private firms constructed a second building, a state-of-the-art commercial office complex. Next came the Maui High Performance Computing Center—complete with a very powerful supercomputer, which was important for the success of the MRTP —made possible by funding from the federal government secured by Hawaii's Senator Daniel Inouye. Other installations followed in the mid- and late 1990s.

Still, even with the active involvement of Maui's leaders, it proved difficult to attract tenants. Infrastructure improvements helped, and the MRTP quickly provided satellite uplinks and downlinks, microwave and fiber optic communications, and access to the Internet. A business information center and research library were also attractions, as was the supercomputer. Nonetheless, the MEDB had to undergo a learning process before it succeeded in helping high technology firms develop. A major challenge lay in a dearth of scientists and technicians on Maui. The MEDB took important steps to upgrade scientific education in the island's public schools and labored to try to improve higher education as well. However, the lack of a four-year university on Maui hurt badly.

Only in the late 1990s did the MRTP begin to fulfill its promise. By the winter of 1998, the twenty-some companies, mainly small businesses, and organizations there employed about 350 people. However, high technology companies had not yet become a third leg of Maui's economy. Nor, despite considerable government support, had that occurred elsewhere in the Hawaiian Islands. The Hawaiian Islands lacked many of the factors needed to attract high technology businesses, elements ranging from the possession of a first-class research university to the existence of government policies favorable toward businesses (high tax rates hurt business development in Hawaii, for example). Despite the concerted efforts of the MEDB and others, in 1999 *Forbes* magazine ranked Honolulu 160th out of 162 regions in the United States as a desirable place in which to conduct high technology businesses.

Success and Failure in High Technology Businesses

As developments in Hawaii, New Jersey, and Texas demonstrated, it was not a simple matter to replicate the successful development of Silicon Valley. Many factors had to come together in a "hot mix" for high technology districts to succeed. Having many flexible, entrepreneurial small firms seemed a necessary factor, but they were not, by themselves, enough to guarantee success. Governmental spending, such as the defense spending so important for Silicon Valley firms during the 1950s and 1960s, helped. So did the presence of a nearby top-ranked research university, such as Stanford University, especially if researchers from that institution interacted with high technology entrepreneurs. Even so, success was not guaranteed. In Japan, governmental efforts to bring together relocated national (that is, public) universities, government laboratories, and private firms in the 1970s and 1980s to create new "technopolises" were only partly successful because of an inability to mesh well the people from the three types of institutions. They had grown up in different social cultures and found it difficult to cooperate.

Additional Reading

Annalee Saxenian, *Regional Advantage: Culture and Competition in Silicon Valley and Route 128* (Cambridge, Mass.: Harvard University Press, 1994), looks at the development of Silicon Valley as a high technology region and compares its evolution to that of the area around Boston. David Kaplan, *The Silicon Boys and their Valley of Dreams* (New York: Harper Collins, 1999), is an informed, journalistic account that stresses the personalities. Leslie Berlin, "Robert Noyce and Fairchild Semiconductor, 1957–1968," *Business History Review* 75 (Spring 2001): 63–102, is an excellent account of Noyce's importance. Stuart Leslie and Robert Kargon, "Selling Silicon Valley: Frederick Terman's Model for Regional Advantage," *Business History Review* 70 (Winter 1996): 435–472, looks at Terman's efforts to replicate Silicon Valley in New Jersey, Texas, and Korea; the authors make much the same argument in Leslie and Kargon, "The Obsolescent University? Reconfiguring Higher Education for Regional Advantage," in Karen Merrill, *The Modern Worlds of Business and Industry* (Turnhout, Belgium: Bradstreet, 1998), 121–40. Thomas Heinrich, "Cold War Armory: Military Contracting in Silicon Valley," *Enterprise & Society* 3 (June 2002): 247–84, stresses the importance of military spending. On efforts to create high technology districts in Japan, see Sheridan Taber, *The Technopolis Strategy: Japan, High Technology, and the Control of the Twenty-first Century* (New York: Prentice Hall, 1986); and Michael A. Cusumano, *Japan's Software Factories* (New York: Oxford University Press, 1991). Mansel Blackford, *Fragile Paradise: The Impact of Tourism on Maui, 1959–2000* (Lawrence: University Press of Kansas, 2001), ch. 1, explores high technology efforts in the Hawaiian Islands.

CHAPTER 8

Small Business in Modern
America, 1972–2000

Writing in 1987, the head of the Small Business Administration noted, "Employment growth in industries dominated by small firms continued to outpace the growth in those dominated by large firms," and observed further that in the 1980s "job creation in the economy has been largely an outcome of small business activity, especially activity by firms with fewer than twenty employees." Waxing more eloquent, the *U.S. News & World Report* asserted in late 1989, "To a far greater extent than most Americans realize, the economy's vitality depends on the fortunes of tiny shops and restaurants, neighborhood services and factories." Small business concerns had, in fact, penetrated the popular consciousness by this time. In Columbus, Ohio, for example, the automobile bumper sticker, "There's no business like a small business AND There's no business like your own business" could be seen on city streets. As these statements suggested, small businesses seemed to experience something of a revival in the 1970s and 1980s.

This chapter examines the realities of small business development, which were often at odds with such rosy rhetoric, in the three decades beginning in the early 1970s. After examining the ups and downs of small businesses in various fields, the chapter looks directly at the roles small businesses played (and did not play) in America's economic development during that period, especially in job generation. If developments in the high tech firms in California's Silicon Valley during the 1950s and 1960s seemed to emphasize the importance of being flexible and fast-moving for small business success, the economic problems that American businesses faced from the 1970s on seemed to underline the significance of those qualities for businesses of all sizes across the nation.

Small Business and Big Business in Modern America

Reversing their earlier long-term decline relative to big businesses, small firms increased in importance in the 1970s and into the 1980s. Of the 20.5 million businesses filing federal tax returns in 1991, only 7,000 employed more than 500 workers. Some 14.3 million of the firms were sole proprietorships, with another 1.7 million organized as partnerships and 4.5 million as corporations. In the decade after 1974, the proportion of full-time nonagricultural workers who were self-employed rose from 10.7 percent to 12 percent for men and from 3.2 percent to 4.7 percent for women. Between 1976 and 1984, firms with fewer than 500 workers increased their share of the nation's total employment from 51 percent to 53 percent.

Several reasons accounted for this turn of events. The end of the Bretton Woods Agreement in 1971 heightened global economic insecurity by abolishing fixed currency exchange rates and allowing national currencies to "float" against each other. A worldwide recession, the worst since the Great Depression of the 1930s, further upset economic matters in the early 1970s, as did hikes in energy prices. At the same time, the growth of strong national economies in Japan, West Germany, and other nations, fully recovered from World War II, produced large multinational firms capable of competing with — and, in some cases, surpassing — their American counterparts in mass-production sectors. With the great increase in international competition — made possible by advancements in communications and transportation, everything from jumbo jets to satellites and computers — many U.S. big businesses, especially those in manufacturing, seemed to falter as engines of growth. Between 1974 and 1984, employment in *Fortune* 500 companies declined by 1.5 million. As this situation unfolded, many Americans looked to small firms for economic rejuvenation. Seen as nimble, able to respond quickly to opportunities in the unstable global economy, small business won widespread admiration.

Even more was involved. The recession of the early 1970s (and another one in the early 1980s) hurt big businesses, especially firms dependent upon world trade, more than it did smaller companies. Then, too, people often form small businesses when they lose their jobs in larger firms. As we have seen, this situation prevailed in the early 1930s, and it may have been important again in the last decades of the century as well. However, structural changes in America's and the world's economies probably were more responsible for furthering the development of small business at the end of the twentieth century. A partial shift in the American economy away from manufacturing, in which big businesses had been most important, to services, which historically had been dominated more by small companies, may also have been a factor. In the final analysis, it is likely that no single element explained the surge in small business development. As D. Storey and S. Johnson noted in their detailed and comprehensive study of small manufacturers in Birmingham, England; Boston, Massachusetts; and Bologna, Italy in 1987, "No single explanation offers a fully satisfactory explanation of this widespread movement [the growth of small business]." Instead, they concluded, small businesses rose to prominence in each of the three regions by different paths and for different reasons.

An increasing number of small businesses depended partially upon foreign sales for their livelihood. Once the almost exclusive domain of big business, overseas markets became more and more important for smaller concerns. Federal government legislation helped. In 1983, Congress enacted a law making it easier to set up export companies, and by early 1989 some 4,180 had been formed, many of which handled the products of small firms. The revolution in communications and transportation allowed small firms to compete on more nearly equal terms with businesses abroad, and by the late 1980s and early 1990s more small firms than before exported a significant proportion of their output. Of the 243,000 American companies that exported directly through their own sales offices in 1989, 88 percent had fewer than 500 employees; and one-half of the businesses exporting through third parties, such as brokers and trading companies, were small businesses. Altogether, small firms accounted for about 21 percent of U.S. manufacturing exports in 1989. A growing number of small businesses also set up their own production facilities overseas, either by themselves or in joint ventures with foreign firms.

This apparent resurgence of small business was short-lived, however. By the close of the 1990s, it was becoming clear that small firms would not be America's economic salvation. For the most part, restructured, more efficient, large companies seemed to be carrying the day. Numerous indicators suggested this turn of events. After dropping steadily throughout the 1980s, America's gross domestic product per company climbed in the early and mid-1990s, showing that companies were growing in size. Moreover, the share of self-employed workers in America's nonfarm workforce, after rising from the mid-1970s through the 1980s, fell throughout the 1990s — to just 9.9 percent in 1999.

The role of the federal government in aiding or hindering the growth of small businesses at the end of the twentieth century was of less significance than economic factors. The SBA continued to work for small business development through loan programs, set-asides in government contracts, and advisory programs. Nonetheless, the SBA came under increasing criticism for not adequately meeting the needs of small businesses, for favoring minority business people over all other groups, and for its involvement in a growing number of scandals. Eager to end what he viewed as the overregulation of the economy by the federal government, President Ronald Reagan proposed abolishing the SBA. The ability of the SBA to survive this attack and then grow in size during the 1990s despite its many problems serves as a poignant example of the longevity of federal government agencies. Another action of the federal government was of some importance, even before Reagan became president. Responding to complaints from small business groups, Congress passed the Regulatory Flexibility Act (RFA) in 1980. This legislation encouraged federal agencies to impose lighter regulatory burdens upon smaller businesses than upon larger ones—in effect, to create tiers of regulatory burdens according to the size of firms. Even before the passage of the act, however, tiering was occurring. For example, the Toxic Substances Control Act of 1976 exempted small chemical companies from various testing and reporting requirements that continued to be required of larger companies; the Office of Federal Contract Compliance exempted businesses with fewer than fifty employees from filing affirmative action plans; and the Occupational Safety and Health Administration exempted firms employing fewer than twenty employees from its regulations. Just how important, then, was the RFA? While of significance in certain fields, its overall importance was limited. The most detailed study yet made of the differential impacts of federal government regulations on large and small firms revealed that, contrary to popular opinion and the outcries of small business people, "regulations have not generally placed smaller businesses at a competitive disadvantage" and concluded that, for the most part, the RFA was unnecessary.

Small Business in Manufacturing

The field of manufacturing offered the clearest example of the renewed importance of small and medium-size businesses in the last quarter of the century. Between 1976 and 1986, firms with fewer than 500 employees increased their share of the total manufacturing output of the United States from 33 percent to 37 percent. Even in larger firms, plant size decreased. A study of 410 leading manufacturers revealed that plants constructed before 1970 but still operating nine years later employed an average of 644 workers; for new plants opened in the 1970s, the average number of employees was only 241.

The flexibility that smaller companies and plants had in meeting the challenges of the rapidly changing business environment of the 1970s and 1980s accounted for much of their growing importance. As in earlier times, small firms proved adept at exploiting niche markets with specialized products based upon short production runs. By the 1970s and 1980s, however, more was involved. The ability of small businesses to react quickly to alterations in markets and fluctuating exchange rates in an increasingly unstable economic world helped explain their growing significance. Then, too, the use of computers in computer aided design, computer aided engineering, and computer aided manufacturing allowed small, independent firms to perform tasks that once only larger businesses could accomplish. Realizing the benefits that could be derived from the flexibility inherent in small-size operations, some large companies disintegrated their work, coming to rely more heavily than before upon subcontractors for the production of major components for their finished products. What developed in some fields in the 1980s and 1990s were congeries of small industrial firms, sometimes operating as subcontractors but often also producing on their own. Often located near each other in specific regions, the small firms supported each other and in some fields offered viable alternatives to mass industrial production by big businesses — much as had occurred in the industrial districts described in Chapters 2 and 3.

Nowhere was the growing importance of small industrial businesses more apparent than in America's metalworking (or engineering) industries. Many small companies began operations during this period. Between 1972 and 1982, the average number of employees in an American metalworking company declined by 13 percent, despite an 11 percent increase in both employment and real output in the metalworking industries as a whole. How did this situation occur? The introduction of numerically controlled machine tools beginning in the 1940s and 1950s permitted small and medium-size production runs and favored, as economist Bo Carlsson has explained, "the manufacture of complex, non-standardized parts rather than simple, standardized parts in mass-production systems." The result, he noted, "is that restructuring of this sort is likely to lead to the establishment of new plants with more flexibility and lower total employment, at the same time as employment is reduced in older facilities."

Much the same trend developed in the very different industry of moviemaking. From the 1920s into the 1950s, seven major studios dominated moviemaking. Vertically integrated, they owned chains of theaters, and in cities of 100,000 or more controlled 70 percent of first-run theater capacity. From the late 1940s onward, however, the economic situation within the movie industry changed. In 1948, a federal antitrust action forced the studios to divest their theaters, and in the 1950s, television introduced a new element of competition. (This legal decision, like the slightly later one forcing DuPont to give up its holding in General Motors, was based on the notion that vertically integrated firms restricted competition.) Nonetheless, in the 1950s and 1960s the major studios continued to dominate movie production. In the 1970s and 1980s, however, vertical disintegration occurred, as studios subcontracted more and more work and as more independent producers grew up. Hundreds of very specialized small firms — production companies, rental studios, editing businesses, lighting firms, film processing outfits — developed in southern California, the heart of the movie industry. This flexible specialization of many different types of businesses engaged in the various steps of moviemaking offered a workable alternative to large vertically integrated studios and eventually largely replaced them. Located in one area, this agglomeration of small companies allowed producers to reap economies of scale without forming big businesses.

However, the very success of large American corporations in restructuring their operations in the 1980s and 1990s — such as in their disintegration in moviemaking — limited opportunities for smaller firms in many fields as the twenty-first century opened. Large manufacturers divested themselves of peripheral operations, returned to their "core capabilities," and put in place more efficient, "lean and mean" management structures and production methods — well ahead of their Japanese and, for the most part, European competitors. It seemed that, although small manufacturers would be more important than they had been in the 1950s and 1960s, they would not, after all, replace their larger brethren as America's primary engines of economic growth.

Many commentators observed the changing relationships among manufacturers of different sizes. In a close look at this situation, the British journal the *Economist* asked in 1995, "What is going on?" The magazine replied to its own question, "Part of the answer is that small firms are being driven out by large firms which are starting to behave more like their smaller brethren . . . pushing decision-making down through management ranks, restructuring themselves around teams and product-based units, and becoming more entrepreneurial." Then, too, the periodical observed, small firms were merging and becoming larger. "High-tech enclaves such as those in Silicon Valley or in Seattle can help firms achieve critical mass," the *Economist* noted, "but as big companies have become more nimble, small firms have to do more than just huddle together." Instead, the journal concluded, "What has started rolling, says Bill Sahlman of the Harvard Business School, is 'a wave of small-company consolidation across every imaginable industry.'" In his well-regarded *Lean and Mean: The Changing Landscape of Corporate Power in the Age of Flexibility*, published at about the same time, Bennett Harris made much the same point. He argued that large companies had recently succeeded in becoming more flexible in their uses of labor and capital by subcontracting with smaller firms. Large manufacturers, Bennett maintained, created global production networks to avoid government regulations and to battle unions. Thus, far from achieving independence in recent decades, small manufacturers had become ever more dependent on large companies.

Small Business in Sales and Services

In 1994, a decade-long campaign against Wal-Mart, America's largest retailer, exploded. Protesters chanting, "One, two, three, four—we don't want your Wal-Mart store," opposed the opening of new stores across the United States. A self-employed clothing designer in Fort Collins, Colorado, summed up what was on the minds of many, "I really hate Wal-Mart. Everything's starting to look the same, everybody buys all the same things—a lot of small-town character is being lost. They disrupt local communities, they hurt small business." It mattered little to such protesters that Wal-Mart brought lower prices to consumers. In fact, however, that concern was what mattered to most consumers. While sympathizing with the protesters, most Americans continued to shop at Wal-Mart.

Sales, especially retailing, presented, at best, a mixed picture for small business people. Challenged by mail-order houses, department stores, and chain stores in earlier years, small retail outlets encountered growing competition from discount stores from the 1970s on. Suburban shopping malls and, a bit later, upscale downtown malls, both of which grew enormously in popularity, were another threat, for they usually provided little space for small merchants—as one observer noted, just "an odd kiosk or two." One advantage of big businesses lay in the rents they paid. The large anchor stores, often Sears outlets or other nationally known department stores, paid much less rent per square foot of space than did their smaller competitors. As a result of these developments, the share of total retail sales made by single-shop stores with twenty or fewer employees dropped from over one-half in 1958 to just one-third by 1977. By the mid-1980s, the nation's fifty largest retailers accounted for one-quarter of America's retail sales. Similarly, the continued development of large supermarkets, which often stayed open twenty-four hours a day, further eroded the positions of small mom-and-pop grocery and convenience stores. These developments led retailing scholar Stanley Hollander to conclude in 1980, "The outlook for small retailing may be described as somewhat discouraging but not totally unnerving."

This trend became even more pronounced during the 1990s. Between 1987 and 1993, the market share of America's top ten supermarket chains rose from about 23 percent to nearly 30 percent; the market share of the top ten specialist clothing chains increased from roughly 24 percent to 30 percent; the market share of the top ten home improvement chains rose from 17 percent to about 27 percent; and the market share of the top ten department store groups increased from 42 percent to 53 percent.

Services, a fast-growing segment of the American economy, remained more of a stronghold for small firms. The number of people working in service establishments rose from about 3.1 million in 1919 to 8.7 million in 1957 and continued to rise in subsequent years. Despite a tendency toward firm concentration in areas such as real estate, insurance, and banking, most service companies were small. Restaurants (despite the rise of fast-food chains beginning in the 1920s), plumbing companies, auto repair shops, barber shops and beauty salons, shoe repair shops, and so forth all tended to be single-owner proprietorships or small partnerships.

Despite a drift toward bigness, the fields of law and medicine long remained homes for small businesses. (Although lawyers and doctors are certainly professionals, they are also business people charging for their services.) The number of lawyers (and judges) in the United States rose from 108,000 in 1900 to 184,000 fifty years later and continued to increase in later decades, as Americans became more and more litigious. While about 100 large law firms had developed in New York City as early as 1904, such big firms were the exception, not the rule, in the legal profession as late as the 1970s and 1980s. In the mid-1970s, fifty law firms, each with more than 100 lawyers, employed a total of about 6,500 attorneys. By 1993, some 67,000 lawyers worked in some 250 large law firms. Even so, attorneys laboring in these large law "factories" represented only 8 percent of the lawyers in America. The number of physicians in the United States rose from about 146,000 in 1920 to roughly 195,000 in 1950 and increased still more later in the twentieth century. A rising proportion of these doctors found employment in organizations such as hospitals and universities, but even in 1973, 42 percent were self-employed, down from 55 percent a decade earlier.

In banking, the trend toward growth in firm size was more pronounced. While the United States still possessed around 15,000 commercial banks in the mid-1980s, about the same number as fifty years before, large bank groups accounted for a growing share of America's financial business, particularly during the 1990s. Branch banking, which grew rapidly in importance, was made possible, in part, by the development of computerized communications and transactions. In investment banking a host of discount brokers and hundreds of new mutual funds developed. Operating nationwide, they undercut local and regional investment banking houses. The story was somewhat similar in real estate: the same revolution in communications and computers that permitted the resurgence of small business in manufacturing threatened small firms. Large real estate companies, often working through franchise systems, expanded from regional bases to nationwide operations, all held together by advanced communications systems.

In both sales and services, franchising was of increasing importance. The franchise movement boomed in the 1960s, experienced a slow-down in the early 1970s (the result of a recession and of government investigations revealing widespread fraud in some franchise industries), but picked up steam again in the late 1970s and the 1980s. In 1980, 442,000 franchise outlets made $336 billion in sales in the United States, and by the mid-1980s franchise outlets accounted for more than one-third of the total value of the nation's retail sales. As before, Americans viewed franchising as a way to fulfill their dreams of becoming independent business people, while at the same time securing the benefits of belonging to large supportive organizations.

Tensions had existed from the earliest days of franchising, but they exploded in the late 1980s and early 1990s. On the one hand, franchisers ranging from Kentucky Fried Chicken to Holiday Inn sought to tighten controls over their franchisees, particularly by forcing them to upgrade their often out-of-date facilities. Increasingly, however, franchisees rebelled against the demands of their franchisers, sometimes successfully. Burger King franchisees blocked an attempt by Pillsbury to sell off its fast-food subsidiary as part of a defense against a takeover by Grand Metropolitan.

Arby's franchisees mounted an attempt to buy the chain when the company took actions they did not like. Franchisees in the Straw Hat Pizza chain purchased the chain's trademark, trade name, and other materials from Marriott when that company tried to sell the chain to the Saga Company; the franchisees then proceeded to form their own cooperative to replace their arrangement with Marriott.

The nature of the franchisee was changing in important ways. Fewer franchisees were small-scale, mom-and-pop business people operating on a shoestring. As franchising matured as a form of business organization, more franchisees were experienced business people, often operating on a large scale. Just how much room was left in franchising for small budding entrepreneurs was problematic. An article in the *Wall Street Journal* in the 1990s captured well the changes taking place: "The profile of the typical franchise owner is changing. A growing number of cash-rich investors and companies are sinking money into several franchises — or buying rights to an entire state or foreign country. Some big-business executives have turned to franchise ownership after being caught in the corporate-restructuring squeeze. Independent store owners are converting to franchises to gain advertising clout. And experienced franchisees are snapping up franchises in other industries in order to diversify. . . . There has been a marked shift recently toward more-sophisticated buyers with proven business skills and deep pockets."

Agribusiness and the Family Farm

If sales and services presented some hope to aspiring small business people, agriculture offered little encouragement. The decline of the family farm, which had begun earlier, continued unabated. By 1986, only 2.2 percent of the nation's working population was engaged in agriculture, and by one estimate just 650,000 commercial family farmers remained in the United States. Problems faced by small and medium-sized farmers, already apparent in the 1950s and 1960s, deepened. Temporarily aided by high prices for their crops, many farmers purchased new farmlands and equipment in the late 1970s, hoping that crop prices and land values would keep rising. However, the rosy future they hoped for failed to materialize, when foreign markets for American farm products collapsed. The loss of these markets was catastrophic, for in the 1980s foreign sales took one-third of the production of America's farms. Unable to pay the interest on their mortgages, many family farmers lost their land. Some small, marginal farmers were able to hang on by taking part-time or full-time jobs in nearby cities, a strategy they had pursued since the 1930s. The major winners, to the extent that there were any, were big corporate farmers raising specialty crops. As was already occurring by the 1950s and 1960s, they often operated as parts of large vertically integrated enterprises — agribusinesses — that made their profits more in processing and marketing food than in growing crops. The trend toward consolidation continued through the 1990s. Soaring energy and fertilizer costs, along with falling farm prices, hit farmers hard, especially at the close of the decade.

Only federal government payments, which continued despite some efforts at deregulation aimed at weaning farmers away from dependence on the federal government, and jobs outside of farming (by one account 90 percent of the income earned by farmers came from nonfarm jobs by the year 2000) kept many farmers in business. Even federal government farm aid failed to help small farms much. Most of the subsidies went to large farms. In the late 1990s, the largest farms, just 1 percent of the nation's farms, received 15 percent of the payments. The top 20 percent accounted for 79 percent of the subsidies.

International Comparisons of Small Business

The picture of small business was rosier in many other nations than in the United States. Newly favorable public attitudes and government policies, together with the development of new production and management methods, reversed the decline of small firms in British manufacturing. In fact, the growth of small industrial companies in Great Britain, firms with no more than 200 employees, was remarkable: from 71,000 (of a total 75,000) manufacturers in 1971 to 133,00 (of a total 135,000) just seventeen years later. Looking beyond manufacturing revealed a similar situation: in 1986, small and medium-size firms (those with no more than 500 employees) accounted for 71 percent of Britain's private-sector employment, up from 57 percent seven years before. In Japan, truly small-scale businesses, those having no more than 20 employees, made up 78 percent of Japanese companies in 1987 and employed 31 percent of the nation's workers. In 1993, small and medium-size companies (those with no more than 300 employees) accounted for just under three-quarters of Japan's industrial employment and one-half of its manufacturing output. Moreover, reversing a past trend, many were independent firms, not serving as subcontractors for larger enterprises; in fact, 40 percent did no subcontracting at all. Cross-national comparisons of small business — whether based on employment, output, or some other measure — proved notoriously difficult for scholars.

However, by many reckonings, small firms in other advanced nations accounted for a higher percentage of economic activity than did small firms in the United States. Whether this situation really meant that small businesses were healthier in those other nations was debatable. Many European observers argued to the contrary, insisting that government regulations made the small business sectors in their countries static and inflexible, when compared to the more dynamic, flexible conditions in the United States.

Innovation and Job Creation

In the late 1980s and the 1990s, two closely related topics of particular interest to many Americans, especially to policymakers, were the roles of small businesses in innovation and job creation. As large United States businesses seemed to lose their competitive edge to their foreign counterparts during the 1970s and 1980s, many Americans came to celebrate small firms for their abilities to achieve technological breakthroughs and create new jobs. A close examination of the roles of small businesses in these fields reveals, however, a spotty record.

Although big businesses spent much more than small firms on research and development, small businesses remained important sources of innovation. In the early and mid-1980s, big businesses accounted for about 95 percent of the corporate-financed research and development conducted in the United States. The fifteen largest spenders carried out about 40 percent of the total. Nonetheless, small firms excelled in conducting research and development projects that required low amounts of capital and high degrees of specialized knowledge. In the twentieth century, small companies introduced new products as varied as the aerosol can, biosynthetic insulin, double-knit fabrics, quick-frozen food, zippers, and computer software.

Numerous studies identified small firms as sources of innovation in the nation's business system. One conducted by the U.S. Office of Management and Budget showed that companies employing fewer than 1,000 employees accounted for about one-half of the innovations made by American businesses between 1953 and 1973. Similarly, an examination of product innovations in 121 industries during the 1970s found that small firms were responsible for 40 percent of them. Recent studies show the continuing importance of small firms as sources of innovation but demonstrate as well that their contributions have been more significant in some fields than in others. After examining the sources of 8,074 innovations made by American businesses in 1982, economists Zoltan Acs and David Audretsch concluded, "Our results are unequivocal—industry innovation tends to decrease as the level of concentration rises." In other words, industries composed of many small businesses generated more innovations than those dominated by a few large ones. They found, moreover, marked differences in the circumstances under which large and small firms were likely to be innovative. "Industries which are capital-intensive, concentrated, and advertising-intensive," they observed, "tend to promote the innovative advantage in large firms. The small-firm innovative advantage, however, tends to occur in industries in the early stages of the life-cycle, where total innovation and the use of skilled labor play a large role, and where large firms comprise a high share of the market." Small, flexible companies were also often able to commercialize their findings (or those of other firms) faster than big businesses. The study of product innovations in 121 industries in the 1970s showed that firms with 500 or fewer employees brought their innovations to market in 2.2 years, considerably faster than the 3.1 years needed by larger companies. In their ability to respond more speedily, small firms offer one of their most valuable services to society.

If investigators established with some clarity the continuing significance of small businesses in the development and commercialization of innovations, they did not do so with regard to the generation of new jobs. In fact, the question of precisely how important small businesses were in creating new jobs in modern America was a very controversial topic, one rife with significance for government policy decisions.

Much of the controversy revolved around the work of the scholar and consultant David L. Birch. Like many business writers and economists, Birch saw in small business the most vibrant engine of growth in the modern American economy. "[John Kenneth] Galbraith and others who think that big business is the American economy," Birch observed, "don't seem to realize that the bubbly, yeasty, creative segment is the small business segment." Birch and scholars like him characterized big businesses as unexciting, stagnant firms that contributed little to the economic growth of the United States. In his initial study of the role of small businesses in job generation, Birch claimed that 80 percent of the new jobs created in America between 1969 and 1976 were in companies employing fewer than twenty workers. Later, Birch backed off from that assertion a bit, being content to note, "The small-firm share of job creation varies a great deal. The time period and location will affect the outcome dramatically."

Many soon disputed Birch's findings. Using much the same type of data that Birch deployed, economists for the SBA found that for the years 1982 through 1986, companies with fewer than 100 employees accounted for just 52 percent of America's new private-sector jobs, and that firms with no more than 20 employees were responsible for only 37 percent. Similarly, SBA investigators discovered that for the years 1985 and 1986 firms with fewer than 100 employees accounted for only 44 percent of the new jobs created in the United States. "Birch is a chorus of one," concluded Thomas A. Gray, the chief economist for the SBA. Scholars also offered thorough critiques of Birch's work. British investigators D. Storey and S. Johnson found in 1987 that Birch "probably overestimated employment growth in small firms" and suggested, "revised figures yield a small business share of employment growth of 50 percent." They reached a cautious conclusion about the roles small businesses could be expected to play in global economic growth: "Whilst it is difficult, because of data problems, to be satisfied that the international comparisons are fully adequate, there appears to be no evidence to support the view that, once the extreme values of the UK and Japan are excluded, countries which have a higher proportion of employment in small firms perform better than those with a low proportion in such firms." They concluded, "There also appears to be no evidence to support the view that those countries in which small firms increased their share of employment most rapidly performed better than other countries."

A study prepared for the U.S. National Bureau of Economic Research in 1993, by far the most comprehensive look at the roles small firms have played in job generation in the United States, reached similar conclusions. In its examination of job generation and destruction in American manufacturing between 1972 and 1988, the report found that firms with fewer than 500 employees were better than larger companies in *gross* job creation. However, the report also found that small firms went out of business more frequently than their larger counterparts, thus destroying many more jobs. On balance, the study concluded that small manufacturing firms were no better than larger ones at *net* job creation. By the late 1990s, however, the terms of the debate had shifted a bit, as small business analysts argued that what mattered was how easily small firms could grow to become larger enterprises. Preliminary research suggested that there were, indeed, fewer barriers to growth in the United States than in other nations, making America's small business sector a very real "seedbed" for big business development.

The Small Business Person

Despite the continuing high mortality rate of small businesses—in the 1970s, 1980s, and 1990s one-half to two-thirds of all newly formed businesses, mainly small firms, failed to reach their fifth birthday, and four-fifths disappeared as independent enterprises by their tenth year—the world of small business continued to attract newcomers. (Of course, not all of these firms failed. Some merged with other companies, others voluntarily disbanded, and still others changed their forms by adding new partners.) The dreams of independence and profits that had motivated those founding businesses in the past have remained potent in recent decades.

It is important to realize, however, that many people starting small firms were not interested primarily in rapid growth. The vast majority sought a modicum of independence to do what they wanted while earning a reasonable income, an income to replace what they left behind in jobs previously held with larger companies. In a sense this may be an urban substitute for the old ideal of having a "good" life for one's family on the farm. Indeed, it was this situation of modest success and growth that developed in most of those small firms that succeeded. According to an estimate by David Sexton and Nancy Bowman-Upton, in the early 1980s "only about 650,000 firms [of some 17 million companies] in the United States qualif[y] as growing firms and . . . the top 5, 10, and 15 percent of those growth firms create 83, 93, and 98 percent respectively of all gross new jobs."

Small business ownership offered increasing opportunities for women. From the late 1970s through the 1990s, women formed new businesses, nearly all of which were small, at a much higher rate than men. During the decade of the 1980s, the number of women-owned firms rose at an average annual rate of 13 percent, compared to 6 percent for male-owned businesses. As in previous decades, businesses owned by women clustered in services and sales; however, there was a growing diversity in the types of businesses owned by women. Substantially more were found in construction and transportation than in earlier times. As an SBA investigator noted in 1988, "the industry distribution of women-owned nonfarm sole proprietorships is becoming more diverse as women make significant inroads into industries traditionally dominated by men." During the 1990s, women continued to advance as business owners. By 1996, almost 8 million companies, nearly all of which were small businesses, were owned by women, up from 4.5 million in 1987. This 78 percent growth rate dwarfed the 47 percent growth rate for the number of all U.S. firms. Sales made by women-owned businesses soared 236 percent in the same period, rising from $681 billion to $2.3 trillion. By 1996, one of every four American workers was employed by a business owned by a woman.

For minorities, small business ownership offered fewer opportunities than for whites, but the degree of opportunity varied considerably by minority group. The number of minority-owned firms more than doubled between 1972 and 1982. Nonetheless, even in the late 1970s the participation rate of minorities in business ownership was only one-fifth that of whites. In 1977, for example, whites owned 63 businesses per 1,000 members of their ethnic group, Asians 29, Hispanics 20, and blacks 9. Immigrants to large cities in America—and to other large cities around the globe—found opportunities in forming small firms. High-tech cities needed low-tech service businesses to support them; and here immigrants, lured by networks of families and friends, sometimes found possibilities. These opportunities, however, like so many small businesses throughout American history, entailed long hours, low returns, and disappointments. The variations in business involvement among the minority groups, including immigrants, were due mainly to differences in the rates at which their members started new businesses, for the business closure rate for each group was about the same.

What accounted for the varying degrees of business formation by the different minority groups? Probably numerous factors. A detailed 1988 report by the SBA showed that blacks had less access to financial capital than did Asians or Hispanics and that blacks could depend upon fewer and less well-developed support groups for help in times of need. Black-owned businesses remained clustered primarily in central cities, and were particularly hard-hit by the flight of capital to the suburbs, as the building of suburban malls proliferated. More than other groups, blacks also experienced difficulty in finding markets beyond other members of their race, a circumstance that may have retarded business formation and growth, given the relatively limited incomes of most black customers. Difficult to assess, but no doubt important, in explaining the relative backwardness of blacks in the formation of new businesses have been human elements, such as the lack of role models. When compared to other minority groups, for example, a lower proportion of blacks worked for close relatives who owned businesses.

This situation began changing in the 1990s. The number of black-owned businesses increased by 46 percent between 1987 and 1992, rising to 620,000 in the latter year, about the same rate of increase as that for nonblack businesses. Most were small businesses: 56 percent had annual receipts of under $10,000 in 1992 (and only 3,000 boasted receipts of more than $1 million). Concentrated, as in the past, in retail sales and services, black firms composed 3.6 percent of all businesses in the United States, but accounted for just 1 percent of the their sales and receipts.

Small Business in a New Millennium
Small businesses remained part of the American scene as the twenty-first century opened. While not contributing as much to the nation's employment picture as the rhapsodies of some pundits had suggested in the 1970s and 1980s, small firms generated a significant share of America's new jobs. They also remained important as sources of innovation, particularly in the commercialization of new processes and products. As always, the world of small business remained complex, defying easy generalization. The complexity of that situation could be seen in the world of book publishing and book selling, as shown in Chapter 9. These two industries underwent tremendous technological and economic changes in the late twentieth century, and those alterations endangered the continued viability of small firms in the fields.

Additional Reading
Bennett Harrison, *Lean and Mean: The Changing Landscape of Corporate Power in the Age of Flexibility* (New York: Basic, 1994); and Gordon Donaldson, *Corporate Restructuring: Managing the Change Process from Within* (Boston: Harvard Business School Press, 1994), provide valuable introductions to the recent restructuring of American business. Steven Soloman, *Small Business USA: The Role of Small Companies in Sparking America's Economic Transformation* (New York: Crown, 1986); and William Brock and David Evans, *The Economics of Small Businesses: Their Role and Regulation in the U.S. Economy* (New York: Holmes & Meier, 1986), reach different conclusions about the importance of small business in postwar America. See also Richard Judd, William Greenwood, and Fred Becker, eds., *Small Business in a Regulated Economy: Issues and Policy Implications* (Westport, Conn.: Quorum, 1988). David Storey, "Symposium on Harrison's 'Lean and Mean': A Job Generation Perspective," *Small Business Economics* 7 (1995): 337–40, compares small businesses in the United States and Europe. D. H. Whittaker, *Small Firms in the Japanese Economy* (Cambridge, Eng.: Cambridge University Press, 1997); and John Stanworth and Colin Gray, eds., *Bolton 20 Years On: The Small Firm in the 1990s* (London: Paul Chapman, 1991), are valuable national studies. Bo Carlsson, "The Evolution of

Manufacturing Technology and Its Impact on the Industrial Structure: An International Study," *Small Business Economics* 1 (1989): 21–37, examines small companies in metalworking. On changes in moviemaking, see Michael Storper and Susan Christopher, "Flexible Specialization and Regional Industrial Agglomerations: The Case of the U.S. Motion Picture Industry," *Annals of the Association of American Geographers* 71 (1987): 104–17.

Zoltan J. Acs and David B. Audretsch, *Innovation and Small Firms* (Cambridge, Mass.: MIT Press, 1990); and Roy Oakley, Roy Rothwell, and Sarah Cooper, *Management of Innovation in High Technology Small Firms* (Westport, Conn.: Quorum, 1988), are both sophisticated treatments of the contribution of small business to innovation. David L. Birch, *Job Creation in America: How Our Smallest Companies Put the Most People to Work* (New York: Free Press, 1987); D. Storey and S. Johnson, *Job Generation and Labour Market Change* (London: Macmillan, 1987); and Steven J. Davis, John Haltiwanger, and Scott Schuh, "Small Business and Job Generation: Dissecting the Myth and Reassessing the Facts," Working Paper No. 4492 for the National Bureau of Economic Research, October 1993; and Zoltan J. Acs, *Are Small Firms Important? Their Role and Impact* (Boston: Kluwer, 1999), reach different conclusions on the issue of job creation. On the importance of immigrant businesses worldwide, see Jan Rath, ed., *Immigrant Businesses: The Economic, Political and Social Environment* (London: Macmillan, 2000), especially the essays by Ivan Light and Richard Staring.

Historians have written little about the legal and medical professions as businesses, but see Philip Scranton's essay in Konosuke Odaka and Minoru Sawai, eds., *Small Firms, Large Concerns* (Oxford: Oxford University Press, 1999); Kenneth Lipartito, "What Have Lawyers Done for American Business: The Case of Baker & Botts of Houston," *Business History Review* 64 (Autumn 1990): 489–526; Kenneth Lipartito and Joseph Pratt, *Baker & Botts in the Development of Modern Houston* (Austin: University of Texas Press, 1991); and Marc Galanter and Thomas Palay, *Tournament of Lawyers: The Transformation of the Big Law Firms* (Chicago: University of Chicago Press, 1991).

9

Independent Bookstores in a Time of Consolidation

The dimming prospects for independent bookstores in recent decades illustrate well some of the challenges facing small businesses in American retailing. Since the 1970s, and especially since the 1990s, independent bookstores have encountered growing threats to their profits and, indeed, to their very existence. The rise of large nationwide bookstore chains, and the spread of mass retailers, which often used books as loss leaders, dramatically cut into their sales. So did the development of bookselling on the Internet, particularly by Amazon.com. Additional developments hurt independents—changes in reading tastes among Americans, alterations in publishing, and other changes. Consequently, many independents failed. Others, however, showed remarkable staying power. By exploiting niche markets, by embedding themselves in their local communities, and by other means, some independents, mainly small businesses, found they could coexist and compete successfully with their larger brethren. This chapter examines the changing nature of America's book business, especially selling, and how one independent bookstore—K&M Books of Cleveland, Ohio—tried to deal with the many changes buffeting its industry.

Consolidation and Competition in Bookselling

Demographic changes lay behind many of the alterations in bookselling across the United States. Of prime importance was the movement of Americans into suburbs after World War II. Shopping centers based on automobile travel grew up in the suburbs, and with that development came the first chain bookstores. City department stores had long subsidized book departments as conveniences to attract customers, but as the department stores moved into suburban shopping malls, they dropped their unprofitable bookshops. In 1969, two midwestern department store chains—Carter, Hawley, and Hale; and Dayton, Hudson—spun off their bookshops as the bookstore chains of Waldenbooks and B. Dalton. Stranded in the cities—few moved to the suburbs—most major independent bookstores were left behind.

Emphasizing high turnover and volume sales to cover the relatively high rents they had to pay in the shopping malls, the two bookstore chains began changing the bookselling business. They stressed selling a relatively small number of best-sellers and carried few backlist books for publishers, a trend that continued through the 1990s. Between 1986 and 1996, the share of all books sold in the United States represented by the top thirty best-sellers nearly doubled, and just six authors wrote 63 of the 100 best-selling titles.

Borders and Barnes & Noble took this approach further, profoundly changing the nature of bookselling. The development of these two nationwide chains greatly increased competition in bookselling and, in fact, transformed the business. In 1994, for the first time, chains made more sales of adult trade books than did independents. Borders and Barnes & Noble were not alone, however, in putting pressure on independent bookstores. Other new retail outlets for books also grew up. Grocery stores and Sam's Club (an offshoot of Wal-Mart) were very important in eroding the market share of independents, as was the development of Internet selling from the mid-1990s.

In 1971, Leonard Riggio, the son of a New York prizefighter, purchased Barnes & Noble, a struggling New York company with a single store. From that base, he expanded through the purchase of shopping mall chains such as B. Dalton and Doubleday, acquired in 1986. Humorous television advertisements, discounting, and comfortable lounge chairs invited shoppers into his growing number of stores. In 1989, Riggio bought the Texas chain Bookstop, which had put up a number of superstores; and he was soon building his own Barnes & Noble superstores across the nation. A successful public offering of stock in his company provided needed funds for expansion in 1993. By the fall of 1996, Barnes & Noble boasted about 400 superstores; a year later the chain had 454 such outlets. At about the same time, the company shut down many of its smaller mall stores. In 2001, Barnes & Noble operated 520 superstores and 470 smaller B. Dalton outlets.

Barnes & Nobles's large, well appointed stores did for bookselling what upscale department stores had done for general retailing in the late nineteenth and early twentieth centuries: the stores turned buying books into a luxurious experience, replete with coffee bars. At the same time, the company made books part of America's consumer culture. Gone were the sometimes cramped stores carrying only a limited number of titles at inconvenient locations. Gary Hoover, the founder of Bookstop, captured well the appeal of Barnes & Noble. "Barnes & Noble understood the social implications of a bookstore," he observed in 1996. "They understood the role of coffee, high ceiling heights, the sofas, the chairs." However, this comfortable atmosphere was only part of the story. So was massive advertising. As Hoover observed, "no one knows like the Riggios how to blow out a best-seller," because "they come from the high-volume, intense New York publishing environment."

The brothers Tom and Louis Borders started what would become the Borders Group with a single used-book store near the University of Michigan's campus at Ann Arbor in 1971. They had dreamed, recalled one early-day employee, of owning a "utopian bookstore"; and the "early atmosphere" was, according to one reporter, "loose and distinctly counterculture." The development of an electronic inventory-tracking system that followed each book from order to sale allowed Borders to expand—a system developed, according to company lore, by Louis when he was working with a computer program to pick winners in horse races. Like Barnes & Noble, Borders was soon building stand-alone, luxurious superstores; and Tom and Louis brought in Robert DiRomualdo to help with a nationwide expansion in 1989. When the brothers sold Borders to Kmart in 1992, DiRomualdo, who had once run Hickory Farms, stayed in charge of the book chain. (Kmart already owned Waldenbooks, which it had acquired in 1984.) In 1995, Kmart, under pressure to return to its core businesses, sold its bookstore chains—Borders and Waldenbooks—to the public under the Borders name.

Since then, Borders, like Barnes & Noble, has emphasized its freestanding superstores over its smaller mall stores. The chain possessed about 130 superstores in 1996, and 340 by early 2001 (there remained about 860 Waldenbooks locations open in shopping centers). About 25,000 square feet each, the superstores were considerably larger than most independents. Still, Borders sought to perpetuate the idea that its employees were "book people," not simply retail sales clerks. In the mid-1990s, test questions for those applying for sales positions asked who wrote *Mrs. Dalloway* and *Thus Spake Zarathustra*. Those at Barnes & Noble derided such claims, as the two chains jockeyed for position in city after city. "The misconception is that we aren't literary," observed Riggio. To the contrary, he asserted, "We are full of literary people."

The rise of Amazon.com as a book retailer further complicated the bookselling industry for independents. Named after the large South American river and adapted to mean "river of text," Amazon.com was started in mid-1994 by Jeffrey Bezos. The senior vice president of a Wall Street fund, Bezos was well versed in computers and did not want to be left out of high technology opportunities. In the early 1990s, he drew up a list of twenty types of products that he thought could be sold on the Internet but soon settled on books, reasoning that not even the largest physical bookstore could carry more than a fraction of the 50,000 or so new books printed in the United States each year. Quitting his Wall Street job, he moved to Seattle, a location he chose because it possessed—thanks to Microsoft's presence there—a large number of high technology professionals, ideal potential customers for Internet sales. By the summer of 1995, Bezos had raised several million dollars from private investors for Amazon.com (he discarded an earlier name of Cadabra because it was too close to Cadaver), moved out of the garage in which he had earlier begun business, and relocated in a 400-square-foot office. As book orders from Internet customers swelled, he and a growing number of employees moved into larger offices several times over the next year.

The key to Amazon.com's operations lay in the fact that it carried very little in the way of book inventory. Rather, the company purchased most books only after customers ordered them by accessing its database on the Internet. That database was originally based on the volumes carried by the Ingram Book Group, a large book wholesaler. Initially, that electronic database held about 1.1 million titles, but by 1997 it contained 2.5 million. In a 1996 interview, Bezos stated that because Amazon.com did not order most books until after the company had sold them, it was able to turn over its small physical inventory, mainly bestsellers, about 150 times a year—compared to about 4 times a year for brick-and-mortar bookstores. Sales soared, until by 2000 Amazon.com had amassed a customer base of about 20 million people and had expanded beyond books into music, videos, and other consumer goods. These sales and the funds generated by the rapid turnover were what allowed Amazon.com's phenomenally rapid growth.

The spread of chain stores and the growth of Internet selling were more in a long line of challenges that independent bookstores had faced in their tumultuous history. In fact, the history of independents was relatively short in the United States and contained no "Golden Age," free from problems. In the colonial period and well into the nineteenth century, few independent bookstores existed. Instead, most were controlled by printers or publishers, who used them as captive outlets for their presses. Not until the 1920s did many independent bookstores appear, and they led far from easy lives. Competition from department stores, the ravages of the Great Depression of the 1930s, and the development of paperback book sales after World War II all threatened their profits, as did the chains that grew up with the first shopping centers. New forms of entertainment — movies, the radio, and television — threatened to woo readers away from books altogether.

Yet, the difficulties independents encountered in the 1990s were of a new dimension. Competition from the chains, Amazon.com, and other mass retailers bit deeply into their sales. Particularly harmful was the discounting of book prices introduced by the chains. At the same time, changes in American culture, which placed a premium on speed and instant gratification, hurt independent stores. As an independent bookstore owner in New York City explained, "Books were slow, while computer games, TV, MTV, everything else was fast." In 1995–96, the sales of adult trade hardcover books, the mainstay of independents, fell — a first in recent American history — for a two-year decline of 10 percent.

Changes in the world of publishing also unsettled independent bookstores. As in sales, the trend was toward consolidation. What one writer called an "acquisition frenzy" affected publishers beginning in the 1970s, "when large communications corporations driven by illusions of media 'synergy' suddenly felt they needed a publishing company." An "enormous number of acquisitions," he noted, "followed in the eighties." By the late 1990s, a handful of major media empires dominated publishing in the United States: Bertelsmann (a German firm) owned Random House; Holtzbrinck (another German company) possessed St. Martin's and Farrar, Straus & Giroux; Longmans, Pearson (based in London) owned Viking, Penguin, Putman, and the Dutton Group; Robert Murdoch's News Corporation (a British firm) owned HarperCollins and William Murrow; Viacom included Simon & Schuster and Pocket Books among the companies it owned; and AOL Time Warner controlled Little, Brown as well as its own Warner Books.

Like so many conglomerates that had expanded during the 1960s and 1970s, these firms were soon surprised to learn that consistent profits in their new acquisitions were elusive. More concerned than earlier generations of publishers with making annual profits, these media and communications giants consequently did all they could to squeeze the last dollar out of their book offerings—a logical business strategy perhaps, but one that increased pressure on independent bookstores. There remained room in the United States for some narrowly focused niche publishers to make profits, but doing so was more and more difficult.

Not surprisingly, the number of independent bookstores in the United States declined in the face of these challenges. In 1990, there were 6,996 general-interest bookstores in America. In 1995, bookstore failures as a proportion of total stores overtook failures in all other retail categories. By 1996, the number of bookstores had climbed to 7,090. However, since about 800 of the new stores were chain superstores, it would seem that about 700 smaller independents closed. The American Booksellers Association (ABA), a trade group composed of independents, saw its membership fall from 5,132 in 1991 to 4,047 in 1998; and during those same years, according to the ABA, 221 independent members of the association went out of business. (Many independents did not belong to the ABA, and still others dropped their membership.)

The same trends were apparent in market share figures. In 1991, independents sold 32.5 percent of the books marketed in the United States, four years later just 19.5 percent. In 1999, independents accounted for only 15.2 percent of the books sold in America, chains were responsible for 24.6 percent, Amazon.com and other Internet retailers sold 5.4 percent (up from just 0.4 percent in 1997), with book clubs, food and drug stores, department stores, and other retail outlets selling the rest, well over half of the total. It was sales made by the mass retailers, even more than those made by the chain bookstores, that disturbed independents. The chain bookstores also saw their market share erode slightly in the late 1990s. According to a respected account by Jason Epstein, only seventy-five major independent bookstores (those with at least 100,000 titles in stock) remained in the United States in 2000.

The growing competition and changing reading habits of Americans affected all retail outlets for books in the late 1990s, not just independents, and led to further changes in the industry. Faced with slight declines in their market shares, the chains began selling online over the Internet, a response to the rise of Amazon.com. Barnes & Noble started Internet service in 1997, followed by Borders, far less successfully, about a year later. The chains also started publishing some of the books they sold, a form of vertical integration. In 1999, Barnes & Noble also sought to purchase the

Ingram Book Group, one of the nation's largest wholesalers of books—a move thwarted by opposition from the ABA, whose members feared that such an action would deprive them of one of their major sources of books to sell.

As of 2001, Amazon.com, for all of its success in increasing its sales, had never earned a full year's profit. Between 1996 and 1998, the company lost $162 million on sales of $774 million, and losses continued into the new millennium: $168 million of losses on sales of $668 million in the first quarter of 2001 alone. Amazon.com found it necessary to become more like brick-and-mortar stores and opened warehouses and distribution centers across the United States, thus increasing greatly the number of its employees and its operating expenses. Faced with sagging stock prices and poor credit reports and needing additional capital, Amazon.com accepted an infusion of $100 million from AOL Time Warner in mid-2001.

As the 1990s closed, Internet book sales, in general, had not become profitable. In 2000, Barnes & Noble.com lost $102 million on its Internet sales of $202 million. In 2001, continuing Internet losses at Borders led the firm to enter into a cooperative Internet selling venture with Amazon.com, by which Amazon.com became the distributor for books sold by Borders on the Internet. It was only in the fourth quarter of 2001 that Amazon.com reported its first profits: just $5 million, a scant 1 cent per share of common stock.

Responses of Independent Bookstores

On occasion, independent bookstores took collective action to address their problems. In 2000, many members of the ABA launched their own Internet sales outlet, called Booksense.com. Initially using the inventory of the Ingram Book Group—and later that of Baker & Taylor (one of America's largest book wholesalers and a major competitor of Ingram) as well—as its database and source of books, Booksense.com offered customers an alternative to purchasing from Amazon.com or other online sources. The ABA also successfully sued to prevent chains from extracting from publishers larger discounts than those given to independents. And, as mentioned earlier, the ABA fought efforts by Barnes & Noble to buy the Ingram Book Group. Such unified actions were relatively rare, however. Like most small business people throughout American history, bookstore owners prized their independence and did not usually work well together in groups. Instead, independents got ahead, when they did succeed, by serving niche markets, by providing superior customer service, and by becoming community institutions—as can be seen in short sketches of several independents.

Begun in 1984 in Washington, D.C., by Carla Cohen and Barbara Meade, Politics and Prose benefited from its location in a neighborhood described by one reporter as "abounding with journalists, academics, diplomats: along Connecticut Avenue, just inside the D.C. [subway] line from Maryland, where people not only read serious books but wrote them." A monthly newsletter, readings, and other literary events, created, the reporter thought, a "sense of community" among the store's customers. Still profitable as the 1990s closed, Politics and Prose offered its titles for sale over the Internet as well as in its store.

Carrying a million new and used volumes in 68,000 square feet of retail space in 2000, Powell's City Books in Portland, Oregon, had what one reporter described as "a funky atmosphere" for people browsing its shelves, but it also began selling on the Internet as early as 1993. Started by Walter Powell, the store had unusual origins. Walter's son, Michael, had borrowed $3,000 from him in 1970 to open a bookstore in Chicago, where he was a graduate student. A retired painting contractor, Walter visited his son's store, fell in love with bookstores, and decided to establish one in Portland, which he did in 1971, housing it in a defunct automobile dealership's building. By carrying many editions, new and used, of the same titles, Powell's differentiated itself from chains by offering its customers more choices. Being located in a particularly literate city also helped, as did having a downtown site well served by public transportation, which many "green" Portlanders used. Even the weather may have contributed to Powell's success. "People have to do something all those rainy days," Walter observed in an interview.

For nearly twenty years, 1978 through 1997, Jeannette Wilson owned and operated one of the best known independent bookstores in the United States, Books & Co., located in New York City. As she explained in the late 1990s, "We achieved our imprimatur from the books we carried—unusual books, literary fiction, university press books, books people couldn't find elsewhere." Her store maintained, she said, a "consistent focus on art, literature, poetry, and philosophy." In other words, Books & Co. engaged in niche marketing—a situation made possible by its location in New York City, a mecca for literate Americans. Customer service was also important. The staff knew many customers by name and catered to their wishes, which could, at times, be frustrating. "Running a bookstore was occasionally like doing social work," said Wilson. "Some of the people who came in were lonely and just needed to talk, and sometimes genuinely crazy people wandered in." Good customer service was typical of independents. In the 1990s, independent stores spent roughly twice as much on their sales staff as the superstores; while the superstores offered more books, independents offered more staff to talk to. Moreover, Wilson succeeded in turning her store into a community institution. Books & Co., observed writer Lynne Tillman, "was a nexus for literary achievements and hopes, for readerly proclivities, for human interactions—from a child's love of writing to a novelist's debut, a chance encounter to a love affair."

Yet, not even Books & Co. was particularly profitable. At its highest point, according to Wilson, the store had annual sales of $1.4 million, allowing her to take out $2,000 per month as salary. Hit hard by growing chain store competition, especially discounting, Books & Co. faced poor prospects by the 1990s. "I had to put money in each year," Wilson noted, referring to her store's last seven years. Like most small business owners, Wilson found the demands on her time almost overwhelming. "I wanted to do everything, and in a way, like many women, I tried to," she remembered. Between her work at the store, raising her children, and serving on the boards of foundations and other groups, Wilson became stressed out. When disputes arose between her and the leaseholder for the building in which Books & Co. was located, Wilson decided to go out of business.

In closing her store, Wilson was increasingly typical. As Michael Powell observed, "There's lots of reasons people close bookstores. They get poor, they get tired, they're not making any money, and they want to do something else." Such, he thought, had long been the case. What had changed in the 1990s, he believed, was that "no one's opening new stores." He was only partly correct. Entrepreneurs and book-lovers continued to start some independent bookstores as new businesses, as can be seen in the case of K&M Books.

K&M Books of Cleveland, Ohio

"I think we'll have no problem having room for all of the books we are planning on and having a little sitting area," Kim Neath e-mailed her parents in mid-May 1997, "I am very excited." Neath was describing the retail space she had just rented in a Cleveland strip mall for the bookstore she planned to open that coming summer. "I think we'll run Borders out of town in about a year, maybe less," she exclaimed two weeks later. In Neath's preparations to start up an independent bookstore, an abiding sense of entrepreneurship merged with a love of books, with excitement and optimism the order of the day.

From the outset, Neath envisioned her store as a community institution. Its business plan stated that K&M Books, as her business came to be named, would be "a small community-oriented general bookstore in Shaker Heights, Ohio." (The preparation of a 20-page business plan was needed to secure bank financing for the store.) It would be, an early advertisement said, "the kind of place where we're on a first name basis with our customers . . . a family bookstore that is part of the fabric of the community." The store would be "a neighborhood store that will become a destination spot for educating and entertaining local residents." Appropriate book selection and superior customer service, Neath thought, would be important elements in her store's success. In an interview published in a local magazine, she observed, "Independent bookstores are special. We can hand-pick titles that our customers want, rather than titles that a corporation in New York thinks they want." In something of a manifesto for independents, she declared, "I don't want to live in a world where a handful of chain bookstores dictates what books get published."

Thus, according to its business plan, K&M Books was "intended to fill a gap in Cleveland's existing book market." Cleveland's bookstores were mainly large national chains, Borders and Barnes & Noble, located in the city's far outer suburbs. Only a very few scattered independents remained, along with a Waldenbooks in the downtown area. K&M Books would be "an alternative—a local store with quality service and neighborhood feel." Sited in one of Cleveland's inner suburbs, it would "compete against chain bookstores (including book superstores) by offering superior service, community-specific merchandise and events, and a well-managed inventory-control system." Filling a gap—niche marketing—would soon become more important to her store than Neath initially imagined.

At the age of twenty-seven, Neath knew books and the book business well. She came from a family that valued books highly; her mother was a librarian, her father a university faculty member in history. Neath's education in the liberal arts at Oberlin College reinforced her interest in books. After graduating with a degree in political science in 1993, Neath moved to Chicago, where she worked for three years in the Water Tower outlet of Rizzoli Books, an Italian chain, becoming the merchandise manager in charge of the store's $900,000 inventory. Moving to Cleveland in 1996, she served as a manager of several stores in the Bookseller Group, a local chain that went out of business in the spring of 1997. That failure cost Neath her job and catalyzed her decision to strike out on her own. Convinced that she could do better than the stores in which she had been employed, she decided to open her own bookstore. Neath was not alone in this venture. She had married another Oberlin student, Mark Neath, upon graduation and moved with him to Chicago, when he went there to study law. She accompanied him again when he accepted a position in a major law firm headquartered in Cleveland. A specialist in corporate tax law and something of a whiz with computers, Mark provided much of the technical expertise needed to get the bookstore up and running. The name Kim and Mark chose for their store, K&M Books, reflected the deep personal interest each had in its success.

Asked by a magazine reporter about her decision to open her own store, Neath replied, "It's a very different thing to say 'I want to own a bookstore,' and actually doing the things involved in running it." She was right; in fact, much needed to be accomplished, all in just a few months' time. Neath had to secure financing for her business, select a location, furnish the store, select and purchase books, advertise her new company, and hire employees.

The Neaths organized K&M Books as an Ohio limited liability company. This legal form gave investors the same protection from the company's liabilities as incorporation would have (that is, investors could lose their investment in the firm, but could not be held personally responsible for the company's debts), but it had the advantage of being treated for federal income tax purposes as a partnership. Funds to start the business were of two types. A seven-year, variable-interest-rate, commercial bank loan provided $80,000. Backed by all of the Neaths' limited assets, the loan was co-signed by Kim's parents. Equity investment roughly equal in amount to the bank loan came from the Neaths, both sets of their parents, and Kim's brother. Approaches to the Small Business Administration for funding proved fruitless. As has been typical for small businesses throughout American history, family members provided the funding for this new business venture.

Even as they were securing funding for their new store, the Neaths looked for a viable location. Eager to avoid direct competition with the large chains, they stayed away from Cleveland's outer suburbs. Instead, they chose space in a strip mall, Shaker Towne Center, in the inner suburb of Shaker Heights. Having two solid anchor stores, about twenty other retail outlets, and plenty of parking, the mall seemed to be a good location. Part of the decision hinged on the Neaths' personal observations. They "spent one afternoon on the benches of the center," Kim later explained to a reporter, "asking shoppers and passersby what they were looking for in a bookstore." Living in the neighborhood themselves, the Neaths thought the demographics of the area would support their proposed store. Their business plan described Shaker Heights accurately as a "diverse 'inner' suburb;" and, in fact, a growing number of middle-class African Americans was making the district their home. Over time, African American books would become an important niche for the store. So would children's books, which reflected the ages of many living in the region; an increasing number of young couples were moving into the area.

Preparing the store for business required a lot of effort. Neath rented 1,800 square feet of space in the shopping mall in a five-year lease, which called for a large security deposit and several months' rent paid in advance. Then began the task of turning that space into a store. Once Neath had devised her floor plan, the shopping center management put in the walls. (One element of the location in the mall that appealed to Neath was that her store had two sides that fronted on the mall's parking lot, giving her two areas in which to put up displays to attract shoppers. After some argument with the shopping center management and city government, Neath also won permission to put up two neon signs pointing in different directions, rather than just one, advertising her store.) For furnishings Neath chose wood for her shelving and chairs, designed to give her store a "cozy" feel. Two computers linked to each other ran the cash registers and, through the use of Booklog software, allowed Neath to keep accurate track of her inventory and sales. Telephone and security systems had also to be selected and installed. Designing and placing advertisements in local newspapers and magazines were also part of the immediate task at hand. Doing so involved selecting a company logo designed by a friend, one featuring a black cat modeled upon her own cat, Dizzy, who would soon feature in some of the store's activities.

Even before her store opened, Neath hired an employee to assist with the preparations. She chose Mary Alice Beck. Like Neath, Beck had been a manager for Booksellers, the Cleveland chain, and it was through their work together at one of the chain's stores that Neath and Beck had gotten to know each other. Neath offered a relatively high salary to attract Beck, and she consistently paid her growing list of employees more than they could earn in chain stores. She did not, however, offer any benefits.

At the same time that she was hiring Beck and turning empty mall space into a store, Neath had to deal with the city government, securing vendor's licenses and having every aspect of the construction of her store examined and approved. She was required, for example, to have a drinking fountain installed, which required inspection of the plumbing. Like many small business people, Neath found her city government to be anything but supportive of her business effort.

Neath also needed to choose and purchase books. After perusing book catalogues, meeting with many publishers' representatives, and consulting with Beck and others, she selected quite a diverse inventory of books, a full line of fiction and nonfiction, as the stock with which to begin business. The books came mainly from the Ingram Book Group. To obtain the highest possible discount, 42 percent, Neath had to purchase a minimum of $50,000 worth (wholesale value). Simply shelving the approximately 5,000 books as they arrived proved to be a major undertaking, one in which family members shared.

At last the opening day for K&M Books arrived—September 20, 1997—delayed several months because of hitches that had developed in construction and other matters. Hundreds of people attended, attracted by the advertising, which included fliers delivered to all of the houses within about a mile or two of the store. "Our grand opening was a success," Neath noted a few days later. "Saturday was a really fun day, and we sold over two thousand dollars worth of books," she wrote. Since bookstores, like many retailers, make a large proportion of their annual sales in the fall, and especially during the weeks right before Christmas, Neath was relieved to have her store open in time for that busy season.

Over the next few years, those involved in K&M Books worked hard to make their store a profitable community institution. They offered discounts on individual books sold to teachers and librarians. For the general public, they discounted books that appeared on the *Cleveland Plain Dealer*'s list of bestsellers. They also discounted staff favorites each month. Neath actively sought off-site book sales. K&M Books held workshops to bring together librarians and teachers with publishers' representatives, and they worked with schools, churches, and businesses in managing their book fairs and other events. Sales made beyond the store's premises eventually became an important source of revenue. Monthly, at times weekly, children's events—everything from Halloween parties to book readings to special events featuring Dizzy, Neath's cat—brought parents and their children into the store. Neath had worked as a playground supervisor during three summers when she was a high school and college student; and her empathy with children aided her in her store work.

Book signings with local and national authors also helped establish the store within the community. Especially important were signings by children's authors Tomie De Paola and Jan Brett. Well-known national authors, they each attracted over 400 customers to the store. Along the same lines, the establishment of several book groups that met at the store, including a young adult fiction group, helped embed K&M Books in its community. To reinforce the presence of her store, Neath sent out a monthly newsletter featuring notices of upcoming events and short book reviews to all of her store's customers. K&M Books reached out to customers in other ways. From its opening day, K&M Books maintained a website on the Internet, and the store was soon adding email supplements to its newsletter; by 2000, the store's entire newsletter was available online. Moreover, K&M Books was one of the first independents to join in the creation of Booksense.com, the online selling tool of the ABA. As the new millennium began, however, online sales remained only a small fraction of the bookstore's sales, less than 5 percent.

As the Neaths had hoped, most sales came from people in Shaker Heights who came to the store. K&M Books moved ahead by offering its customers books sold by knowledgeable staff in pleasant surroundings. By 2000, the store had three part-time employees in addition to Kim, who worked full-time, and her husband who helped out on weekends and who handled the store's tax and legal matters. Sales and revenues mounted year by year, running ahead of the projections of the venture's original business plan. By 2000, K&M Books carried an inventory of about $200,000 worth of books (retail value), about twice as much as the inventory with which the store had opened for business.

This growth did not come easily. Long hours of hard work were involved, as was some unpaid help by family members. Unexpected situations arose, and some aspects of the store's activities changed over the years. The store originally offered customers free coffee in a comfortable sitting area, but stopped that practice when homeless people moved into that section of the store. Then, too, the customer base of the store turned out to be a bit different than what had been expected. Her computer system allowed Neath to compare easily her sales and inventory of books by subject matter; and she soon found herself making alterations in the titles that she carried in response to what her customers were purchasing. Children's books and African American books accounted for higher proportions of her store's sales than she had initially expected, and she built up her listings in those areas. Unexpected competition surfaced. City Books, an independent about three times as large as K&M Books, opened about two-and-a-half miles way. Plagued by poor management and inadequate financing, that store went out of business within a few months, much to the relief of those at K&M Books.

By 2000–2001, K&M Books had become a successful small business, only to face new challenges that clouded its future. Most distressing was the opening in the fall of 2000 of a very large independent bookstore, Joseph-Beth Booksellers, part of a chain based in the South, only two miles down the street. Featuring an upscale coffee bar and restaurant and having about 30,000 square feet of space for 120,000 book titles and an extensive offering of music CDs, the store bit deeply into the sales of K&M Books. Book buying had changed dramatically over the past few decades. Most book purchases were made by people in the top quartile of income, individuals who expected book buying to be a "yuppie" experience replete with latte coffee. Joseph-Beth, which spent $5 million in renovating the building in which it was located and which received major tax abatements from the city of Cleveland, could afford to offer such amenities. K&M Books could not. Asked about the impact of Joseph-Beth's sales on her store's viability in early 2002, Neath ruefully observed, "We had four real good years and one bad one. . . . During the past year business went down to nothing . . . people just stopped coming in."

Faced with rapidly declining sales, K&M Books closed its doors. It could not deal with the competition from Joseph-Beth. Other factors were also involved in the closing. An economic downturn that gripped the United States, and especially the Cleveland area in 2001, made a bad situation worse. Books are a discretionary consumer item, among the first type of purchase to be cut out in hard times. In addition, Kim Neath had her first child in the late summer of 2001, and she came to question whether she wanted to spend the same long hours and tremendous amounts of energy on her store that she had expended in the past. As she explained in a newspaper interview, "It's a huge amount of work to own a business, and I just don't care to be in that situation ever again, especially having a baby now." In the winter of 2002, Neath liquidated K&M Books and moved with her husband away from Cleveland.

Success in Bookselling

As the example of K&M Books suggests, success for independent booksellers had become difficult in the new millennium. Several elements seemed to be necessary: a thorough knowledge of the book business, something Kim Neath obtained from her earlier jobs; adequate financing, made possible by the support of family members; a capacity for sustained hard work for long hours; an acceptance of the most recent technological advances (K&M Books embraced the use of computers and the Internet in making and tracking sales); a good location, which provided a reasonable customer base; and an ability to change operations as needed, a flexibility in viewing the future. Such factors had long been important to small business success in retailing—and, indeed, in most forms of success in small business. Even so, the story of K&M Books is a cautionary tale. At no point could the store succeed in going head-to-head with superstores. It could not offer the type of experience many customers wanted and in the end had to close its doors.

Additional Reading

Jason Epstein, *Book Business: Publishing Past, Present and Future* (New York: W. W. Norton, 2001), is an insider's account of changes in publishing. See also Andre Schiffrin, *How International Conglomerates Took Over Publishing and Changed the Way We Read* (London: Verso, 2000). Lynne Tillman, *Bookstore: The Life and Times of Jeannette Watson and Books & Co.* (New York: Harcourt Brace, 1999), looks at the development of one independent bookstore. Walter Powell, "Competition versus Concentration in the Book Trade," *Journal of Communication* 30, no. 2 (1980): 89–97, provides a look at the changes that began in the last two decades of the twentieth century. See also Paul Watkins, "That Wonderful Book," *Torch Magazine* (Winter 1999–2000): 24–27. Articles in the press were essential sources for this chapter, especially *Forbes*, March 8, 1999; *Inc. Tech* 2 (1997): 57–61; *New York Times*, May 30, 1997, and December 16, 2001; *New Yorker*, October 6, 1997, 50–63; and *Wall Street Journal*, May 16 and 29 and September 3, 1996; March 15, June 3, September 2, and November 4, 1997; March 12, 1998; September 4, 1999; June 26 and July 17, 2000; and June 21 and July 24, 2001. The websites for Borders, Barnes & Noble, and Amazon.com were also valuable sources of corporate information. My daughter, Kim Neath, was the founder and owner of K&M Books, and she graciously gave me access to information about her store. Published articles on K&M Books may be found in the *Cleveland Plain Dealer*, May 23, 1999, and June 16, 2000; *Crane's Cleveland Business*, January 8–14, 2001; *Shaker Magazine*, January/February 1998, November/December 2000; and the *Sun Times*, January 17, 2002. For a valuable look at small businesses in one neighborhood of New York City, see Tom Shachtman, *Around the Block: The Business of a Neighborhood* (New York: Harcourt Brace, 1997).

Scholars understand much more about the development of small business in the United States than was the case just a generation ago. The work of historians, political scientists, economists, sociologists, and others has begun to illuminate this previously little-known field. Despite all that recent research has accomplished on the history of small business, however, much remains to be learned. I hope my study has provided a broad survey of the contours of change in the evolving world of small business, but I realize that it is far from the last word on the topic. If anything, I hope my volume stimulates further research on the history of small firms and the many roles they have played in America's development.

The Evolution of Small Business in America

Small business development in the United States has been complex, as has its impact upon American politics and culture. That complexity is an indication of the centrality of small business to American life. From the founding of the first colonies to the present day, small business has been of great importance to the majority of Americans, as the dominant form of business enterprise in their nation and as a symbol for their socioeconomic aspirations.

The position of small business in America's economy and culture has changed over time. In the colonial and early national periods—in fact, up until about 1880—few large businesses existed in America, and small firms decreed how the nation would develop economically. In these years there developed a business ideology based upon individual opportunity and grounded in the idea of small business ownership (with farms thought of, in part, as businesses). Challenges to small business arose in manufacturing—and, to a lesser degree, in other fields—with the emergence of large industrial complexes between 1880 and 1920. These challenges intensified during the fifty years following World War I. Small family farms came under increasing pressure from agribusinesses. Retailing, long a stronghold of small business, faced competition from chain stores and other institutions. Despite public attitudes that favored the continuance of small business development and sporadic efforts by the federal government to take action that reflected those attitudes, most forms of small business declined in economic importance relative to big business into the 1970s.

Of course, not all small businesses went into decline. Even in manufacturing, my study shows, many continued to prosper by coexisting with their larger brethren. Some joined together in industrial districts: the Philadelphia textile makers and the iron and steel companies in Pittsburgh, for example. Others made a go of it as independents, as did Buckeye Steel Castings and Wakefield Seafoods. The key to success, to the extent that there was a single key factor, seemed to lie in producing a specialty product for a niche market, whether that was cast-steel railroad couplers or frozen king crab meat. Here lay the major element of continuity in small business success: creating specialized products or services for niche markets. In this way, small business owners partially insulated their firms from direct competition with big businesses. Whether for a small-scale cotton textile manufacturer during the 1880s or for a small-scale producer of computer software a century later, specialization, combined with flexibility, seemed to offer the most fruitful strategy for coexistence with larger concerns. In manufacturing, this strategy often entailed development and use of the most up-to-date technologies and employment of well-trained and educated workers, workers able to innovate and improve their work processes.

Over the past several decades changes in the nation's and the world's economies opened some new opportunities for some forms of small businesses, especially those in manufacturing. The instability of the global business system from the early 1970s on seemed to beckon especially to small, nimble firms. However, those opportunities, as events in the 1990s showed, were limited. Flexibility and specialization did not work in all cases. Large companies restructured and regained their competitiveness, especially in the United States. Nor did government actions help most small enterprises very much. As a consequence, small firms never fully developed as engines of economic growth or job creation.

Mixed motives lay behind the entrance of Americans into the world of small business. Small business owners have long seen their firms as vehicles for their socioeconomic advancement. Profits and economic growth have always been important goals for those starting small businesses in America. Significantly, however, they have not been the only, or perhaps even the dominant, goals. As much as they have sought rapid individual economic ascendance, small business owners have also sought independence, combined with a comfortable economic life for their families. Few attained all that they desired. Small businesses have always led perilous lives, with relatively few lasting more than about five years.

Research Needs

Despite the progress made recently in increasing our understanding of the place of small business in American life, scholars need to do still more. We need both a general reassessment of the evolving place of small firms in America's business system and work on specific aspects of the development of small businesses in the United States. For business and economic historians, in particular, the field of small business promises to be a fertile one indeed.

We need to know much more about the historical evolution of small firms and their changing contributions to the economic development of the United States. The manufacturing sector of our economy has long attracted historians, but relatively few have looked at small industrialists. We need more information about their roles in the industrial growth of the United States. Just how common were small, flexible firms such as the ones Philip Scranton and John Ingham have studied? How did they relate to larger enterprises in their fields? Precisely what roles are small flexible companies playing in the present-day transformation of American industry, especially the movement away from vertical integration, once a hallmark of American manufacturers? How widespread is this trend? Our lack of knowledge is even more pronounced in the service and sales industries. Broadly defined, service businesses — many of them small firms — now employ about two-thirds of all Americans. Yet, we have less knowledge about them than about manufacturing enterprises. Exactly what is happening in the service sector, as the American economy becomes more and more integrated into the global economy? What are the ramifications, for instance, of the recent merger movement among American banks?

More generally, we need to understand better how the management of small firms was handled in the twentieth century, particularly in the years after World War II. Are most small firms run as informally as they once were? Or have the demands of the SBA, commercial banks, and other organizations that loan to small businesses perhaps forced the firms to become more bureaucratic? K&M Books had to prepare a very detailed business plan to secure its bank loan. The nature of small businesses may have changed significantly in the 1980s. Proportionally fewer may operate as truly independent enterprises than was the case in earlier times. A larger share may have become subservient to big businesses as subcontractors or as franchise outlets. As historian K. Austin Kerr has recently suggested, more may have become tied into "technical systems of analysis, bureaucratic values, and reporting required by larger, more powerful organizations." This possible trend deserves a full exploration by scholars.

Closely related to the topic of management style is the issue of innovation. Several recent historical investigations of the sources of innovation in America's business system have focused upon big businesses — General Electric, DuPont, and AT&T. Yet it is unclear just how important big businesses have been in fostering technological innovation in the United States. Much of the early industrial research conducted by large firms aimed mainly at market control. Moreover, as we have seen, in the early 1980s small businesses were the source of innovations in many fields. What of times past? We need to know much more about product and process innovations originating in small and large firms throughout American history before solid conclusions can be reached.

We also need to learn more about how small firms have interacted through their organizations. To what degree have trade associations and other types of organizations been important to the evolution of small firms? To what extent have small businesses taken part in the organizational thrust that has swept through much of American society since about 1870? In particular, it would be valuable to learn more about how small companies have banded together to deal with larger firms on something approaching an equal basis. How common, for example, have retailer-owned wholesalers been in America? How successful?

And, what about government actions and small business? Certainly an important policy matter has been understanding the roles of small businesses in creating opportunities for business management and ownership among women and minorities. To the extent that they have gotten ahead in American business at all, women and minorities have, at least until very recently, generally done so in small businesses. Scholars have begun to study this phenomenon, but more remains to be done. It appears that the progress of women into middle- and top-level management ranks in big businesses may have slowed in the mid-1980s; at the same time, women formed new small businesses at a rate much faster than did men. Perhaps it was precisely because their progress into the middle and upper ranks of management in big businesses was slower than they had anticipated that women left large firms to start their own small businesses. Small companies may also have offered women a better fit in their lifestyles, such as the flexibility to balance childbearing and careers, than did large businesses. We need to know more about this situation, as well as the entire topic of the roles small businesses have played for women over time. Similarly, some minorities have advanced through small business opportunities. However, it is important to recognize, as scholars have recently stressed, that those opportunities have varied considerably by racial and ethnic group and by type of industry.

Beyond these specifics, scholars need to reassess how they have viewed the roles played by small firms in the development of America's business system. As noted earlier, it is important to realize that there have been many different types of small businesses in America's past and that, as in the case of their larger counterparts, the nature of these firms has changed over time. The world of small business has not been a static world. It may well be propitious, too, to question the labels often applied to small businesses by scholars and what those labels imply. Should small businesses be called "traditional" businesses, with big businesses pictured as "modern"? Have small businesses composed a "peripheral" segment of the business system of the United States, with larger companies at the "center"? Many recent studies suggest that some small firms may make up the most dynamic part of our modern economy. What, then, of times past? As historians examining industries as diverse as textiles and steel have recently demonstrated, scholars may have long underestimated the significance of small and medium-sized firms in America's economic evolution. A fruitful way to approach a reassessment of small business in America's past might be to take the comparative approach. I have hinted at some international comparisons throughout this volume, but scholars need to do much more along those lines.

Additional Reading
Douglas A. Farnie, Tetsuro Nakaoka, David J. Jeremy, John F. Wilson, and Takeshi Abe, eds., *Region and Strategy in Britain and Japan: Business in Lancashire and Kansai, 1890–1990* (London: Routledge, 2000), shows how valuable the comparative regional approach can be in studying business history. This work illustrates how small firms were of great importance

in the economic development of both Northwest England and the area around Osaka in Japan. For another comparative regional study that provides insights into small business development, see Mary Rose, *Firms, Networks and Business Values: The British and American Cotton Industries since 1750* (Cambridge, Eng.: Cambridge University Press, 2000).

44–45, 108, 109; colonial and ante-
bellum limitations on, 13, 14; and
industrialization, 14; as small busi-
ness, 64–65, 152. *See also* Chain stores;
Wholesalers
Doubleday, 184
Drug stores, 4, 19, 75, 97
Dual economy. *See* Center vs. peripheral
companies
Du Bois, W. E. B., 72
Dun and Bradstreet, 66–67
DuPont Company, 103, 134, 137–38, 170,
202
Dutton Group, 187

Eisenhower, Dwight D., 134, 135, 136
Elkins Act (1903), 50
England. *See* Great Britain
Entrepreneurship, 7, 8, 21, 37, 154, 170–71
Epstein, Jason, 188
Equitable of New York, 67
Europe: industrial districts in, 6, 28–
29, 58, 84; American trade with, 21,
22; cult of domesticity in, 33–34;
relative lack of vertically integrated
firms in, 52; immigrants from, 71–
72; competition for U.S. businesses
from, 170; government regulations and
small business in, 176. *See also specific
countries*

"Fairchildren," 158
Fairchild Semiconductor, 158
Family businesses: country stores as, 18;
retail enterprises as, 22, 38, 143; manufacturing companies as, 24, 56–57, 82,
84, 85, 86, 87, 88, 105, 140; among artisans, 25, 27; in early industrialization,
27; banks as, 32; small businesses as,
37–38; women's businesses as, 71; minority businesses as, 71, 72. *See also*
Family farm

Family farm, 21, 22–23, 38, 58–64, 76, 113,
14, 147, 174–75, 199
Farming: decline of small business in,
3, 63, 113–14, 147–48, 152, 174–75, 199;
importance of small business in, 11,
43, 76; innovation in, 12, 23, 59–60,
147; down to 1880, 13, 17, 20–24; as
small business, 13, 21, 38, 58–59 (*see
also* Family farm); commercial, 13, 21–
22, 23, 24, 60, 61–62, 63–64 (*see also*
Agribusiness); and country stores,
17, 23, 66; relative value of, 20–21, 22,
51–52, 59; and tenancy, 21–22, 113;
community involvement of, 23–24,
61, 114; and artisans, 24; women in,
33, 114; big business in, 43, 46, 113, 114
(*see also* Agribusiness); government
regulation of, 51; in 1880–1920, 58–
64; specialization in, 59, 60–61, 64,
113, 114–15, 147, 175; African Americans
in, 73, 113; and chain stores, 111, 112;
and sharecropping, 113–14; in 1921–
1945, 113–15; in 1946–1971, 147–48; in
1972–2000, 174–75
Farrar, Straus & Giroux, 187
Federal Reserve Act (1913), 50
Federal Reserve System, 50–51, 68, 97
Federal Trade Commission (FTC), 49–50
Federal Trade Commission Act (1914),
49–50
First National Stores, 108–9
Flour milling, 30, 53
Ford Motors, 102, 103, 138
Foreign competition, 6, 141–42, 153, 159,
166, 176
France, 29, 33, 52, 58, 142–43
Franchising, 74, 153, 173–74, 202
Free blacks, 34, 35
Furniture making, 53, 57

Galbraith, John Kenneth, 177
Geelhoeld, Bruce, 146

Independent Grocers Association (IGA), 110, 143

Independent retailers, 9, 66, 108–13, 144, 146, 171–72, 183–98 passim

Industrial districts: small businesses in, 6, 8, 29, 39, 43, 53, 54–58, 76, 81–85, 106–8, 157, 159, 162, 169, 200; in Europe, 6, 28–29, 84–85, 142–43; importance of for small business, 6, 53, 54, 81; in Japan, 6, 106–8; and economic development of United States, 28, 57–58, 74, 142; big businesses in, 57–58

Industrialization, 12, 25–26; and business specialization, 13; merchants and, 13, 20, 26; technological innovation and, 14, 26, 44; and market expansion, 14, 44; in Japan, 20; capital for, 20, 26, 27; role of small business in, 24, 29–30; and artisans, 24–30; and rise of big business, 43–47; and service sector, 66

Ingham, John, 88, 201

Ingram Book Group, 186, 189, 195

Innovation. *See* Technological innovation

Inouye, Daniel, 161

Institute of Social Research (University of Michigan), 93

Insurance companies, 31, 66, 70, 151; as minority businesses, 35, 71, 73; government regulation of, 51; growth of into big businesses, 67, 145, 172

Intel, 158

Internet retailing, 184, 186, 188, 189, 190, 196, 198

Interstate Commerce Act (1887), 50

Interstate Commerce Commission (ICC), 50

Iron and steel making, 8, 33, 44, 57–58, 81–86, 89, 94, 200

Italy, 58, 107, 143

Jackson, Andrew, 18, 32

Japan: industrial districts in, 6, 58, 106–7; merchants, shopkeepers, and peddlers in, 20; antibusiness attitudes in, 36–37; relative lack of vertically integrated firms in, 45; banking in, 67; small industrial firms in, 106–7, 142, 175, 178; small retailers in, 113, 146; competition for U.S. businesses from, 142, 153, 169, 166, 170; efforts to create "technopolises" in, 162

Japanese Americans, 61, 71, 150. *See also* Asian Americans

J. C. Penney, 108

Jefferson, Thomas, 38

Job creation, 7, 157, 160, 165, 176, 177–78, 181, 200

Johnson, Lyndon, 137, 152

Johnson, S., 167, 178

Jones, John Beauchamp, 11, 18, 37

Joseph-Beth Booksellers, 197

Juniata Iron, 82

Justice Department, 133–34, 137–38; Antitrust Division, 134

K&M Books, 8–9, 183, 191–98, 201–2

Kane, James and Archibald, 18

Kargon, Robert, 158

Kentucky Fried Chicken, 173

Kerr, K. Austin, 202

Kirk, Charles B., 143

Kirk's hardware store, 143

K. J. Brown, 146

Kmart, 185

Korea, 160

Korea Advanced Institute of Science, 160

Korean Americans, 150–51. *See also* Asian Americans

Korean War, 134, 140

Kroger, 108–9

Kwolek-Folland, Angel, 96, 102, 151

Kyoto, Japan, 20

Washington, D.C., 190

Weis, Marc, 144

Westinghouse, 57

Wholesalers: SBA and, 1, 135; colonial and antebellum, 15–16, 19; and retailers, 16–17, 18, 111, 202; specialization among, 19; in Great Britain and Japan, 20; and rise of big business, 45, 64–65; and manufacturers, 86; and Great Depression, 100. *See also* Distribution

William Morrow, 187

Willing, Thomas, 31

Wilson, Jeannette, 190–91

Wilson, Woodrow, 94

Women: importance of small business for, 7, 70–71, 151, 179–80, 202–3; in retailing, 33, 70, 71–72, 96, 179; in service sector, 33, 70, 96, 179; in manufacturing, 33, 102, 105; in farming, 33, 114; as small business people down to 1880, 33–34; and "separate spheres," 33–34, 71, 151; as small business people, 1880–1920, 70, 71; Jewish, as small business people, 71–72; African American, as small business people, 73; business and professional associations for, 74; as small business people, 1921–1945, 96, 102; as consumers, 151; as small business people, 1946–1971, 151; as small business people, 1972–2000, 179–80

Woolworth, 65, 108

World War I, 94–95, 113

World War II, 92, 98, 100–102, 106, 119, 158

Yamasaki, Mamoru, 161

Zeitlin, Jonathan, 58